PARISHES IN TRANSITION

Edited by Eugene Duffy

Parishes in Transition

the columba press

First published in 2010 by
the columba press
55A Spruce Avenue, Stillorgan Industrial Park,
Blackrock, Co Dublin

Cover by Bill Bolger
Origination by The Columba Press
Printed in Ireland by ColourBooks Ltd, Dublin

ISBN 978 1 85607 706 4

Contents

Introduction

It is an understatement to claim that the church in Ireland has been going through a period of intense crisis over the past decade or more. Much attention has focused on the failures of those in leadership, in the priesthood and religious life. This is only part of the crisis that the church is now attempting to face. Meanwhile another seismic shift has been occurring as vocations to priesthood and religious life have plummeted, with the result that the forms of pastoral ministry and parish life that were such staples of the Catholic Church in Ireland for generations will no longer be possible. In the light of this change and in order to contribute positively to the necessary response that is called for, the Department of Theology and Religious Studies at Mary Immaculate College, Limerick, organised a two-day conference, *Parishes in Transition*, in May 2008. The collection of essays in this volume are papers arising from or presented at that conference.

The essays here fall into a number of natural sections, each representing items on the agenda of any parish community or group that attempts to explore possible ways forward in the current climate of change and transition. There are two essays from an historical perspective, each of them in its own way showing how pastoral provision and its structures have changed through the millennia. Indeed they show how fluid and adaptive these were in former times, thus giving warrant and courage to those who will have to make radical changes in the very near future. They will also alert any community considering change to attend to the historical dimensions of its own existence and the need for sensitivity to its heritage and traditions.

Those who are engaged in the reordering of pastoral provision at parish or local level need to be attentive to current geographical, demographic, social and economic factors, as well as to the impact of information technology and its implications for

social networks and relationships. Again, two essays by geo-
graphers and a sociologist address these issues and provide a
template for others who will have to analyse and evaluate these
and similar factors in their own communities. Even though
there has been significant change in the economic situation of
the country in the short time since these papers were first delivered, they nevertheless indicate the type of analysis required if
one is to engage seriously with the realities of community life
and its future development.

In the last number of years, as the need for change has begun
to impact on church leadership, many dioceses have engaged in
a process of grouping or clustering parishes in order to make the
best use of their pastoral resources. This has provided the inspiration for most of the essays on the theological and canonical
dimensions of parish life and its reorganisation. Since the process
of grouping parishes together is not a new phenomenon, two
contributors from mainland Europe offer perspectives that have
been informed by experiences in Holland and Germany. Each of
these alerts us to important theological and canonical foundations that must guide any efforts at reform and renewal. Five
other essays, by Irish theologians, explore a contemporary vision
of parish, the theology and practicalities of clustering parishes,
liturgical provision as the number of ordained ministers declines sharply, the challenges facing the increasingly burdened
pastor and the canonical implications for governing parishes in
this changing environment. While there is no clear blue print for
the clustering of parishes, nor is there yet an adequately developed theological rationale for the process and the resulting
structures, nevertheless, it remains an important dimension of
the task of renewal to continue reflecting theologically on what
is being done and on what is being proposed because pragmatic
responses without sound theological foundations will not serve
the church well.

The final essays in the volume return to some practical considerations. Two sets of reflections from parish clusters, one
rural, the other urban, provide some indication of the variety of
new life and energy that communities have gained by working
in greater partnership. What they have to say offers a stimulus
and grounds for hope to any group of parishes entering into a
clustering arrangement. The last essay is on leadership, an essential
gift and service to any community or group that is to survive the

challenges of the moment. Leadership has always been a valued charism in the church, but it is one that has to be worked upon and which must be open to learning from good practice in other organisations. It is here that good theology and good practice have to meet.

It is hoped that the essays in this volume will provide some further enlightenment, impetus and encouragement for those already embarked on the process of renewal and reorganisation of parish life at this time of significant transition. There are many other dimensions to the task of renewal in need of urgent attention, but let these contributions suffice for the moment.

Eugene Duffy

CHAPTER ONE

The Irish Parish in Historical Perspective

Liam Irwin

This general introduction to the history of the parish and pastoral care in Ireland aims to provide a historical context for the discussion on how the future role and function of the parish might most fruitfully be developed. To range over such a lengthy time span and try to discuss such a complex subject, necessarily involves a very radical selection of material and quite broad generalisations. It is hoped that, however piecemeal such an approach inevitably is, it will at least show the complex and changing nature of pastoral care throughout Irish history and that the radical rethink which now seems necessary is not something that has to be seen as negative, to be feared or even perhaps regretted.

The difficulty of discovering how the early Irish church was structured and organised, and the often less than truly Christian tone of the scholarly debates on the issue, is discussed initially. The lack of clear information on how, if at all, pastoral care was provided for the laity is noted. The implications of the relatively late development of a formal parish structure in Ireland and the consequent impact on the church in the late medieval period is discussed. The impact of the Reformation and the resultant legal and social disabilities in the succeeding centuries are analysed. The forces that created and characterised the modern parish from the nineteenth century until the present day are then highlighted in the context of the challenges now facing that particular model.

The diocesan and parochial structural organisation of the church is derived essentially from the civil administration of the Roman Empire. The word parish comes ultimately from the Greek παροικια meaning literally 'beside (παρά) the house' (οικος) or, in a more modern idiom, the neighbourhood. In Latin the word was confused with *parochus* which was a term for a local official in the Roman provinces eventually becoming, as it remains, to mean the basic unit of a Christian community whose pastoral care is provided by the parish priest or pastor. The term diocese, from the Greek διοίκησις, originally meant the administrative territory of a city and serves to remind us that the first Christian communities were founded in cities, and the early Christian church was essentially an urban one. The liturgy was celebrated by the bishop and his clergy; the few faithful outside the cities went to the city or were visited from time to time by priests from there until the fourth century when there were village groups sufficiently large to be served by resident clergy. While these Christian communities were called *parochiae*, crucially there was no distinction between terms 'diocese' and 'parish' – both terms were used to describe the territory or district of the bishop. As late as the ninth century Pope Leo IV specifically wrote that the area of jurisdiction of a bishop was a parish.

The introduction of Christianity into Ireland continues to be a subject of debate among scholars, as indeed it appears to have been almost from the beginning when one examines the inconsistencies and contradictions in the Irish annals and the early lives of St Patrick. That there was already a significant Christian community in Ireland by the early fifth century is clear from the unimpeachable source of Prosper of Acquitane, who wrote that in 431 the Pope, Celestine, *Ad Scottos in Christum credentes ordinatus a papa Caelestina Palladius primus episcopus mittitur*. The decision to ordain the first bishop for the 'Irish believing in Christ' provides the clearest evidence for the arrival of Christianity in Ireland sometime in the fourth century and presumably well before the arrival of St Patrick. In terms of pastoral care for these Christians, the model, by then universal in the western church, of dioceses or parishes served by secular clergy was presumably introduced even if, as very likely, in an embryonic form. Further evidence in the annals, recording the arrival in Ireland in 439 of Auxilius, Secundinus and Iserninus[1] supports the assumption that there was a consistent Roman mission in the first half of the fifth century. The precise nature, as well as the extent and location, of Patrick's evangelisation remains uncertain but there seems no valid reason to question that it too conformed to the western system as practised in Britain, where Patrick was trained, financed and, it would appear, from where he was supervised.[2]

1. Recorded in both the Annals of Ulster and the Annals of Innisfallen.
2. His *Confessio* was written to defend himself against unspecified charges apparently made to his superiors in Britain.

While it is impossible to discover the extent to which a
parochial system was organised in Ireland, it seems clear that it
was overtaken, relatively quickly, by one based on monastic
paruchiae. There has been spirited debate among scholars in recent times on precisely what this system entailed. It has traditionally been seen as essentially a federation of geographically
dispersed monasteries but at least one scholar equates it simply
to the jurisdictional area of a bishop, similar in fact to the contemporary European concept of a 'parish' as outlined above.[3]
While there has been much discussion on the role of bishops in
the early Irish church, it has mostly been in the context of a discussion of the monastic churches and concerned with their
power *vis à vis* the abbots. The older model of a church exclusively based on the monasteries has certainly been modified by
recent scholarship. It is now accepted that the situation was
more complex, with churches independent of monasteries existing within *tuatha*, as well as episcopal and even minor proprietary churches also functioning to some extent.

It must be noted that there has been a regrettable lack of
interest in, or attention to, the issue of pastoral care in the work
of most academic historians. Where it has been the subject of
some investigation startlingly different conclusions have been
drawn. Richard Sharpe[4] has argued that Ireland had one of the
most comprehensive pastoral organisations in northern Europe,
while Colmán Etchingham[5] on the other hand claims that pastoral care was only provided for the *manaig*, a group whose pre-

---

3. For the principal arguments on this issue see, Kathleen Hughes, *The
Church in early Irish society* (London, 1966); Donnchadh Ó Corráin, 'The
early Irish churches: some aspects of organisation' in D. Ó Corráin (ed),
Irish Antiquity: essays and studies presented to Professor M. J. O'Kelly (Cork,
1981); Colmán Etchingham, *Church organisation in Ireland AD650 to 1000*
(Maynooth, 1999); Dáibhí Ó Cróinín, *Early Medieval Ireland* (Essex,
1995), idem, 'Review of Etchingham, *Church Organisation*' *Peritia*, 15
(2001), 413-20; Richard Sharpe, 'Some problems concerning the organisation of the church in early medieval Ireland' *Peritia*, 3 (1984), 230-70.
4. Richard Sharpe, 'Churches and communities in early medieval
Ireland: towards a pastoral model' in J. Blair and R. Sharpe (eds) *Pastoral
Care before the parish* (Leicester, 1992); idem, 'Some problems concerning
the organisation of the church.'
5. Colmán Etchingham, 'The early Irish church: some observations on
pastoral care and dues', *Ériu*, 42 (1991), 99-118; idem, 'Pastoral provision in the first millennium: a two-tier service?' in Elizabeth Fitzpatrick

cise composition and function are disputed but who may generally be classed as the lay tenants on monastic lands.

The literary evidence for this whole question, principally the annals, early Irish Law and various ecclesiastical documents, is difficult to interpret, which explains this divergence of views. Archaeologists have not been noticeably more successful in reaching a consensus either. A notable feature of many of the surviving early Christian stone churches is their small size. This has been interpreted by some scholars as indicating that the laity were excluded and by others that the church functioned merely as the sanctuary or sacristy (*Sanctuarium* or *Secretarium*) while the laity stood around outside or that only those receiving communion would enter the church (as appears to be indicated in the Life of St Columba). Certainly the facile assumption that the small size of churches can be equated with a lack of provision of pastoral care is not tenable.[6]

Whatever the precise situation had been prior to the twelfth century, the reform which began in 1111 at the synod of Raithbreasail brought about a fundamental change to the structure and organisation of the church in Ireland. The territorial framework of dioceses finalised at the synod of Kells/Mellifont in 1152 was to remain intact for the rest of the medieval period, and indeed is remarkably unchanged both in nomenclature and boundaries to the present day. Parish formation, on the other hand, appears to have been a much slower process and one which varied considerably between dioceses. More rapid progress was made in the Anglo-Norman areas where the establishment of manors went hand in hand with parochial development and the construction of parish churches.[7]

and Raymond Gillespie (eds) *The Parish in Medieval and Early Modern Ireland: Community, Territory and Building* (Dublin, 2006) 79-90; idem, *Church Organisation*.

6. Tadhg O'Keeffe, 'The built environment of local community worship between the late eleventh and early thirteenth centuries' in Fitzpatrick and Gillespie (eds), *Parish in Medieval and Early Modern Ireland*, 124-46; S. Ní Ghabhláin, 'Church and community in medieval Ireland: the diocese of Kilfenora', *JRSAI*, 125 (1995), 61-84; Tomás Ó Carragáin, 'Church buildings and pastoral care in early medieval Ireland' in Fitzpatrick and Gillespie (eds), *Parish in Medieval and Early Modern Ireland*, 91-123.

7. C.A. Empey, 'The Norman period: 1185-1500' in W. Nolan and T.G. McGrath (eds), *Tipperary: history and society* (Dublin, 1985), 83-6; A. J. Otway-Ruthven, 'Parochial development in the rural deanery of Skreen', *JRSAI*, 94 (1964), 111-22.

In Gaelic areas it would appear that the traditional *tuatha* formed the basis for parish boundaries and that progress was slower in the west of Ireland than elsewhere.[8] Many of the former monastic churches appear to have become the churches of the new parishes, while the termon lands became the property of the bishops and were farmed for them as tenants by clans of hereditary *coarbs* and *erenaghs*. A feature of the medieval church was the division, or perhaps more correctly, duality between the native Irish *inter Hibernicos* and the Anglo Normans *inter Anglicos* which was reflected particularly among the religious orders with divisions within houses or increasingly different houses, based on ethnicity. There was a strong hereditary factor, with the clergy coming largely from within clerical families. One of the frequent complaints made about their lifestyles related to their failure to wear clerical dress and having long hair and moustaches. In general, however, they have been given a favourable verdict from historians. While clerical celibacy was certainly not universally practised, it does not appear to have been regarded as a major problem. In the 15th century a Fermanagh priest, Fr Cathal Mac Manus, received praise for being a 'gem of purity and a turtle-dove of chastity' despite his fathering of at least twelve children.[9] Only very basic pastoral care would appear to have been provided: a report on Clogher cathedral in 1517 stated 'Mass is celebrated only on Sunday; one set of vestments; a wooden cross; a chalice; one bell'. In general there was better provision and practice in urban and anglicised areas than in Gaelic areas. There is no evidence of anti-papal feeling and little anti-clericalism. In general the main determinant of the parish in the middle ages was the issue of revenue, whether from tithes, dues and fees for marriages and burials rather than any strong sense of what was best for the pastoral care of the parishioners.[10]

The widespread assumption that 'protestantism' was introduced to Ireland by Henry VIII is of course based on a misunderstanding of the nature of Henry's schism while the Lutheran

8. Patrick Nugent, 'The dynamics of parish formation in high medieval and late medieval Clare' in Fitzpatrick and Gillespie (eds), *Parish in Medieval and Early Modern Ireland, 186-208;* K.W. Nicholls. 'Rectory, vicarage and parish in the western Irish dioceses', *JRSAI*, 101 (1971), 53-84.
9. John Watt, *The Church in Medieval Ireland* (Dublin, 1972), 186.
10. K.W. Nicholls, *Gaelic and Gaelicised Ireland in the Middle Ages* (Dublin, 2003) chapter 5; Watt, *Church in Medieval Ireland*, chapter 6.

inspired changes of his successor Edward VI were too brief and geographically limited to have any impact. Only when the equally brief restoration of links with Rome under Mary I ended with the accession of Elizabeth I did the enduring reformation of Anglicanism become established. This led to a takeover of the existing parochial structure by the Church of Ireland. Historians such as Corish and Whelan argue that this meant that Catholics had to establish a new infrastructure[11] while Duffy, for example, claims that there was simply a continuation of the medieval organisation.[12] Certainly the Council of Trent placed strong emphasis on the parish while the difficult conditions and shortage of priests necessitated that changes be made to suit particular circumstances. This period also saw a divergence within Catholicism in Ireland between the Old English who overwhelmingly adopted the Tridentine reform programme while the majority of the Gaelic Irish appear to have retained much of the forms and trappings of medieval practices.[13] This divergence became more acute in the seventeenth century particularly during the Confederation of Kilkenny in the 1640s where differing political agendas intensified the divisions.[14] The need for unity to cope with the pressures on Catholicism during the Cromwellian era of the 1650s healed this rift somewhat. This was a particularly challenging period for the provision of pastoral care by the bishops and clergy and in most areas this had to be done without a

11. P. J. Corish, *The Catholic Community in the seventeenth and eighteenth centuries* (Dublin, 1981) 58-9; Kevin Whelan, 'The Catholic parish, the Catholic chapel and village development in Ireland' in *Irish Geography*, 16, (1983) 1-15.

12. P. J. Duffy, 'The shape of the parish' in Fitzpatrick and Gillespie (eds) *The Parish in Medieval and Early Modern Ireland*, 37.

13. Tadhg ÓhAnnracháin, 'A typical anomaly? The Success of the Irish Counter-Reformation' in Howard Clarke and Judith Devlin (eds) *European Encounters: Essays in Memory of Albert Lovett* (Dublin, 2003), 78-94; Colm Lennon, 'The Counter-Reformation in Ireland 1542-1641' in C. Brady, & R. Gillespie, (eds) *Natives and Newcomers* (Dublin, 1986), 75-92.

14. Tadhg Ó hAnnracháin, 'Disrupted and Disruptive: Continental Influence on the Confederate Catholics of Ireland' in Alan MacInnes and Jane Ohlmeyer (eds) *The Stuart Kingdoms in the Seventeenth Century* (Dublin, 2002), 135-50; idem, 'Conflicting loyalties, conflicted rebels: political and religious allegiance among the Confederate Catholics of Ireland', *English Historical Review*, 119 (2004) 851-72.

functioning parochial structure. It should be noted, however, that the laity were free from the risk of penalty from not attending Anglican church services as no Act of Uniformity was in operation.[15]

The Restoration period was one of toleration and recovery for the Catholic Church: the execution of Archbishop Oliver Plunkett was uncharacteristic of the period, being a by product of the anti-Catholic hysteria of the Popish Plot scare in England. That Catholics felt secure in this period is shown by the clause on religious liberty in the Treaty of Limerick in 1691 which sought a guarantee of continuation of the liberty enjoyed under Charles II. This of course was a disastrous miscalculation as such freedom had only been at the discretion of the monarch and had no legal basis. This loophole was exploited to the full in the eighteenth century by the Irish Parliament to introduce the wide series of anti-Catholic legislation, commonly referred to as the 'penal laws'.[16]

However, the main focus of these laws was directed against the property and social position of Catholics rather than their religious practice. While bishops and regular clergy were banished the secular clergy who registered, as required in 1704, were free to minister in their respective parishes, though amending legislation in 1709 made their position less secure. In theory, given the banishment of the bishops, the absence of seminaries and the prohibition against education abroad, eventually there would be no parochial clergy left but, if such a result was ever intended, it was tacitly abandoned. There is no evidence of any sustained attempt at conversion nor, it can be argued, at persecution of the laity for actually practising their religion. The popular belief that Mass had to be said in secret locations, such as Mass rocks, has no basis in reality; in so far as popular memory may contain some semblance of historical truth, shortage of churches rather than persecution is the explanation. Most parishes had Mass houses, which varied in size and quality and in general im-

---

15. The best account of this period is P.J. Corish, 'The Cromwellian regime, 1650-60' in T. W. Moody, F. X. Martin & F. J. Byrne (eds) *A New History of Ireland*, vol III, (Oxford, 1976), 353-86.

16. P.J. Corish, *The Catholic Community in the seventeenth and eighteenth centuries* (Dublin, 1981).

17. Maureen Wall, *The Penal Laws, 1691-1760* (Dundalk, 1967) is still the most useful summary of this subject.

proved as the century progressed.[17] It is useful to recall that Carolan, who died as early as 1738, often sang and played the harp at Mass. Parish boundaries, in some areas, do appear to have undergone change in the period, particularly the creation of larger units.

There was also, ironically in light of the absence of seminaries, an over supply of priests and, in particular, candidates for the priesthood which led to the 1742 rescript to the Irish Bishops from the Holy See setting a limit of 12 ordinations in each diocese in any one year. This appears to have been motivated both by concern at the quality of the seminarians, the practice of ordination before formation and training and the burden that too many priests would place on a largely impoverished Catholic population. Further damage was done in 1751 when *Propaganda Fide* forbad the admission of any further novices into any Irish House of regular clergy, a decision which severely damaged all the orders.[18] It is clear that it was poverty rather than persecution which was the main problem faced by the Catholic Church in Ireland during these centuries.

One of the most significant changes in the nineteenth century was the increase in the number of priests, facilitated initially by the opening of St Patrick's College, Maynooth in 1795. In 1800 there were 1,850 priests in Ireland; this figure had risen to 2,150 by 1840, to 3,000 by 1860 and to 3,700 in 1900. The large increase in the post-famine period coincided with a substantial fall in population so that the ratio of priests to people increased even more dramatically from one priest for every 2,100 Catholics in 1800 to one priest for every 900 by the end of the century. The relationship between priest and people had been cemented in the campaigns for Catholic emancipation and the abolition of tithe and was further strengthened in the Land War and the Repeal and Home Rule campaigns, in which the clergy often played significant leadership roles. This was accompanied by significant changes in the fabric, structures and role of the parish. New churches were built at an increasing rate and in ever more impressive materials and styles ranging from simple barn, t-shaped and cruciform examples to large neo-Gothic and Hiberno-Romanesque structures. With the increased population chapel villages grew up around churches erected in new locations.

---

18. Hugh Fenning, *The undoing of the Friars of Ireland: a study of the novitiate question in the eighteenth century* (Brussels, 1972).

Large parochial houses began to be built and with the advent of national schools, a greater emphasis on the parish as a unit began to emerge.

There has been much debate on the so-called 'Devotional Revolution' in the post-famine Irish church. This concept was originally proposed by the American historian Emmet Larkin[19] and supported by scholars such as Seán Connolly[20] and David Millar. It argued that the Irish only became consistently practicing Catholics after the famine and Millar claimed that average Mass attendance in the pre-famine period had been as low as 40% on average.[21] This thesis has been subjected to detailed and in some cases devastating criticism by Desmond J. Keenan, Donal Kerr and Thomas G. McGrath.[22] It now seems clear that many of the devotional practices were already well established before the famine but their popularity and geographical extent was increased in the later nineteenth century.

The parish in twentieth-century Ireland became a central and pivotal feature of Irish life. Apart from its pre-eminent role in the pastoral care and the religious life of the people, it took on a wider one of vital social significance. People's sense of identity came to be increasingly associated with their parish, reinforcing the traditional Irish attachment to locality. Sunday Mass in the parish church was the main meeting place for most rural dwellers, where news and gossip were exchanged, social events arranged and community activities discussed. The construction of parish halls, providing a venue for new social and cultural organisations such as Muintir na Tíre, Macra na Feirme, the IFA

---

19. Emmet Larkin, 'The Devotional Revolution in Ireland, 1850-75' *American Historical Review*, lxxvii (1972), reprinted in *The Historical Dimensions of Irish Catholicism* (New York, 1981).

20. Seán Connolly, *Religion and Society in Nineteenth-Century Ireland* (Dundalk, 1985).

21. D. W. Millar, 'Irish Catholicism and the Great Famine', *Journal of Social History*, vol. ix, no 1 (1975), 81-98.

22. Desmond Keenan, *The Catholic Church in Nineteenth-Century Ireland: A Sociological Study* (Dublin, 1983); D.A. Kerr, *Peel, Priests and Politics: Sir Robert Peel's Administration and the Roman Catholic Church in Ireland 1841-6* (Oxford, 1982); Thomas G. McGrath, 'The Tridentine Evolution of Modern Irish Catholicism: A Re-examination of the "Devotional Revolution" Thesis,' in Réamonn Ó Muirí (ed), *Irish Church History Today* (Armagh, 1991), 84–99.

and the ICA increased its centrality in the life of the people. The GAA also played a formative role in this regard, with its structure firmly based on the parish unit.[23]

The priests both benefitted from and became prisoners of this reality. High social standing and deference were paid for, in terms of providing community leadership, advice and responsibility for much tedious organisational detail which had little direct relevance to their primary pastoral role. Even before the decline in religious vocations made some change in this dynamic inevitable, a clear shift had begun to occur in this social and perhaps mental world. More fundamental change is certain to occur and the challenge facing the church in Ireland is how to plan for, adapt to, and even benefit from this inevitability. Historians do not claim that the past provides answers but we suggest that an understanding of the collective experience of our predecessors is a valuable, indeed indispensible, guide to help plan for the future. Even where that future seems uncertain or possibly threatening, history can point to the long experience of survival, adaptation to circumstances and, not least, proud achievement, which above all characterise the story of the Catholic Church in Ireland and thereby boost morale in whatever difficult and challenging decisions may lie ahead.

---

23. Kevin Whelan, 'The Catholic parish, the Catholic chapel and village development in Ireland'. *Irish Geography*, xv (1983) 1-16; W. J. Smith, 'Continuity and change in the territorial organisation of Irish rural communities', *Maynooth Review*, vol 1, no 1 (1975), 51-78.

CHAPTER TWO

Early Irish priests and their areas of ministry AD 700-900

Catherine Swift

Sometime before the year 725 AD, when Charles Martel was beginning to put together the series of European conquests which resulted eventually in the Carolingian empire, and the Venerable Bede was working away in the tranquillity of the library at Jarrow, a great compilation of church law was put together by two churchmen from either end of the Gaelic-speaking world. Their names were Ruben of Dair-inis (on the river Blackwater, north-west of Youghal) and Cú Chuimne of Iona (at the central crossing point of the Hebridean sea-lanes). Their massive work consisted of 67 books arranged according to topic, beginning with a discussion of the clerical grades of bishop, priest and deacon and following this with consideration of issues such as fasting, prayers, rules of burial and less obviously Christian topics such as kingship, lot-casting, rules of inheritance, hospitality, leadership of barbarians and curses. Each book was divided into short paragraphs (entitled chapters), consisting of quotations or paraphrases of a variety of sources including both the Old and New Testament, the writings of early church fathers such as Augustine or Jerome and canon laws taken from various church synods held in the Middle East, Africa and France.

Some of the quotations in these various chapters are attributed to an 'Irish synod' but, unfortunately, no further details are given. We cannot tell, therefore, how many 'Irish synods' were involved, nor where they were held and we have no idea of the particular circumstances which caused them to be called. We do know, however, from a story in one of the early Lives of St Brigid, that at least some synods were held at the communal festivities known as *óenaig*. These were seasonal assemblies or fairs at which tenants offered up their animals and foodstuffs as rent; horsemen, chariot-drivers and sporting enthusiasts came together to run races and play games; kings and lords fought over the minutiae of political alliances; poets and musicians recited their latest compositions; merchants traded foreign goods and young men sought wives.[1] The deliberations of the churchmen, therefore, were but one strand in the complex web of negotiations and contracts which bound together early Irish society.

One quotation from an 'Irish synod' is listed in the second book of the collection, entitled *On presbyters and priests*. Chapter 25 deals with correct punishment to be meted out to priests who are absent from their churches:

> *An Irish synod* decrees that a priest should refrain from being away from (his) church for a whole day; if for two days, he must do penance for seven days on bread and water; if however a dead man should be brought to the church and he is absent, he must do penance for he owes compensation to the dead man. *Same source*: If he should be absent one Sunday from church he does penance for twenty days on bread and water; if absent for two or three, he should be removed from the honour of his grade.[2]

This is a relatively rare example of concern about a priest's ministry in this particular source. The other twenty-six chapters in the book concern the nature of the priest's role, their Old Testament precursors, the nature of sacrifice, the rituals of ordination and (by far the greatest area of concern with ten separate chapters), the rules governing clerical income. The emphasis on the dead in the quotation above is further reflected in the fact that another three chapters deal with the inner meaning of the last rites, the entitlement of a priest to a mortuary due and the fact that this is capped at a maximum of one milch cow. There is also an interesting chapter (again attributed to an Irish synod) on the nature of the church's sacramental role:

> An Irish synod: Now the Church offers in many kinds to the Lord, first through it, in itself, secondly through commemoration of Jesus Christ, who says 'Do this in memory of me' and thirdly through the souls of the dead.[3]

1. Catherine Swift, 'Óenach Tailten, the Blackwater valley and the Uí Néill kings of Tara' in *Seanchas: studies in early and medieval Irish archaeology, history and literature in honour of Francis J. Byrne*, ed. A. P. Smyth (Dublin: Four Courts Press 2000), 116-118.

2. Hermann Wasserschleben, *Die Irische Kanonensammlung* (Darmstadt: Scientia Verlag Aalen, 1966), 19.

3. Wasserschleben, *Kanonensammlung*, 14-15, (59).

Priestly concern for the dead in this early period of Irish Christianity should be understood in the light of contemporary social norms, for recent research has begun to reveal the limited extent of church authority over burial at this time. Archaeological excavation has made it clear that not everybody was buried in Christian graveyards and has indicated how some much older monuments, of pre-Christian date, continued to be used on occasion. In Knoxspark in Sligo, for example, two cairns containing Iron Age cremations were surrounded by some hundred extended inhumations with heads orientated to the west. At least one of these burials was dated by the excavator to between the eighth and tenth centuries AD.[4] At Ballymacaward in Donegal five slab-lined graves of the fifth century AD were inserted into a cairn of prehistoric date while other inhumations, in unprotected graves, were inserted into the same monument in the seventh century AD.[5] Working from textual sources, Elizabeth O'Brien has argued that the practice of Christian burial around churches was still only making gradual headway in Ireland during the eighth and ninth centuries against a more widespread system of kin-based secular cemeteries.[6] In such a context, it makes sense that the eighth-century canon lawyers would stress the particular value attached to Christian burial and emphasise the concern felt by church authorities and their continuing prayers for the dead.

In yet a third chapter from *On presbyters and priests*, the distinction is drawn between the sacramental role of priests and bishops and emphasis is laid on their mutual roles in celebrating the Eucharist and in preaching. Here the authority cited is the sixth-century Spanish churchman Isidore of Seville whose work was held in particularly high esteem by the Irish church. J. N. Hillgarth has pointed out that while *De officiis* and *Sententiae* are the most frequently cited of Isidore's works, *Quaestiones, Epistola*

4. Charles Mount, 'The promontory fort, inhumation cemetery and sub-rectangular enclosure at Knoxspark, Co.Sligo', *A celebration of Sligo: first essays for the Sligo Field Club*, ed. M. A. Timoney (Carrick-on-Shannon: Sligo Field Club 2002), 103-116.

5. Elizabeth O'Brien, 'Ballymacaward', *Excavations* 1998, ed. I. Bennett (Dublin: Wordwell Press, 2000), 26-7

6. Elizabeth O'Brien, 'Pagan and Christian burial in Ireland during the first millennium AD: continuity and change', *The early church in Wales and the West*, eds N. Edwards & A. Lane (Oxford: Oxbow Books, 1992), 130-7.

ad Massonam, Chronica and the *Etymologiae* are all quoted at some stage by Ruben and Cú Chuimne.[7]

> *Isidore* says about priests: The management of the ministry of God is entrusted to them just as indeed to bishops. For they preside over the church of Christ and in arranging of the divine body and blood, they are partners with bishops, just as in the apostolic doctrine and in the office of preaching; only the higher authority required for the ordination and consecration of priests is reserved etc ... (sic).[8]

The evidence for the duties and functions of priests and their role in Irish society is not limited to *On presbyters and priests* but can also be found scattered through other books within the collection. In Book 21, for example, *On judgement*, a priest is identified as a suitable person to be a judge, along with fourteen other social categories including a bishop, a king, a legal scholar, a kinsman (on issues concerning his own kin), a craftsman (on matters pertaining to his own craft), the old, the poor and the wise.[9] This incidental material dealing with the social role of priests is widely scattered throughout the work, however, and full consideration of it will probably have to be deferred until the forthcoming edition and translation of the entirety of Ruben and Cú Chuimne's compilation by Roy Flechner.

The text which provides the closest parallels to *On presbyters and priests* is a law tract written in Old Irish entitled *Ríagal Phátraic*. It is also of approximately similar date, having been dated to the eighth century on the basis of its language. There are slightly different variants in the different manuscripts but I quote here the translations offered in the most recent discussion of its pastoral provisions:

> He selects a surety on their behalf from the *manaig* of each church which is his responsibility with respect to a proper stipend, comprising the price of baptism, the due of communion and of chanting the requiem of all the *manaig*, both the living and the dead and Mass every Sunday and every chief solemnity and every chief festival and celebration of each canonical hour and singing the three fifties [i.e. the psalms]

7. J. N. Hillgarth, 'Visigothic Spain and Ireland in the seventh century,' *Peritia* 3 (1984), 9, fn 4.

8. Wasserschleben, '*Kanonensammlung*,' 13 (§ 4).

9. Wasserschleben, '*Kanonensammlung*,' 62-3 (§ 2).

every canonical hour unless instruction or spiritual direction
i.e. unction and baptism prevent him.[10]

The exact definition of the *manaig* is, as discussed elsewhere
in this volume, at the root of current debates about the extent to
which all Irish people were practising Christians at this stage.[11]
Whatever the size of the congregation, this extract makes it clear
that a priest might have responsibility for more than one church
('the *manaig* of each church which is his responsibility'.) For
these churches, weekly celebration of the Eucharist on Sundays
in addition to Masses on feast-days was considered the norm.
This extract also redresses the balance left missing from the quotations already considered in that it includes baptism as one of
the key duties of the priest. Provisions in early Irish penitentials
also make it clear that baptism was considered a key duty of the
clergy – if a child died without having been baptised and the
fault lay with the cleric involved, he must do penance on bread
and water for six months (if he was not of the same locality) or a
year (if he was).[12]

Requiring the priest to recite the entirety of the Psalms every
canonical hour (as is the literal meaning of the Irish in *Ríagal
Phátraic*) is rather more difficult to envisage. Our sources specify
that between six and eight canonical hours were celebrated in
any twenty-four hour period.[13] The Rule of Monks (*Regula
Monachorum*) attributed to St Columbanus has a lengthy discussion of the number of psalms which it was reasonable to ask a
religious community to perform and specifies that shorter summer nights require a smaller number otherwise 'it causes not so
much weariness as exhaustion'.[14] Though the Latin is difficult to
understand precisely, the rule appears to be 75 psalms or half

---

10. Colmán Etchingham, *Church organization in Ireland AD 650 to 1000*
(Maynooth: Laigin Press, 1999), 253-4, translating Daniel Binchy, *Corpus
Iuris Hibernici* (Dublin: Dublin Institute for Advanced Studies, 1979),
2130:23-8.
11. See Liam Irwin, 'The Irish Parish in Historical Perspective', in this
volume.
12. Ludwig Bieler (ed), *The Irish Penitentials, Scriptores Latini Hiberniae*,
(Dublin: Dublin Institute for Advanced Studies, 1963), 92 § 48, 116 § 33,
224 § 11.2
13. *Dictionary of the Irish Language* T (Dublin: Royal Irish Academy,
1913-76), 275 (henceforth DIL).
14. G. S. M. Walker, *Sancti Columbani Opera Scriptores Latini Hiberniae* 2
(Dublin: Dublin Institute for Advanced Studies, 1954) 128-133.

the Psalter on Saturday and Sunday nights between November and January with 36 psalms on other nights of the week. These decrease to 36 psalms on weekend nights around the time of the summer equinox and 24 on other nights. Even this seems something of a tall order. At the very most, it seems unlikely that a priest would be required to do more than recite the entire 150 psalms in any given 24-hour period and indeed, it may be more plausible to visualise him chanting a much smaller number.

In a provision that seems remarkably relevant to modern-day Ireland, the author of *Ríagal Phátraic* goes on to consider the problems posed by a possible lack of available clergy:

> If indeed, it be on account of the scarcity of ordained men in the communities, [it is proper?] that there be three churches or four in the cure of each ordained man, provided that he can offer communion and baptism for the souls of all and Mass on solemn days and feast-days on their altars.[15]

The word translated here as 'cure' is *cubus* – literally the 'conscience' of the priest and the word identified as the neutral-sounding 'communities' is *tuatha*, often translated as kingdoms or (in older translations) as tribes. Here it seems to be being used as a general word for secular society as a whole. As I understand this provision, the idea is that the three or four churches must be geographically close in order to allow the priest to travel from one to another and still celebrate Sunday Mass in each. Colmán Etchingham, in contrast, understands this to imply that 'Mass and communion – and perhaps pastoral services in general – would not necessarily be offered every Sunday but on a priestly visitation at the time of the great feast-days'.[16]

Etchingham's interpretation seems to me to be at odds with the stipulation in the Latin canon laws discussed above, namely that a priest who was missing from his church on Sunday must do penance for twenty days and that, if it happened on a regular basis, he should demoted from his status as priest. This could hardly be articulated as a general rule if Mass was only celebrated irregularly at the great feast-days. It is also counter-intuitive – since the priest must still get to all four, he could hardly offer Mass on feast-days unless the churches were within easy reach

---

15. Etchingham, *Church organization*, 254, translating Binchy *Corpus* 2130:28-31
16. Etchingham, *Church organization*, 254.

of one another. The only way in which Etchingham's model would work would be if the priest was only offering Mass in one church per single 'great feast-day'. Such a severely limited system of pastoral care is nowhere attested in our sources and seems to be incompatible with the rules concerning baptism and burial mentioned above which require a priest to be easily available to the laity at short notice.

It is clear from *Ríagal Phátraic* itself that within the confines of a single *tuath*-kingdom, there would be a number of different churches within contemporary use:

> Any church, of the small churches of the *tuath* as well as the great churches, in which there is an ordained man, owes the stipend of his order i.e. a house and a precinct [?] and a bed and clothing and food which may suffice him without exemption, without neglect of anything that is in the power of the church i.e. a bushel of corn with its condiment and a milch cow every quarter and food at the festivals.[17]

The duty here is from the church authorities to the individual priest. Ruben and Cú Chuimne cite Old Testament precedent to the effect that, just as Aaron was given his vestments by Moses and others, so too should the necessities required by an Irish priest be provided by his *princeps* or church superior.[18] This word *princeps* is somewhat ambiguous as its literal meaning 'leader' does not specify whether we are talking about episcopal or monastic superiors and it can, in fact, be used of both, particularly in their role as governors and controllers of economic resources.[19] It therefore seems reasonable to assume that, just as with the contemporary Frankish and Anglo-Saxon churches, the authority to appoint priests could fluctuate between the two different systems of authority, depending on the relative status and power attached to each in a specific area.[20]

---

17. Etchingham, *Church organization*, 252-3 translating Binchy, *Corpus*, 2130: 19-23

18. Wasserschleben, *Kanonensamlung*, 15 (§ 11). I am grateful to Dr Jessie Rogers for identifying the source of this statement as Exodus 28:esp vv 1-3.

19. Etchingham, *Church organization*, 50-59

20. *Les Canons des conciles mérovingiens (VI-VII siècles)*, ed. J. Gaudemet & B. Basdevant, Sources Chrétiennes 353 (Paris 1989), I 113, 219, 271; John Steane, *The archaeology of medieval England and Wales* (University of Georgia Press 1985), 82.

Previous discussion of this paragraph has concentrated on the precise nature of the great churches (*móreclais*) and here I would agree with Richard Sharpe that the most likely explanation is that this phrase refers to the larger ecclesiastical settlements which in many (most?) cases would be monasteries or have a monastic component.[21] I would understand this rule to state that a priest, whether or not he was living within a community of professed religious, is always entitled to the wage proper to his status. That wage appears to be allocated to him from the tithes of the faithful rendered to the church authorities (and subsequently transmitted to the individual cleric) but it also would seem to have included items such as the mortuary due paid directly by the bereaved to the man officiating at the burial.

The key point for the discussion here, however, is that both the small churches (*mineclais*) and the great churches (*móreclais*) are given in the plural whereas *tuath* is used in the singular. In other words, the author of *Ríagal Phátraic* would appear to be describing a norm in which there would be a number of priests operating at any one time within a single *tuath*. There is nothing problematic, therefore, in assuming that the three or four churches which might represent the responsibility of one individual would all have been located within the boundaries of a single *tuath*-kingdom.

If a *móreclais* should be considered as a large ecclesiastical community, what then was a *mineclais* or small church? The seventh-century Bishop Tírechán from north Mayo, who wrote a retrospective account of journeys by St Patrick across Ireland, makes it clear that many churches in his day were headed by secular clergy of various grades. In his account of the saint's activities in the region of modern-day Roscommon, for example, Tírechán identified churches where Patrick was thought to have left bishops, others where he left priests, still others deacons and even, in more remote and poorer districts, *barbari* (barbarians) without any clerical grade at all.[22] As a general rule, Tírechán's

21. Richard Sharpe, 'Some problems concerning the organization of the church in early medieval Ireland', *Peritia* 3 (1984), 260. For examples of monastic establishments attached to episcopal settlements, see C. Etchingham 'The idea of monastic austerity in early Ireland', *Luxury and austerity* ed. J. Hill & C. Lennon (Dublin: University College Dublin Press, 1999), 14-29

22. Ludwig Bieler, *The Patrician texts in the Book of Armagh*, *Scriptores Latini Hiberniae* 10 (Dublin: Dublin Institute for Advanced Studies, 1979), 138 (§19), 140 (§20, §23) 140 (§ 27) 144 (§28, 29).

arrangement appears to list one church per individual community or region while the status of the cleric left behind reflects
the political power of the community in which he was based –
large over-kingdoms had episcopal or even arch-episcopal churches
while smaller kingdoms had churches headed by priests or deacons.[23]

Since Tírechán is only concerned to identify churches associated with the cult of Patrick, we cannot assume from his account
that he is visualising a system whereby there is only one functioning church per region. In fact, he makes it clear that this is
not the case for in some of his summary accounts of Patrick's activities, he lists multiple foundations associated with a single
district: 'From Mag Tochuir, he [Patrick] came to Dul Ocheni
and built seven churches there.'[24]

The most detailed account of an individual church settlement in this work is that of Tírechán's own church by the western banks of the River Moy. He describes this as *aeclessia magna
Patricii*, 'the great church of Patrick' and identifies it as the location of 'the wood of Fochloth' from which the call had gone
forth to persuade the saint to leave his family and take up his
Christian mission in Ireland. It was also the location of Patrick's
celebration of his second Easter in Ireland and indeed, the focus
of Tírechán's entire work is the description of Patrick's travels
from the *aeclessia magna Patricii* of Meath[25] where Patrick con-
verted the Uí Néill rulers of Tara to the *aeclessia magna Patricii* of
north Mayo.

Tírechán's description of the site, though short, makes it
clear that it was composed of a number of different elements. It
held the relics of the first bishop appointed by Patrick, St Mucneus,
as well as the 'seven books of law' donated to Mucneus at the time
of his ordination. This was the Heptateuch or the first seven books
of the Old Testament used by Irish canonists as their primary
source of inspiration and it seems that Tírechán's church also functioned as a centre for legal learning and a clerical court.

There were also satellite churches in the near vicinity including *Cell Róe Mór* where Patrick fought with pagan druids and

23. A detailed discussion of the evidence for this proposition is put forward in my D Phil thesis: Catherine Swift, *The social and ecclesiastical
background to the treatment of the Connachta in Tírechán's seventh-century
Collectanea* (Oxford 1994)
24.Bieler, *Patrician texts*, (§48)
25. Now Donaghpatrick between Kells and Navan.

which later became the church of Macc Ercae, the place of two female saints which later became *Cell Forgland* and what Tírechán describes as an 'earthen church' (possibly originally a prehistoric monument) on the ceremonial assembly site of the local rulers. In addition, Tírechán specifies that there was another church owned by the community, on a peninsula guarding the crossing of the Moy at Bartragh and a free-standing cross which seems to have been the focus of a major cemetery. These various sites were located in a scattered penumbra around the episcopal church proper and analysis of the evidence for their placenames suggests that they occupied some ten square miles.[26]

It is clear that in cases of settlements headed by bishops and over-bishops, churchmen with various roles were, at the very least, closely associated with the church claiming episcopal authority. Tírechán does not specify whether, in the case of his own settlement, these subordinate churches were manned by secular or monastic clergy and we should, perhaps, envisage a mixed community involving both. The church associated with the female saints should probably be understood as an establishment for female religious for Ruben and Cú Chuimne specify that such communities were under the direct control of the local bishop.[27] Equally, however, the distinctive nature of the placenames associated with each individual would imply that their homes and churches were dispersed across a wider landscape rather than existing in nucleated proximity to a central church.[28]

Thus the domestic arrangements of Tírechán's own episcopal establishment conforms to the specification in *Ríagal Phátraic* that each priest is entitled to his house (*tech*) and precinct or yard (*airlise*).[29] In terms of domestic arrangements, then, it appears that the early Irish secular clergy normally lived apart as individuals rather than, as in Merovingian France or early

---

26. Swift, *Connachta*, 317-340.
27. Wasserschleben, *Kanonensammlung* 114 (§14).
28. Catherine Swift, 'Forts and fields: a study of monastic towns in seventh and eighth-century Ireland', *Journal of Irish Archaeology* 9 (1998), 105-126.
29. *Airlise* is identified in Ó Clery's Irish glossary (DIL A 226) as a synonym for *garrdha*, a loan from Old Norse *garð*. This has been identified by Patrick Wallace as the word for the house plot (with vegetable gardens) surrounding individual dwellings in Hiberno-Norse cities. Patrick Wallace, '*Garrda* and *airbeada*: the plot thickens in Viking Dublin', *Seanchas*, ed. A. P. Smyth (Dublin: Four Courts 2000), 261-3.

Rome, as members of an episcopal household. Rules concerning a priest's right to labour from his congregation also stress the separate nature of his establishment: e.g. a standard's day ploughing each year and its seed and corn-land as well as a half measure of clothing – was due to each *fer gráid* (ordained man – literally man of rank) from members of his congregation.[30] The title *fer gráid* here comes from the usage of Pope Gregory the Great who, in his work *The Book of Pastoral Rule* written c. 590, identifies priests with the Latin word *ordo* or rank.[31]

An interesting insight into the problems that such a dispersed clergy might pose to church authorities is indicated in the First Synod of St Patrick which decreed that a British cleric should not be allowed minister without some form of letter granting permission 'even though he lives amongst the lay population'. Elsewhere in the same text, this is elevated into a general rule – no *clericus vagus* 'wandering cleric' should be allowed to settle amongst lay people.[32] At the same time, it is clear that in reality priests did in fact operate independently to a great extent – for other rules from the same source state:

> If a priest has built a church, he shall not offer the holy sacrifice in it before he has his bishop (*pontifex*) come to consecrate it for so it is proper.
>
> If a newcomer joins a community, he shall not baptise or offer the holy sacrifice or consecrate or build a church until he receives permission from the bishop (*episcopus*). One who looks to laymen for permission shall be a stranger.
>
> Any cleric who is a newcomer in a bishop's community is not allowed to baptise or to offer the holy sacrifice or to perform any functions; if he does not abide by this, he shall be excommunicated.[33]

It is an oft repeated precept in legal scholarship that if a law is passed on a frequent basis, it implies not only that the authorities want to enforce it but also that they are having trouble in so doing. The fact that this rule is repeated three times within the

---

30. Binchy, *Corpus*, 2130:31-3.
31. Bruno Judic, *Grégoire le Grand: Règle Pastorale Tome I* (Paris: Les éditions du Cerf, 1992), 68. Gregory is quoted in *On presbyters and priests*, Wasserschleben, *Kanonensammlung* 13 (§5).
32. Bieler, *Penitentials* 54 (§3), 58 (§ 33).
33. Bieler, *Penitentials* 56 (§23), 58 (§ 24), (§ 27).

single text of the First Synod is a clear pointer to the fact that priests enjoyed a good deal of *de facto* independence from episcopal authority. The word translated by Bieler as 'community' is the Latin *plebs* or people and this has generally been held to be the equivalent of the vernacular *tuath* or kingdom.[34] It seems clear from these provisions that the priests, while under the jurisdiction and authority of their bishops, lived apart from them and within the lay community, just as Irish priests and secular clergy do today. This goes some way to explaining the concern, expressed in two different penitentials, that a *clericus plebis* (churchman of the *tuath*) should not be mourned with *bardigium/bardicatio* – two Latin loan words which appear to be calques on the native Irish word *bairdne* – or bardic poems. Anyone reciting such poems to mark the death of a priest is condemned by the canonists to twenty days fasting on bread and water. While this looks harsh, it is in fact less than half the penalty for mourning a lay person in the same way – which implies that the authors felt it reasonable, though reprehensible, that the local priest would be honoured by his congregation in this manner.[35]

In short, examining the different sources from the seventh and eighth centuries, one must infer that the *mineclais* or small churches of *Ríagal Phátraic* were those of the secular clergy, living apart from other professed religious or episcopal authorities, amongst the ordinary people of the *tuath*. It seems logical therefore, that the three or four churches which might be on the conscience of an ordained man would, in many instances, belong to this category. What remains to be explored is the precise size of the individual *tuatha* and what this might imply for the extent of pastoral provision in early Ireland.

Uraicecht Becc is a legal text which, like the others considered here, has been dated to the eighth century although the most recent commentator, Liam Breatnach, suggests a rather wider dating range, extending from the eighth up to the early tenth century.[36] In this, the king of a single *tuath* is identified as one who has access

---

34. Kathleen Hughes, *The church in early Irish society* (London: Methuen, 1966), 50; Thomas Charles-Edwards, *Early Irish and Welsh kinship* (Oxford: Oxford University Press, 1993) 138, 143; Etchingham, *Church Organisation*, 134-142.

35. Bieler, *Penitentials*, 162 (§ 28), 230 (§6.4).

36. Liam Breathnach, *A companion to the Corpus Iuris Hibernici* (Dublin: Dublin Institute for Advanced Studies 2005), 316.

to an army of seven hundred warriors, and subsequent commentators have added the gloss that this figure represents the sum
total of the king's clients.[37] If one assumes that the bulk of these
warriors are likely to have had wives and families, we are left
with a *tuath*-population in the region of 1400 adults. If we include the possibility that the warriors may have had adult children who were not themselves clients and the various categories
of unfree adult who were not entitled to be clients and who are
classified under various headings as *fuidir*, *mug*, *sen-cléithe* or in
the case of females, *cumal* and *ancilla*, we end up with rough ap-
proximations of 2000 to 3000 adults within the average *tuath*.
This is probably a grossly minimalist figure, assuming as it does
that all free males who were blacksmiths, chariot-builders, poets,
lawyers, historians and merchants were also available and qualified to hold arms. Still, even given all the necessary caveats, it is
an interesting figure to bear in mind when trying to evaluate
Ríagal Phátraic's provision that there might be a number of both
mineclais and *móreclais* within the borders of a single *tuath*.

    This is an approach which seeks to define a *tuath* in terms of
its population size but it gives us little idea of the actual geographical extent of a *tuath*, especially as it seems clear that early
medieval Irish settlements and cleared land were surrounded
by large quantities of unoccupied land consisting of bogs, woods
and mountain-tops.[38] The common approach to identifying the
actual acreage of individual *tuatha* has been to examine later administrative units such as modern baronies, their Anglo-Norman
predecessors, and medieval rural deaneries. Many of these units
incorporate early medieval population names which has led
scholars to suggest that they represent the territories occupied
by those populations in the pre-Viking period. The problem
with this approach is that continuity of placename does not necessarily mean continuity of administrative unit or consistency in
boundaries over time. This problem is compounded by the fact
that in many parts of Ireland our first detailed account of land
units and their acreage stems from seventeenth-century maps
and surveys. This can make it difficult to assess the precise relationship between the recent unit and their medieval predecessors. In fact, detailed local studies in regions where we do have

37. Binchy, *Corpus* 1602:4ff.
38. Fergus Kelly, *Early Irish Farming*, Early Irish Law series Vol iv
(Dublin 1997), 406-8.

sources to investigate have made it clear that the boundaries have indeed changed over time as land reclamation and improvements have altered the local landscape.[39]

Another problem has been to identify precisely the exact correlation between a *tuath* and a particular population group. Most early Irish kingdoms are named after ancestor figures as in the case of the Cenél Conaill (the kindred of Conall), otherwise known as Tír Chonaill (the land of Conall) in modern Donegal or the Cenél Eógain/Tír Eoghain of Tyrone. Others are named after areas of cleared land such as Mag mBreg or Brega in Meath and north Dublin or Mag nAí in Roscommon. Rarely, if ever, are these kingdoms called *tuatha* in our early medieval sources. Instead *tuath* is a word which is generally limited to the general regulations and social descriptions found in law codes. This introduces yet another element of uncertainty into our attempt to delimit early medieval *tuatha* on the ground.

Modern placenames which include the word *tuath* include the parish of Tuosist in Co Kerry (Túath Ó Síosta), Touaghty parish in Co Mayo (Túath Aitheachta) or Tuogh and Tuoghcluggin parishes in Co Limerick.[40] These parishes cover 39,340 acres, 3,067 acres, 6,518 acres and 2,093 acres respectively. Such a degree of variation, even allowing for differences in land quality, would seem to suggest that here we are dealing with the survival of a *tuath* placename into modern times rather than an ancient unit which has survived intact from the early medieval period.

It might be more reasonable to look at the use of *tuath* during the period of the Anglo-Norman colonisation where the evidence is much closer in date to the pre-Viking era considered here. In the charters and inquisitions of the thirteenth century, the spelling is often Latinised as *theodum, theudum, theode* and others but it is later rendered in local placenames by spellings such as Toghe (in Limerick) or Tovo- (in Co Offaly). Paul MacCotter

---

39. See, for example, C. A. Empey, 'The cantreds of medieval Tipperary', *North Munster Antiquarian Journal* 13 (1971), 22-9; ibid., 'The cantreds of the medieval county of Kilkenny', *Journal of the Royal Society of Antiquaries of Ireland* 101 (1970), 28-34.

40. Deirdre & Laurence Flanagan, *Irish placenames* (Dublin: Gill and Macmillan, 1994), 158; Edmund Hogan, *Onomasticon Goedelicum* (Dublin: Four Courts, 1993), 651; *General Alphabetical Index to the townlands, towns, parishes and baronies of Ireland* (Baltimore: Genealogical Publishing 1986), 956.

suggests that in Tipperary and Kilkenny, the *theodum* is largely replaced by the Anglo-Norman economic unit known as the manor while in Limerick, many manors were smaller and appear to be based on half-*theoda*.[41]

Canon Empey, in a number of detailed studies of the first phases of Anglo-Norman colonisation, has approached the matter differently. Working on the same material from Tipperary and Limerick as used by MacCotter, C. A. Empey has suggested that the Norman cantreds coincided with the rural deaneries as well as reflecting 'the boundaries of the great "capital" manors'.[42] Thus, for example the cantred of Elyocarroll was equivalent to the manor of Dunkerrin (with some 100,000 acres) and the cantred of Eliogarty was another way of describing the manor of Thurles, with a roughly comparable area.

In the case of the manor of Thurles, we have a charter by Theobald Walter compiled c. 1192. Within this unit, Theobald refers to a number of *theodum*s including the *theodum* of Kenelfenelgille, the *theodum* in which Thurles itself was situated and another *theodum* of Corketeny. These various *theoda* holdings all became subordinate fiefs belonging to Theobald's tenants within the cantred. Each of these, in their turn, was the equivalent of a medieval parish of the Norman period. Again one should note that in these the word *theodum* occurs frequently. A charter of Radulf le Bret from 1190-1200, for example, grants the tithes of the parish of Cooleagh in south-east Tipperary to the Hospital of St John the Baptist in Dublin and this church is stated to be the equivalent of *teudum de Oros*. Similarly c. 1200, Simon de Leminster granted the tithes of the *theodum* called Kenel Rathonere to the Hospital while Mannasserus Arsic included the tithes of the *theodum* called Gortcorki.[43] In terms of size, these could be relatively small – Cooleagh, for example is a mere 2,557 acres.

In some parts of Offaly on the borders of the Anglicised

41. Paul MacCotter, *Medieval Ireland: territorial, political and economic divisions* (Dublin: Four Courts Press, 2008), 21-2.

42. C.A. Empey, 'The Norman period 1185-1500', *Tipperary: history and society* ed. W. Nolan (Dublin: Geography Publications 1985), 73; ibid., 'The settlement of the kingdom of Limerick', *England and Ireland in the later middle ages*, ed. J. Lydon (Dublin: Irish Academic Press, 1981) 2.

43. Mark Henessey, 'Parochial organisation in medieval Tipperary', *Tipperary History and Society*, ed. W. Nolan & T. McGrath (Geography publications) 62-3.

areas, the area identified as a *tuath* could be much larger. A Tudor map of 1563 depicting the lands of Brian Ua Conchobuir identifies *Tovogeishel* which has been identified by Alfred Smyth as an early *tuath* kingdom. This, however, is only attested in the pre-Norman era by the name *Mag Géisille*.[44] In the 1302 taxation lists which provide us with the best coverage of the later medieval church within Ireland, this unit appears to be represented by the Deanery of Oppaly (=Offaly) which incorporates six churches within its borders. Of these, the church of 'Gesel' and its associated Vicarage are identified as the richest. The modern civil parish of Geashill is identified in the Townland Index of 1851 as containing 43,309 acres and as being divided between the two baronies of Geashill (with 30,874 acres) and Upper Phillipstown. In this instance, therefore, what is recorded in the Tudor period as a *tuath* corresponds to a medieval rural deanery and a single modern (civil) parish.

We have seen, in the case of the Tipperary churches, that the tithes from these parishes were granted by their Anglo-Norman rulers to external church bodies. This pattern represents the norm: a charter of c. 1195-1200, for example, indicates that the tenant, one Thomas de Hereford, donated all the tithes to the abbey of St Thomas in Dublin. The tithes of the *theodum* of Thurles, similarly, were donated to the church of Abingdon in Oxfordshire. Empey argues that this wholesale attribution of tithe-income to newly founded establishments of Anglo-Norman origin, indicates that the pre-Norman *tuath*, underlying the later *theodum*/manor, did not have a parish structure of its own and that this was an innovation of the Normans themselves. The ecclesiastical unit corresponding to the cantred as a whole was the rural deanery, in the charge of a rural dean or archdeacon and Empey further notes that these men are always given Norman names in the sources, indicating yet another innovation in church organisation established by the in-comers.[45]

Whatever about the rural deaneries, the argument concerning the tithes is not entirely convincing. We have seen above that in the early period, tithes were paid to the local *principes* of the church, be they episcopal or monastic. To say that the Anglo-Norman lords in places like Tipperary had chosen new ecclesi-

44. Alfred Smyth, *Celtic Leinster* (Blackrock: Irish Academic Press 1982), 70-71, 75.
45. Empey, *Tipperary*, 85.

astical foundations to be the beneficiaries of the tithe income from their estates is not the same as saying there was no such thing as tithes or parishes in the preceding era. The old *tuath* kingdoms may have, in many instances, been the equivalent of the secular manors in the newly founded colony but the people who governed the latter and who benefitted from their agricultural surpluses were invariably the Norman settlers. It is not unreasonable that in terms of ecclesiastical organisation, a similar transfer of assets from pre-existing units to newly established authorities and ecclesiastical foundations may also have taken place.

Indeed, as Mark Hennessey points out, the normal pattern of the eleventh and twelfth centuries throughout western Europe was that lay patrons were in a position to grant the tithes to a priest of their choice, subject to episcopal agreement and / or that of the monastic house to which the authority to appoint a local priest had been granted.[46] We do not know for certain whether this was also the case in Ireland in earlier periods but the reference quoted above to priests (illegally) seeking the permission of local laymen to build churches make it seem likely. Fragments of the eighth-century law text *Córus Bésgnai* also refer to the *eclais fine griain* (church of the land-owner's family) where, according to the associated commentary, the owner of the land on which the church stood had rights to select successors to the *apdaine*. The latter is normally translated as abbacy but can also mean any form of ecclesiastical ruling office.[47]

Certainly, in parts of Ireland which were not conquered by the Anglo-Normans, we see clear remnants of the older systems by which local tithes were paid directly to the ecclesiastical superior. In describing the system in Gaelic Ulster, Kenneth Nicholls quotes Bishop George Montgomery, writing in 1609:

> The Byshop of Clogher hath beside his lands the fourth part of all tythes throughout his Dyoces, which is called *quarta episcopalis*. The Byshops of Derry and Rapho have the third part and it is called *tertia episcopalis*.
>
> The rest of the tythes are devyded between the Parson and Vicar. In Clougher the Parson hath two fourth parts, the Vicar hath one. In Derry and Rapho the Parson and Vicar

---

46. Mark Hennessey, 'Parochial organisation', 62.
47. Binchy, *Corpus*, 1821:20-1, DIL A 363.

have each of them one third part ... The Vicars are tyed to perpetuall residence and service of the cure and beside their portion of tythes, have the benefit of all oblations and other small dueties at burials and christenings to themselves alone for attendance of the service ... The parsonages and vicarages through all theise Dyoceses have byn ever collated by the Byshops of theise Sees without contradiction or challenge of any person.[48]

This structure is identical to that described in the eighth-century Latin canon laws, down to the fact that the person attending services for the dead receive a mortuary fee directly while their main income, although based on tithes, comes to them from their ecclesiastical superiors. What we see in 17th century Ulster, therefore, is the direct successor of the early medieval system as described by our original authorities, Ruben and Cú Chuimne.

In the province of Tuam and that part of Killaloe diocese west of the Shannon, however, there appears to be somewhat different and, at first sight, rather more confused arrangements. To quote Nicholls:

On the one hand, we may find the rectories of a number of parishes united as a single benefice, often bearing a territorial name rather than that of a church, on the other hand, we hear of two rectories in a single church and of distinct rectories 'in lay fee' and 'in ecclesiastical fee' within one church.[49]

As an example of the unification of rectories, Nicholls cites, amongst others, the unit known by the territorial name of Okassyn or Ogashin. This name reproduces the name of one particular group of descendants from Brian Boru's family who were known in Irish as the Uí Caisin and were based around Quin in the modern baronies of Upper and Lower Tulla in Co Clare. In this particular example, by the time of the seventeenth century Visitations, the unit comprised eight separate parishes. It was a benefice held 'in lay fee' and the right to appoint the priest or rector was held by the O'Brien king of Thomond. They

---

48. *Ordnance Survey of the County of Londonderry I Parish of Templemore* (1837), 50 quoted by K. W. Nicholls, 'Rectory, vicarage and parish in the western Irish dioceses', *Jn Royal Society of Antiquaries of Ireland* 101 (1971), 54-5

49. Nicholls, 'Rectory', 53.

also had the right to appoint priests to the other great rectories of Clare named respectively Tradry (Tradraighe) and Omulled (Uí mBloid).[50] In terms of size, these rectories were far larger than the individual parishes of eastern Ireland: Okassyn, for example, was approximately 175,000 acres.[51]

Kenneth Nicholls' conclusions about these rectories in lay fee are particularly interesting:

> It seems to me that in these great rectories which covered a group of parishes, we have a survival not so much of a pre-parochial stage of organisation as of an intermediate stage in which the tribal state or territory was taken to constitute a parish and acquired, therefore, an incumbent, the predecessor of the later rector. One may instance the case of Mael Isa mac an Easpaig Uí Maoilfhaghmhair, 'parson of Uí Fiachrach and Uí Amhalgaidh', whose obit is recorded by the annals in 1224. John O Ceandubhain, rector of Castleconnor, is styled in his annalistic obit (1416) 'parson of Tír Fiachrach Muaidhe' showing that his great rectory of Castleconnor (which in 1417 and after covered three parishes) bore this alternative territorial designation.[52]

In fact, what Nicholls is identifying is once again a direct reflection of the situation as described in the early Irish sources. As already discussed, the seventh-century Bishop Tírechán mentions individual churches within distinct geographical districts whose leaders varied in clerical rank – one district might have a church headed by a deacon, another by a priest or a bishop. *Ríagal Phátraic* says that where sufficient clergy were not available, the individual would have responsibility for neighbouring churches. Just so, did the fifteenth century John O Ceandubhain as rector have responsibility for the three churches within his district of Tír Fhiachrach Muaide although in his case, he was able to put vicars into these parishes to man the individual churches concerned. (As an example of the ebb and flow of church settlement over time, it is worth noting that Bishop Tírechán recounts a story of Patrick blessing a member of the Uí Fhiachrach Muirsce who later became a bishop although it

---

50. Nicholls, *Rectory*, 59, 78-79.
51. Townland Index, 968.
52. Nicholls, *Rectory*, 61.

should be noted that the exact location of his settlement is no longer known.)[53]

It is interesting that the great western rectories, incorporating numerous parishes, often coincide with the local rural deanery and indeed, were often known by the same name.[54] In the colonised areas, these deaneries usually coincided with the Anglo-Norman cantreds which themselves, as we have seen, were often made up of a number of early medieval *tuatha* or *theoda*. In terms of size, however, the eastern rural deaneries were often considerably smaller then those of the west – compare the 175,000 acres of Okassyn with the 100,000 odd acres of individual cantreds and manors within Anglo-Norman Tipperary.

The rural dean was essentially an officer of the bishop whose duties included supervision of the local clergy, upkeep of local churches and the holding of monthly chapters in which the bishop's mandates could be conveyed to his subordinates.[55] The point at which this office developed in Ireland is not clear and requires further research but it is worth noting Katherine Simms' point that there seems to be a steady growth of episcopal power between the synod of Rathbreasail in 1111 and the early thirteenth century and that this increase in political importance led to the transfer of all unassigned church lands to the diocesan bishops.[56] Given Empey's argument that the early deans in the conquered areas all have Norman names, it seems likely that this particular official was introduced into Irish church structures during the twelfth and thirteenth centuries.

A separate strand in the organisation of the later medieval parochial system were the establishments located on church lands. The normal pattern was that these formed separate parishes where the tithes were divided up between the resident vicar (the man who in most cases was the actual minister living locally) and the 'rector' who, in this case, was normally a member of a cathedral chapter. Where this type of parish church was

53. Bieler, *Patrician texts*, 158 §45; Swift, *Connachta*, 340-343.
54. Nicholls, *Rectory*, 59.
55. C. A. Empey, 'The Anglo-Norman diocese of Ossory', *A worthy foundation: the cathedral church of St Canice 1285-1985*, eds. S. Barry, C. A. Empey & J. Bradley (Kilkenny: Dolmen 1985), 18.
56. Katherine Simms, 'Frontiers in the Irish church – regional and cultural', *Colony and frontier in medieval Ireland: essays presented to J. F. Lydon* (London: Hambledon Press, 1995), 184-7.

found within a large parcel of land owned by the local bishop,
these parishes were often termed 'cross lands' or 'in the crosses'
and could be run entirely separately from the local secular administration. In some cases in the west, however, these 'rectories
in ecclesiastical fee' were made up of individual townlands,
scattered through the normal parish structure in which case the
cathedral authorities would be granted the relevant proportion
of the parish tithe.[57] Examination of sixteenth and seventeenth
century land surveys such as the *Compossicion Book of Connaught*
or the *Books of Survey and Distribution* make it clear just how
much land eventually ended up under such church control.[58]
What is unusual about this system is that the vicar's stipend is
not a sub-set of that owing to the rector as was the case in, for example, medieval England where it was the rector who appointed
the vicar as his local representative.[59] In Ireland, the rector's
share of the local tithe could be allocated to a quite different person or institution without any direct link to the vicar.

Again, the evidence is that these elements in the ecclesiastical
administrative system were well established prior to the establishment of the Anglo-Norman colony. The seventh-century
Bishop Tírechán tells the story of one particularly large estate
which was granted to the church by a local king:

> The said [Bishop] Assicus took refuge in the region north of
> Slíab Líacc and stayed for seven years in a retreat which is
> called Rochuil west of Slíab Líacc and his monks searched for
> him and found him in the mountain valleys with his metal-
> work and his monks took him forcibly with them and he
> died in their company in the solitude of the mountains and
> they buried him in Ráith Cungi in Mag Sereth and the king
> gave him and his monks after his death, grazing for a hun-
> dred cows with their calves and for twenty oxen, as an offer-
> ing for ever.[60]

---

57. Empey, *Tipperary*, 75-6; Nicholls, *Rectory*, 57.
58. A. M. Freeman, *The Compossicion Booke of Conaught*, (Dublin: Irish
Manuscripts Commission, 1936); *Books of Survey and Distribution*, ed. R. C.
Simington Vols 1-IV (Dublin: Irish Manuscripts Commission 1949-1967)
59. John R. Moorman, *Church life in England in the thirteenth century*
(Cambridge: University Press 1955)
60. Bieler, *Patrician texts*, 14 § 22. The fact that the bishop was attended by
monks shows that the Irish had adopted the idea initiated by St
Augustine and promoted by Pope Gregory, that a bishop should live

An indication of the worth of this grant is provided by an account of the Anglo-Norman manor of Inch, north-west of Thurles in 1303:

> The jurors say on their oath that there is at Inch a certain castle standing on a motte surrounded by a broken-down palisade, the greater part of which lies prostrate. And there are in the same manor a new hall, an old wooden chapel and other rooms (kitchen, larder fish-house…) There are 360 acres of arable land in demesne … of which four score and two acres are usually held by [Irish] betaghs and farmers. There are ten acres of meadow … there are sixty acres of pasture without wood or bog … on which the lord can maintain twenty cows, forty pigs and 100 sheep besides 200 sheep on the demesne.[61]

It is clear from the pre-Norman charters that land-grants would normally include all the elements required for a (largely) self-sufficient agricultural estate: an eighth-century estate purchased by the nun Cummen included, for example, land 'in wood, plain and meadow, with its enclosure and its herb-garden.'[62] The grant to Bishop Assicus probably, therefore, included wood and arable land as well as the pasture required for the cattle and it may even have been rather larger than the manor of Inch. Such an estate would, in all likelihood, have had a considerable human population whose pastoral care, therefore, would be directly controlled by the church without the intervention of lay authorities.[63]

Smaller units could also be donated to the church as is indicated indeed by the estate of Cummen. The charter describing this grant is written into the front of the small gospel book known as the *Book of Armagh* and the value of the land is given as seventeen ounces of silver, together with a silver vessel and a gold necklace. Seventeen ounces of silver was seen as the equiv-

---

with a community of monks in order to safeguard his spiritual well-being. See B. Colgrave & R. B. Mynors, *Bede's Ecclesiastical History of the English People* (Oxford: Clarendon Press, 1969), I 27.

61. Empey, *Tipperary*, 80

62. Bieler, *Patrician texts*, 175.

63. This again bears on the vexed question of church tenantry or *manaig* – in the model proposed by Etchingham, pastoral provision in early Ireland was limited to the inhabitants of such church lands but this is disputed by scholars such as Sharpe and Ó Corráin. See Liam Irwin, 'The Irish Parish in Historical Perspective'.

64. Kelly, *Early Irish farming*, 58.

alent of seventeen milch cows[64] so this donation would appear to be considerably less than that given to Bishop Assicus.

Eleventh-century Clonmacnoise provides us with an example of estates given to clerical families attached to the great ecclesiastical centres. According to an entry for 1031 in the *Annals of the Four Masters* an estate called Ísel Ciaráin was linked to the name of Conn na mBocht, 'the person responsible for the Céli Dé and the anchorites at Clonmacnoise'. In the next generation, Conn's descendants were said to be resident on the land and were being taxed by the local king even though they continued to be officials of Clonmacnoise. By 1089, however, the family had purchased the rights to the land from the local king and the leaders of Clonmacnoise who, at this stage, certainly included bishops.[65] Here, therefore, we have an example of an estate whose owners were officials attached to a centre with episcopal authority just as Nicholls describes for the rectories 'in ecclesiastical fee'. Interestingly, a Middle Irish Life of St Ciarán refers to the particular estate of Ísel and states that the people living on it included *uasalsacairt* (noble priests), *cléírig* (clerics) and *bráithre* (brothers).[66]

References to the Céli Dé at Armagh include a single reference of AD 921 and they then disappear from the historical record until the later fourteenth century when they reappear as a separate and distinct community within the body of regular canons attached to the cathedral. Their head appears to have been particularly important in the chanting of the liturgy: the head acting as precentor while the rest of the community of 'Colidei' performing the office of vicars in the choir. There were six of these men in total (one prior and five brethren) and they held various lands including the rectories of Aghaloo (Tyrone) and Carnteel (Tyrone) and the vicarages of Tynan (Armagh), Kilmore (Armagh), and Drumcree (Armagh). At the Dissolution,

---

64. Kelly, *Early Irish farming*, 58.

65. For discussion of this material, see Catherine Swift, 'Sculptors and their customers: a study of Clonmacnoise grave-slabs' *Clonmacnoise Studies* 2 (Dublin: Dúchas 2003), 116-7. For bishops of Clonmacnoise, see Annette Kehnel, *Clonmacnois – the church and lands of St Ciarán* (Münster: Vita regularis – Ordnungen und Deutungen religiosen Lebens im Mittlealter 8, 1997), 34-5, 268-73.

66. Whitley Stokes, *Lives of the saints from the Book of Lismore* (Oxford: Clarendon Press 1890), 119, 128-9.

they were found to control seven townlands within the parish of Lisnadill (Armagh) as well as seven rectories and their associated vicarages. It is not explicitly recorded in our surviving data but it seems reasonable to conclude that these rights to tithes and appointment of local priests and vicars are a survival from a pre-Norman situation such as is recorded for Clonmacnoise. Comparable studies of the Céli Dé from Scotland, where the records cover the eleventh and twelfth centuries, would appear to bear this conclusion out.[67]

What then are the conclusions to be drawn concerning the early history of priests and their areas of pastoral ministry in Ireland? The first and perhaps the most important is that evidence for the exercise of pastoral care must be drawn from the entire range of sources for the Middle Ages. Irish church history has suffered considerably from the long-standing academic tradition that one is either an early medievalist (generally working in the National University) or a later medievalist (dominated by scholars from the University of Dublin.) This dichotomy has been breaking down in recent years but we are still burdened with its legacy. We therefore have the extraordinary situation whereby early medievalists look at pastoral care through the lens of early canon law while later medievalists look at it through manorial extents, state documents, papal registers and the diocesan records. The former write in generalised and universal terms about a 'system' – the latter comment primarily on the particular, based on localised examples.

It seems clear, even from this brief overview, that this bipartite approach has masked the considerable degree of overlap between the evidence from pre-Norman and post-Norman Ireland. This has been strengthened by widespread acceptance of the idea that parochial structures were introduced into Ireland only with the arrival of the Normans. Where the source for this interpretation is specified, it is normally found to be based on a particular article by Jocelyn Otway-Ruthven on the parishes of Skreen, published in 1964.[68] When evaluating her conclusion, one must bear in mind that while a superb scholar in many ways, Otway-Ruthven was very much a product of the bi-polar university structures described above. In her book, *A history of*

---

67. William Reeves, *The Culdees of the British Isles* (Dublin: Gill, 1864), 6-58.
68. A. J. Otway-Ruthven, 'Parochial development in the rural deanery of Skreen', *Journal of Royal Society of Antiquaries of Ireland* 94 (1964), 111-22.

medieval Ireland she explicitly acknowledges her lack of knowledge of 'Gaelic' Ireland and thanks Dr Kathleen Hughes for providing her with a basic introduction to pre-Norman Irish society.[69]

It is reasonable to conclude that just as with other parts of Western Europe, the Irish parochial system, in terms of a systematised and tightly controlled administration of the entire landmass of a particular country or state, is a product of the eleventh and twelfth centuries.[70] It is not, however, reasonable to state that there was no system of pastoral care or of local priestly ministry before that date. On the contrary, what can be observed in the evidence from the western and northern parts of Ireland is that the system of parishes in operation there in the later middle ages is the direct inheritance of pre-Norman structures, going back to the seventh and eighth centuries.

Identifiable within this early system are local churches manned by a local cleric resident in the wider community. These men had responsibility for baptism and performance of the last rites (including burial) and also for the celebration of Sunday Mass and for preaching. Their income came in part from their superiors within the church hierarchy (who, in turn, would be drawing on tithes donated by the laity) and in part in specific fees and labour dues proffered directly by their congregations. They could and did build churches without seeking permission but they could not celebrate Mass there until the buildings had been consecrated by the local bishop. Within the limits imposed by the necessity for Sunday Mass, they could find themselves with three or four churches 'on their conscience' but these would, in all likelihood, have been located relatively close to one another.

Using the later medieval evidence as our guide, it seems probable that the right to appointment as minister to these local churches could lie with either the local landowner or king or with the church authorities (both episcopal and, on occasion, monastic). In all cases, however, the local bishop would have ultimate rights over who eventually got the job and the incumbent

69. A. J Otway-Ruthven, *A history of medieval Ireland* (London: Routledge 1968) – foreword.

70. See for example, *Minsters and Parish churches: the local church in transition 950-1200*, ed. John Blair (Oxford: Oxford University Committee for Archaeology, 1988); *Pastoral care before the Parish*, eds. J. Blair and R. Sharpe (Leicester: University Press, 1992).

would owe first loyalty to him as his direct superior. In the later period, we see clear evidence that in many cases the priests would have vicars who would act as their local representatives – it is not clear whether this is also true of earlier times although the fact that Bishop Tírechán refers to churches headed by deacons would make such a suggestion plausible. Again, in the later period, we see an intermediary rank of cleric between bishop and priest known as rural deans – there is no evidence for this particular group in the early canons and it seems likely that this was an innovation established in an era of increased episcopal control during the twelfth and thirteenth centuries. Finally, we can also detect that some of the churches served by the local priests were located within much larger estates of church land and in such instances we can see that a portion of the tithes collected went to pay for the upkeep of the ecclesiastical personnel attached to the bigger churches.

There seems to be no clear standard involved in determining the size of territory which was served by these priests although *Ríagal Phátraic* make it clear that there could be a number of such churches within a single *tuath* or kingdom. Unfortunately the exact size of such kingdoms is still a matter for research but modern units incorporating the placename element *tuath* can range from 40,000 acres to 2,500. Parishes first noted in Anglo-Norman documentation (and therefore mainly found in the south and east of the country) are often at the smaller end of this range.

A key element in interpreting the territorial extent under the local churches will be the rural deaneries, although detailed research into the precise function and origin of these units has still be undertaken. It appears that they are the most important unit in constructing the individual manors of the early Norman conquest and, as such, they appear to be of the order of 100,000 acres. The rural deaneries of the west are rather larger, possibly because the land was, on the whole, less good and the population more widely scattered. While it is impossible as yet for this author to date the development of the rural dean as an office, it does seem likely to belong to the period of episcopal reforms in the twelfth century, and the kingdoms which the rural deaneries seem to reflect appear   , on the whole, to be ones which represent post eleventh-century creations. It is, therefore, difficult to be certain to what degree these deaneries may be the *tuatha* described in our early medieval canons. Like the seventh and eighth century administrative units, however, the deaneries did include a number of churches within their borders and, in the absence of more clear-cut evidence, they appear to be the best candidates currently available for the territories which are described in *Ríagal Phátraic*. If this provisional conclusion is accepted, we are led to the conclusion that the basic structure and organisation of a national system of pastoral provision had been put together by the eighth century and was well-established in both eastern and western parts of the country by the time the rural deaneries were created. In this, as in many aspects of church history, the Irish appear to have been well to the fore within Western Europe.

CHAPTER THREE

Community and Parish in Contemporary Ireland: The Challenge of Rapid Social Change

Desmond McCafferty and Brendan O'Keeffe

1. Introduction

It is now widely recognised that the future of the parish depends to a great extent on the development of an extended role for the laity in parish affairs (Pope, 2004). This recognition is not, of course, entirely new within the Catholic Church, and can be traced back at least to the Second Vatican Council. However, it has been sharpened considerably in recent years as the numbers in the ordained ministry have continued to decline in Ireland and throughout most of Europe. One response to this trend is an increased focus on the development of 'lay ecclesial ministry' (USCCB, 2005) in which a potentially wide range of functions may be delegated to suitably prepared and qualified members of the laity acting in a quasi-professional capacity. But, more fundamentally, it is apparent that the vibrancy of parish life depends on nurturing a strong, socially-cohesive community, whose members are actively engaged in a wide range of more and less structured voluntary activities, both within and without the church. The current debate about the role of the laity in the parish is taking place within the context of wider social debates about issues such as social engagement, volunteering, active citizenship, participative democracy, partnership, and new forms of governance. Underpinning these in turn are the comparatively new concept of social capital, which has received widespread attention from academics as well as from government policymakers, and the much older concept of community development.

This chapter addresses the issue of parish development from a community development/social capital perspective, and enquires both theoretically and empirically as to how recent demographic, social and economic change in Ireland might be understood as impacting on local communities. We begin with a discussion of the concept of social capital, examining its relationship to volunteering and participation. We then outline some key aspects of recent social and economic change in Irish society that might be expected to have impacted both on the stock of social capital and on the level of voluntary activity. These trends, it is argued, together present a challenging context for the growth of participation, and ultimately therefore for community and parish development. Following this, we examine in detail some of the recent evidence on trends in volunteering, as one indicator of social capital. This involves a detailed analysis of both the social and geographical dimensions of voluntary activity, based on new data available from the census of population. The chapter then concludes with a discussion of the implications for the future of the parish.

2. Governance, Sustainability, Social Capital and Volunteering

The development of vibrant parish communities, in which members of the laity play a proactive role in ministry and in the promotion of social justice, can be seen as part of a more general transition in modern liberal democracies from traditional, exogenous or top-down approaches to decision-making, to one that is based on the principles of partnership and equity. In political science and public administration this transition is frequently referred to as the shift from traditional 'government' to 'collaborative governance' (Davoudi, 2005). Where 'government' is associated with the centralised, exogenous, hierarchical and rigid, 'governance' is associated with the local or bottom-up, horizontal structures, shared decision-making and responsibilities, co-operation, flexibility and innovation. Good governance, it is argued, ensures maximum buy-in from interested persons and associations; it encourages creativity, promotes understanding, delivers greater efficiencies, and promotes strategic and longer-term approaches to planning and development (O'Keeffe, 2007). However, adherence to good governance requires time, so that trust can be built-up between those involved in decision-making and so that large organisations can adjust to the needs and issues of individuals and locales (OECD, 2001 and 2006; Stoker and Chhotray, 2008).

Literature on collaborative governance has mushroomed over the past two decades, and in particular since the publication of the United Nations Report *Our Common Future* (World Commission on Environment and Development, 1987). This report outlined the challenges facing humankind due to the over-consumption of the earth's natural resources. In response, it advocated a sustainable development approach, based on achieving a balance between economic, social and environmental objectives. The attainment of this balanced or sustainable approach requires action at the global, national and local levels. At the local level, individuals are challenged to collectively foster the creation of communities that are prosperous, green, healthy, safe, just, inclusive and culturally-rich. While the original UN report on sustainable development does not explicitly mention the spiritual dimension of community life, the complementarity between spirituality and sustainable development has emerged in more recent commentaries (McDonagh, 2007), and is evident in a number of Catholic Church pronouncements and actions over recent years.[1] Indeed, in 2007, The Vatican became the first state to become carbon neutral.

Good governance and sustainability are complementary and mutually reinforcing social and political processes and outcomes. Moreover, both are contingent on community development, whereby citizens organise themselves in collective associations to pursue economic, social and environmental development outcomes. Thus, community and voluntary groups are an essential element in attaining sustainability, and citizens' willingness and capacity to engage on a voluntary basis in community development activity is both a desirable outcome in itself, and an indicator of the health of a community. Modern debates about voluntary associational activity have relied heavily on the conceptual framework associated with social capital, which has attracted a great deal of interest in recent years both from the academic community (across a wide range of disciplines) and from policy makers and governments. The concept is central to the Third Way social and economic policies introduced by the Clinton administration in the US in the 1990s and New Labour in the UK. In Ireland the 2002 Programme for Government (Fianna Fáil and the Progressive Democrats, 2002) committed the government to working 'to promote social capital in all parts of Irish life', while the review of the National Anti-Poverty Strategy lists the development of social capital as one of three key objectives. In addition, the National Competitiveness Council now reports on a number of social capital indicators in

---

1. Irish Catholic Bishops' Conference (2009), *The Cry of the Earth: A Pastoral Reflection on Climate Change from the Irish Catholic Bishops' Conference.*

its annual competitiveness report (National Competitiveness Council, 2008).

The popularisation of social capital as a means of understanding the health of community life is largely due to the work of the American sociologist Robert Putnam (2000), building on earlier contributions from Pierre Bourdieu (1986) and James Coleman (1988). According to Putnam (2000) social capital consists of the networks, norms and generalised trust that enable individuals and groups to engage in co-operative activity for mutual benefit. He identifies three distinct types of social capital. Bonding capital consists of the links to family, close friends and neighbours that often provide important practical and emotional support for individuals on an informal basis. Bridging capital consists of links between socially heterogenous individuals and groups, such as often exist in sports and special interests clubs. Linking capital consists of connections to the sources of power in society, including those in the public realm, such as governmental bodies, as well as private sector institutions. A common finding in studies of local social capital is that bonding capital is often strong in disadvantaged communities, but bridging and linking capital are stronger in middle class or better-off communities.

Social capital as conceived of by Putnam is both a public good, and intended to be used for the public good (Johnston and Percy-Smith, 2003). The Taskforce on Active Citizenship (2007a) describe it as one of the key resources underpinning community development. It exists in a reflexive relationship with voluntary activity: on the one hand it is maintained and renewed by voluntary activity, on the other hand both the level and type of voluntary activity in the community are influenced by the level and type of social capital present. This is the neo-Durkheimian view elaborated by Hardill *et al* (2007) who suggest that bridging social capital may result in quite 'instrumental' forms of volunteering, in which individuals see volunteering as a means of improving their labour market or social status. On the other hand bonding capital may be more likely to result in volunteering that is aimed at community or neighbourhood improvement where 'the principal benefits to the volunteer are less about opportunities for getting on than about opportunities for participation in the shared life of the group' (400).

One of the advantages of using social capital as a means of

understanding voluntary activity is that recent empirical research on social capital can yield insights into current and likely future trends in volunteering and associational activity. In particular we can draw on a number of comparative cross-national studies that have attempted to identify some of the correlates of social capital. Newton (1997) among others has suggested that one of the factors promoting social capital formation is strong and stable family ties, while Fukuyama (1997) argues that a lack of social capital may be related to factors such as the breakdown of the nuclear family (through divorce and extra-marital births), crime, child abuse, alcoholism, and drug abuse. Other factors that have been identified as inimical to social capital development include social and political inequality (Boix and Posner, 1998; Knack, 1999) and social and ethnic divisions (Whiteley, 2000). If these factors can indeed be regarded as causal or explanatory of social capital (or its absence) then by examining recent trends in them we may be able to gain some insights into the prospects for social capital formation, voluntary activity and community develop- ment in Ireland. Such an account is furnished in the next section.

3. Recent Social Change in Ireland

Irish society has undergone profound change in recent years, much of which has been driven by economic restructuring and the significant improvement in overall living standards pro- duced by the economic boom that emerged in the early to mid- 1990s. It seems reasonable to suggest that many of these changes will impact on levels of social capital at both the national and local (community and parish) level. Here we focus on changes that seem likely, on the basis of factors identified in the relevant literature, to have such an impact. The period covered in the dis- cussion varies according to the availability of appropriate statist- ical data, but in most instances extends to 2006 or 2007.

Perhaps the single most positive feature of the boom was that, following the sustained high levels of unemployment of the 1980s, the numbers out of work fell in both absolute and rel- ative terms. The unemployment rate declined from 10 per cent in 1997 to under 4 per cent in 2001, and while it rose slightly to 4.6 per cent in 2007 it remained consistently below the EU aver- age throughout this period. In 2007 the Irish rate was under two-thirds the EU average, and the sixth lowest among all 27 countries. In parallel with this drop in unemployment the phenomenon of 'jobless households' (i.e. households in which no one has paid employment) also declined, as indicated by the reduction in the proportion of the population aged 18-59 years living in such households from 12.5 per cent to 7.8 per cent in the decade from 1997 to 2007 (Central Statistics Office, 2008a).

This economic improvement was based on foreign direct investment (FDI) to a large extent, one of the key phenomena associated with the increasing globalisation of the Irish economy. Globalisation has also led to increased immigration, and consequent cultural and ethnic diversity in what was for a long time one of the most homogenous populations in Western Europe. In the course of the 1990s the State not alone experienced its highest ever level of population growth, but a change in the driver of growth to net migration rather than natural increase, which had been the main source of growth since the foundation of the State. In the twelve months leading up to census day in 2006, 121,700 persons migrated into the State. Of these migrants, 55 per cent were not Irish born, among whom the main countries of birth were Poland (33,400), the UK (22,600), and Lithuania (7,400). These one-year data reflect an on-going trend established in the late 1990s, the outcome of which was that by 2006 non-Irish nationals constituted about 10 per cent of the usually resident population (Central Statistics Office, 2006).

While increasing cultural and ethnic diversity is among the more dramatic and visible forms of change in the Irish population in recent years, it has taken place against a background of profound demographic change that had been on-going over a considerably longer period of time. One of the most significant aspects of this is the decline in the Total Fertility Rate (TFR) which is a measure of the number of children that would be born to a woman in the course of her reproductive lifetime if she experienced the national age-specific fertility rate at each year of age. The TFR fell from 2.12 in 1990 to 1.88 in 2005 before increasing somewhat to 2.03 in 2007. However, for every year since 1991 it has been below the replacement level of 2.10, the only period in the history of the State for which this is true (Central Statistics Office, 2008b).

The decline in the TFR is the result of a long-term downward trend in the birth rate, which, combined with on-going decline in the death rate and a corresponding increase in longevity, has resulted in a significant change in the age structure of the population. This is reflected most clearly in the age dependency rates, i.e. the population aged either under 15 years of age (young dependency) or over 65 years of age (old dependency) expressed as a ratio of those in the category 15 to 65 years. As the annual numbers of births dropped from 1980 onwards, and the relatively large numbers born in the 1970s gradually made their way into category aged 15 years and over, the younger cohort contracted in relative terms, leading to a decrease of 31 per cent in the youth dependency ratio between 1991 and 2006 (Central Statistics Office, various). In time, as the 1970s birth cohort ages, the population 'bulge' will be evident in older cohorts. Significantly, the group aged 45-64 (which, as shown later, is the main volunteering group) will expand by approximately 37 per cent by 2021, according to the most recent set of population projections (Central Statistics Office, 2008c).

This change in the age structure has also been favourable for economic growth, yielding the so-called 'demographic dividend' whereby the labour force has been expanded as a result of the high birth rates of the 1970s. Another significant source of labour force growth is the increased participation of females, whose overall participation rate increased from 44 per cent in 1998 to 53 per cent in 2006. Ireland's expanded and more feminised labour force is by and large more highly educated also, and the numbers aged 15 to 64 with third level education rose by almost 300,000 between 2000 and 2006 (Central Statistics Office, 2008b). Increasingly employment is concentrated in the services sector, part of a long-established sectoral shift from agriculture and manufacturing that in turn has had important consequences for where jobs are located. More than ever, this tends to be in the larger urban centres, and the result is an on-going urbanisation of Irish society over the last decade and a half. Of the total population growth of over half a million between 1991 and 2006, 83 per cent was located in the cities and towns of 10,000 or more population. Even so, the urbanisation of population has lagged behind that of jobs, and this spatial mismatch resulted in a significant increase in commuting to work during the economic boom, which is reflected in the fact that the average commuting distance increased by 42 per cent between 1991 and 2006.[2] Average commuting times have also increased, and the number of commuters travelling for more than one hour to work grew

2. Commuting also includes travel to school and College by students.

by 32 per cent, from 137,706 to 182,351 between 2002 and 2006 (Central Statistics Office, various).

Apart from its effects on the individual, long-distance and long-time commuting is recognised as a stress factor in personal relationships and potentially detrimental to family life. It is notable in this context that the latter years of the economic boom were characterised by a sharp increase in the extent of marital breakdown. The number of divorced persons increased from 35,100 to 59,500 between 2002 and 2006, an increase of about 70 per cent, while the number of separated persons (including divorced) increased from 133,800 to 166,800 (+25 per cent) over the same period. In parallel with increasing marriage breakdown there has been a strong trend towards cohabitation: cohabiting couples accounted for 11.6 per cent of all family units in 2006 compared with 8.4 per cent in 2002, while the number of children living with cohabiting parents increased from 51,700 to 74,500 (+44 per cent) (Central Statistics Office, 2007).

Marital breakdown is one of several factors that have contributed to a high rate of new household formation in Ireland which is reflected in the sharp rise (+43 per cent) in the number of households, from 1,029,100 in 1991 to 1,469,521 in 2006. This increase has outstripped population growth over the same period, resulting in a decrease in the average household size from 3.3 persons per household in 1991, to the latest figure, for 2006, of 2.8 persons, a decline of 12 per cent. Over the same period the number of one-person households grew by 52,000, and these households now account for 22 per cent of all households (Central Statistics Office, various).

Finally, the various changes outlined above have been accompanied by an increasing incidence of a number of social pathologies. Between 2003 and 2007 the number of homicides increased by 62 per cent, controlled drug offences doubled in number, recorded instances of damage to property and the environment increased by 27 per cent, and public order and other social code offences by 34 per cent (Central Statistics Office, 2008d). Although certain other categories of offences (including sexual offences) showed a downward trend over the same period, the number of prisoners also increased, in this instance by 32 per cent between 1997 and 2006 (Central Statistics Office, 2008e).

In summary, the last decade and a half has been one of profound economic and social transformation. While many of the changes have been positive in nature, others have trended in the opposite direction, and it would appear evident that many of these have shifted in a direction that is not conducive to social capital formation. This is most obvious in relation to the increasing rates of serious crime and drug use, and the growing numbers of prisoners. However it may also be true of factors such as urbanisation, increased commuting times and distances, the increase in marital breakdown, and the trend towards smaller households and non-family based households. Against this background, we next examine the most recent data on patterns of voluntary activity in Ireland.

4. Trends in Volunteering and Participation

Ireland is generally perceived as a society that has promoted and valued volunteerism. Many religious orders have been to the fore in promoting volunteerism, and large voluntary bodies such as the St Vincent De Paul Society are closely associated with the church. Several members of the clergy play a prominent role as conveners and leaders of community and voluntary associations, and are among Ireland's leading lights in the promotion of social justice. The European Union has been a strong advocate of volunteerism and community development, and has produced a White Paper on Governance (Commission of the European Communities, 2001). The EU has provided funding and technical support for countless community-based projects, and is to the fore in supporting community-based approaches to peace and reconciliation in Northern Ireland and the border counties of the Republic. National and local government bodies have also taken steps to promote volunteerism. Through Local Agenda 21, city and county councils have engaged with schools, neighbourhood associations and other voluntary bodies in promoting projects to improve citizens' quality of life and the local environment. Area-based Partnerships and LEADER Local Action groups have been extremely active in supporting community and voluntary groups, and in building their capacity to promote an extensive range of projects and actions (Walsh, Craig and McCafferty, 1998; Walsh and Meldon, 2004). At national level the Taskforce on Active Citizenship was launched by An Taoiseach in 2005, and its roles include advising government and public bodies on how they can support community development and volunteerism. As suggested by Table 1, which is taken from one of the Taskforce's reports, these combined efforts appear to be delivering positive results in the form of a net increase in volunteerism in Ireland. These data are consistent with the findings of a 2002 survey for the National Economic and Social Forum (NESF, 2003) that both informal social contact and local community involvement in Ireland are above the European average.

Table 1: Trends in Volunteerism and Community Engagement, 2002-2006

Percentage of surveyed adults who:

	A. Undertook regular voluntary activity		B. Were actively involved in a voluntary / community group	
	2002	2006	2002	2006
All respondents	17.1	23.1	21.7	29.0
Male	18.9	23.7	25.3	31.4
Female	15.4	22.5	18.4	26.7
Source: Taskforce on Active Citizenship (2007b)				

However, a somewhat less optimistic picture emerges from the data on volunteering collected nationally for the first time in the 2006 census of population. The census gives a figure of just 16.4 per cent of the population engaged in at least one form of voluntary activity, considerably lower than that for the same year in the Taskforce report.[3] This figure is somewhat below the EU average, and it compares unfavourably with countries such as Italy and Austria that have long traditions of an active civil society.[4] There is also a strong variation in volunteerism according to age, with the lowest levels among young adults (Figure 1). Less than 4 per cent of persons aged 20 to 34 years are en-

---

3. While the census is based on a survey of every citizen in the state, and deals with a wide range issues, the Taskforce data in contrast are gathered from sample surveys that deal specifically with issues of volunteerism and active citizenship.

4. The Eurobarometer Survey 273 Wave 63.3 records that across the EU, an average of 30% of adults participate in voluntary activity. The countries with the highest levels are Austria (60%) and The Netherlands (55%), while countries such as Italy and Spain are recognised for high levels of volunteerism associated with a well developed social economy and co-operative sector (Douglas, 2006). Former communist counties in Central and Eastern Europe, along with Portugal, record the lowest levels of volunteerism.

gaged in any type of voluntary activity, while less than 2 per cent of those in this age cohort are involved in any church-related activity. The age cohorts with the highest levels of voluntary engagement are 45 to 54 years and 55 to 65 years, with the latter also having the highest level of engagement in church-oriented activities.

Very considerable variations emerge among religious denominations in respect of their members' engagement in voluntary activities. The highest levels of volunteerism can be found among the smaller and newer churches. Among the larger and longer-established churches in Ireland, Methodists, Presbyterians and so-called 'other'[5] Christians have the highest levels of engagement in voluntary activity. In contrast, Roman Catholics and members of the Orthodox Churches are the least likely to engage in any type of volunteerism, and especially in any church-related voluntary activity. Just under 4 per cent of Roman Catholics are involved in a church-related voluntary association, as compared to over 13 per cent of Methodists.

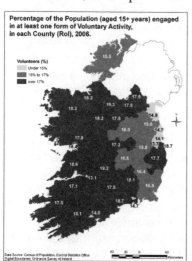

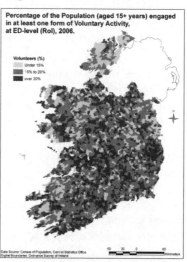

The census data also provide interesting insights into the spatial variations that exist in respect of volunteerism in Ireland. A clear urban-rural dichotomy emerges, with rural areas generally having above average levels of volunteerism and urban areas having lower levels. Western counties, notably Clare, Leitrim,

---

5. The term 'other' is used by the CSO to refer to Christian churches excluding Catholic, Church of Ireland, Presbyterian, Methodist and Orthodox.

Galway and Roscommon, together with North Tipperary record the highest levels of volunteerism in the state. The striking exception in respect of counties along the Atlantic seaboard is Donegal, which has one of the lowest levels. The counties with the lowest level of volunteerism nationally are Fingal (14.7 per cent) and Louth (14.9 per cent), while low levels are also prevalent in the counties of the Dublin commuter belt, namely Kildare, Laois, Carlow, Meath, Westmeath and Wexford. Of the counties in the east of Ireland, Wicklow and South Dublin are the only ones to record relatively high levels of volunteerism, 17.7 per cent and 18.7 per cent respectively – on a par with counties Galway and Kerry.

Urban areas generally have lower levels of volunteerism, and the local authority area with the absolute lowest level is Limerick City, where only 13.1 per cent of the population is recorded as being engaged in any form of voluntary activity. The corresponding figures for Dún Laoghaire-Rathdown (13.7 per cent), Dublin City (14.1 per cent), Cork City (14.0 per cent) and Waterford City (14.7 per cent) are only marginally higher than Limerick's, and are all indicative of low levels of social capital and poorly developed community structures and facilities in Ireland's cities. The figures may be attributed to social polarisation associated with residential segregation based on social class, and to the greater degree of transience in urban populations. Whatever the underlying causes, viewed in the light of the country's on-going urbanisation (as described earlier), the association of lower levels of volunteering with urban living appear to have negative consequences for the national stock of social capital.

While the census figures show clear contrasts between urban and rural areas generally, a further spatial distillation provides greater insights into the dynamics of volunteering within our cities, towns and rural areas. Thus, by disaggregating data on volunteerism at ED level (Electoral District – the smallest spatial unit used by the census), one can capture and analyse patterns at a much more localised level. Although the average level of volunteerism in Limerick county stands at 17.1 per cent, very clear contrasts emerge within the county. Levels of volunteerism are generally higher in the east and south east of the county, and lower in West Limerick. The communities with the highest levels of volunteerism include Galbally, Kilfinnane,

Bruff and Bruree. The LEADER Partnership, Ballyhoura Development, has been active in these communities and throughout East Limerick and North East Cork since the 1980s. Although there are many active community associations in West Limerick, the levels of volunteerism there are noticeably lower that in the east of the county, with the lowest levels being found in the hinterland of Abbeyfeale.

Within Limerick City, there appears to be a correlation between social class and levels of volunteerism, with the higher levels (above 14 per cent) evident in relatively affluent areas such as the North Circular Road, South Circular Road, Caherdavin, Raheen and Corbally. Castletroy also records an above average level of engagement in voluntary activity, which may in part derive from the activities of student bodies and clubs based in the university. In contrast, neighbourhoods that have been classified as disadvantaged (Haase and Pratschke, 2005) tend to record the lowest levels of volunteerism. This is consistent with the findings of Humphreys and Dinneen (2007) who, in a detailed neighbourhood-level study, report comparatively low levels of social capital, other than bonding capital, in the Moyross and King's Island areas as compared to the Castletroy / Monaleen area.

5. After the Tiger: Opportunities and Challenges for Parish Development
The writings of Brien Friel and the late John B. Keane among others provide insights into how the concepts of 'parish' and 'community' became synonymous with each other in 20th century Ireland. Indeed the words 'parish' and 'community' continue to be used interchangeably in the contemporary vernacular of Ireland. Traditionally, the parish has represented much more than an ecclesiastical unit; it is often the forum in which community identity is expressed and the fulcrum around which social events and associations are structured and defined.

The development of vibrant parish life in Ireland is very much tied up with fostering active citizenship, volunteerism, trust and social capital at community level. Thus, progressing the sustainable development of parishes requires that we draw on experiences in community development practice both within church organisations and without. Community development is both an outcome and a process. As an outcome, it implies an active civil society working in partnership with other bodies. As a process it involves informing, animating and empowering people, and in particular those who are most disadvantaged or socially excluded. It implies working with and through existing organisations and structures and, where necessary, reforming them and enabling them to adapt, rather than setting up new, duplicate or parallel structures that waste energy and split resources. Community development requires investment in skills and capacities at local level, and is contingent on training volunteers and community leaders. Community associations need to regularly review and evaluate their efforts and achievements, and to work in collaboration with other communities. Over recent years in Ireland, a number of inter-community networks have emerged. These enable groups of volunteers to share information, resources, expertise and know-how, while ensuring that each constituent group retains and draws on the strengths associated with its own identity and experiences. Parallels exist between these networks and the emergence of parish clusters.

The policy and institutional contexts for the advancement of volunteerism and community development in Ireland have become more favourable in recent years. Considerable expertise exists among many community and voluntary groups, and there are several examples of vibrant community action throughout the island of Ireland. Indeed, many community and voluntary groups have filled gaps in public sector provision and are responsible for the management of services in childcare, eldercare, social housing, mental health, youth development, and life-long education and training. Harnessing these new and emerging energies, skills, commitments and organisational structures presents considerable opportunities for parish development.

However, as this chapter has shown, many challenges need to be addressed. First, there is a clear challenge for the church itself. While clergy generally welcome and encourage lay participation in the liturgy and in aspects of parish administration, collaborative governance remains an elusive goal for many parishes. There is a clear need for strategic planning at parish level, so that all members of the parish community can contribute to the formulation and realisation of a shared vision and mission.

Second, as we have noted above, there is evidence that rapid economic growth and the associated demographic and social transformations of the so-called Celtic Tiger period have placed a strain on social capital. This poses a challenge for the development of participative democracy and governance as well as the maintenance and reinforcement of parish. Change raises questions about what 'community' means to people in contemporary Ireland. There is evidence of increasing individualism and alienation from society, and the Durkheimian concept of 'anomie' would appear to provide a useful way of understanding increasing social pathologies. Our track record in welcoming the new Irish is patchy at best,[6] and we are inclined to judge migrants based on their contributions to our economy, rather than supporting them to enrich our society and community and parish life.

But if the boom raised challenges for community and parish development, the manner of its ending in a sharp economic downturn and an accompanying financial crisis appears only to have intensified these challenges, as new social problems emerge, and as our capacity to address current social ills declines. Our collective self-confidence as a society has been eroded, and we increasingly hear calls for 'leadership' and 'a sense of direction'. Social partnership, which is much in need of renewal, is in fact under considerable pressure, and calls from the government for a new 'patriotism' seem naïve and ineffective at best, such has been the erosion of trust in government that some commentators have labelled them as hypocritical or even cynical. For the church too there are major issues of trust, and Hughes *et al* (2006; 107) observe that 'the exposure of the extent of child sexual and physical abuse perpetrated by members of the religious orders has contributed significantly to the dramatic decline in the standing of the Catholic Church in Irish society.'

It is probably true, then, to say that what social capital theorists refer to as 'generalised trust' appears seldom to have been at a lower ebb in Ireland. Consequently, the social context for community and parish development efforts to have been more difficult. At the same time studies of social capital suggest that the building of trust begins in the locality and neighbourhood and so despite, or maybe because of, the current adverse circumstances there appears to be an opportunity for the parish to emerge at the centre of a new model of social cohesion in Ireland. Parishes need to look to their internal, combined and

---

6. MacÉinrí, P. (2007), 'Ireland: What Models for Integration?' in Fanning, B., *Immigration and Social Change in the Republic of Ireland*, Manchester, Manchester UP.

collective capacity and to bear in mind the words of President
McAleese (2008):

> We need to look to our proven strengths and the resilience
> that comes from having faced tough times before, to find the
> tenacity, self-sacrifice and creativity to see us through the pe-
> riod of retrenchment ahead.

References

Boix, C. and Posner, D. N. (1998), 'Social capital: explaining its origins and effects on government performance', *British Journal of Political Science*, 28 (4), 686–93.

Bourdieu, P. (1986), 'Forms of capital', in Richardson, J. (ed) *Handbook of Theory of Research for the Sociology of Education*, Westport, CT: Greenwood Press.

Central Statistics Office (2007), *Statistical Yearbook of Ireland 2007*, Dublin: The Stationery Office.

Central Statistics Office (2008a), *Measuring Ireland's Progress 2007*, Dublin: The Stationery Office.

Central Statistics Office (2008b), *Statistical Yearbook of Ireland 2008*, Dublin: The Stationery Office.

Central Statistics Office (2008c), *Population and Labour Force Projections, 2011-2041*, Dublin: The Stationery Office.

Central Statistics Office (2008d), *Garda Recorded Crime Statistics 2003-2006*, Dublin: The Stationery Office.

Central Statistics Office (2008e), *Ireland – North and South: A Statistical profile 2008*, Dublin: The Stationery Office.

Central Statistics Office (various), *Census of Population Volumes*, Dublin: The Stationery Office.

Coleman, J. J. (1988), 'Social capital in the creation of human capital', *American Journal of Sociology*, 94, 95-121.

Commission of the European Communities (2001), *European Governance: a White Paper*, Luxembourg: EC.

Davoudi, S. (2005), 'Multi-level Governance and Territorial Cohesion', Presentation to SPAN Conference: Managing Space, Making Place, Dublin: SPAN (Strategic Planning Action Network).

Douglas, D. J. A. (2006), 'Rural Regional Development Planning – Governance and Other Challenges in the New EU.' *Studia Regionalia*, 16.

Fianna Fáil and the Progressive Democrats (2002), *An Agreed Programme for Government*, Dublin: Fianna Fáil and the Progressive Democrats.

Fukuyama, F. (1997), 'Social Capital', *The Tanner Lectures on Human Values* 19, 375-484.

Haase, T. and Pratschke, J. (2005), *Deprivation and its Spatial Articulation in the Republic of Ireland*, Dublin: Area Development Management.

Hardill, I., Baines, S. and 6, Perri (2007), 'Volunteering for All? Explaining Patterns of Volunteering and Identifying Strategies to Promote It', *Policy and Politics* 35(3) 395-412.

Hughes, I., Clancy, P., Harris, C. and Beetham, D. (2007), *Power to the People, Assessing Democracy in Ireland*, Dublin: TASC.

Humphreys, E. and Dinneen, D. (2007), *Evaluation of Social Capital in Limerick City and Environs*, Limerick: Health Services Executive Mid-West Area and Limerick City Development Board.

Johnston, G. and Percy-Smith, J. (2003), 'In Search of Social Capital',

Policy and Politics 31(3), 321-334.

Knack, S. (1999), 'Social Capital, Growth and Poverty: A Survey of Cross-Country Evidence', *Social Capital Initiative, Working Paper No 7*, Washington DC: World Bank.

McAleese, M. (2008), Address to the Northern Ireland Medico Legal Society, Queen's University, Belfast, 18th November.

McDonagh, S. (2007), *Climate Change – the challenge for all of us*, Dublin: Columba Press.

National Competitiveness Council (2008), *Annual Competitiveness Report 2008. Volume 1: Benchmarking Ireland's Performance*, Dublin: Forfás.

NESF (2003), *The Political Implications of Social Capital*, Forum report No 28, Dublin: National Economic and Social Forum.

Newton, K. (1997), 'Social capital and democracy', *American Behavioural Scientist*, 40(5), 575-86.

OECD (2001), *Local Partnerships for Better Governance*, Paris: Organisation for Economic Co-Operation and Development.

OECD (2006), *Partnerships for Better Governance*, Paris: Organisation for Economic Co-Operation and Development.

O'Keeffe, B. (2007), *Local Governance and Citizen Participation – the case of Dún Laoghaire-Rathdown*, NUI Maynooth: SPAN–Strategic Planning Action Newtork.

Pope, S. J. (2004), *Common Calling–the Laity and Governance of the Catholic Church*, Washington DC: Georgetown University Press.

Putnam, R. D. (2000), *Bowling Alone: the Collapse and Revival of American Community*, New York: Simon Schuster.

Stoker, G. and Chhotray, V. (2008), *Governance Theory – a cross-disciplinary approach*, London: Macmillan.

Taskforce on Active Citizenship (2007a), *The Concept of Active Citizenship*, Dublin: the Taskforce on Active Citizenship.

Taskforce on Active Citizenship (2007b), *Statistical Evidence on Active Citizenship in Ireland*, Dublin: the Taskforce on Active Citizenship.

USCCB (2005), *Co-Workers in the Vineyard of the Lord*, Washington DC: United States Conference of Catholic Bishops.

Walsh, J., Craig, S. and McCafferty, D. (1998), *Local Partnerships for Social Inclusion?* Dublin: Oak Tree Press in association with the Combat Poverty Agency.

Walsh, J. and Meldon, J. (eds) (2004), *Partnerships for Effective Local Development*, Charleroi: Universite Libre de Bruxelles.

Whiteley, P. F. (2000), 'Economic Growth and Social Capital', *Political Studies*, 48, 443-66.

World Commission on Environment and Development (UN) (1987), *Our Common Future*, Oxford: Oxford University Press.

CHAPTER FOUR

Migration and Community Building

Eoin O'Mahony

'Everyone thinks of changing the world, but no one thinks of changing himself.' *Tolstoy*

Introduction

In Ireland until recent years, we took a sense of community for granted. It was noted only when it was absent. We took pride in our community's activity and were clear that 'our community' was inextricably linked with 'our' faith. In the last 20 years there have been many challenges presented to this collective, imagined and assumed homogeneity. The in-migration of people from scores of countries has confronted the host society with some significant challenges, some welcome and others not so welcome. Many of the discussions about integration and migration have been more about how Irish identity is changing than the personhood of the new arrival. We use the term 'new Irish' and the word 'newcomers' to describe migrating people when in actual fact we are talking about ourselves and drawing attention to change amongst this assumed community.

This paper explores some of the recent challenges to established notions of communities. In doing so, I provide a profile of Ireland's current population and chart recent trends in migration. Secondly, I discuss the established concept of communities of interest and finally I introduce a model for 'parishes of interest'. Identification with the parish up to now has mostly been about location, a physical space, delineated by rivers and field boundaries. My own proposal is for a reconfiguration of parishes based on communities of interest. It is not just workers who have made the journey to Ireland but people with pre-existing family ties, assumptions about what is right and wrong and a defined need for the organisation of new communities. Their interests may not match the physically-bounded space and yet we are not sure what that is or what that can become. The paper examines what is meant by 'the parish' in a time of significant and continued in-migration. It asks some questions about the integration of members of a society when they are defined by their place in a bureaucratic hierarchy and not by their residence.

A profile of Ireland's population and recent migration trends
To examine a changing sense of the parish, we should examine a quick demographic profile of various places in Ireland. In doing this I am aware of the limitations of the geographical units here as well as the exclusion of people resident in the north east of the island. Looking at place of birth data from the Irish Census in 2006, we note that there is little divergence in the proportions of each area's population of Irish-born people and those born outside of Ireland. In the State as a whole 85% were born in Ireland while in Cavan, Monaghan and Donegal it is just over 82% of the population. You might be surprised to see that the largest non-Irish born group in the State is that of those born in the UK. This includes those born in Northern Ireland and now living in the Republic. Crucial issues arise about the perceptions of problematic groupings which I will turn to later when briefly referring to Iris Young.

Table : Place of birth of those usually resident in the Republic of Ireland 2006.
Source: www.cso.ie/census/default.htm (last accessed July 2008)

Usually resident	Place of birth					
	Ireland	UK	Poland	Lithuania	Other EU 25	Rest of world
Leinster	84.91	5.52	1.57	0.68	2.17	5.16
Munster	87.14	6.20	1.58	0.42	1.66	3.00
Connacht	84.52	8.55	1.46	0.40	1.58	3.48
Ulster (part of)	82.31	12.62	0.83	1.00	1.06	2.18
State	85.32	6.51	1.51	0.59	1.89	4.17

Perhaps one of the reasons why the CSO tabulated Polish and Lithuanian born people in the Census was because of their relatively large proportions in the overall tally. These data present a story about recent migration into Ireland. In the period directly before the accession of ten new states to the EU in 2004, there was a significant migration of Polish and Lithuanian people to the booming Irish economy. There were recruitment fairs by FÁS in the big cities of these European countries and there was a sense in smaller towns in these countries that sufficient work was to be had at such pay levels as to make it worthwhile for people to leave.[1] Because this is what we are talking about: individual decisions to leave, short- or long-term. These are stories of people leaving families and households, moving to Ireland and finding the small things difficult and the big things all-consuming. We can also see that about 4% of the resident population was born outside of the EU area – defined here as a 'rest of the world' category.

So where did the large numbers of UK-born people come from? 7.5% of Clare residents are UK-born. 8.5% of the residents of Connacht are UK-born. What attracted these migrants into Ireland? Was it the availability of work? Perhaps it was pre-existing family ties? Are there migration support groups for UK-born people? Where are the integration opportunities for this group of migrants? I ask these questions facetiously of course but wish to draw attention to the fact that there are far higher proportions of UK-born people living in Ireland than any number of problematised groups of 'others'.

The nationalities present in the State tell another story. The table below shows the nationalities of those usually resident in the Republic. Once again we see a proportion of Poles and Lithuanians living across each part of the State as well as a number of nationals from non-EU states.

Table 2: Nationalities of those usually resident in the Republic of Ireland 2006.
Source: www.cso.ie/census/default.htm (last accessed July 2008).

| Usually resident | Nationality | | | | | |
	Irish	UK	Polish	Lithuanian	Other EU 25	Rest of World
Leinster	87.89	2.18	1.58	0.67	2.08	4.37
Munster	90.00	3.04	1.58	0.41	1.59	2.39
Connacht	89.36	3.79	1.45	0.39	1.48	2.65
Ulster (part of)	91.08	3.60	0.84	1.00	0.98	1.72
State	88.85	2.70	1.52	0.59	1.81	3.45

About 4.5% of Leinster's residents are nationals of 'rest of world' countries. Note as well that a small percentage of those with Irish nationality were not born in the State – there is a 3.5% difference in the proportion of the population declaring Irish

1. FÁS, The Irish Labour Market Review 2004 (Dublin: FAS, 2004) 14-18.

nationality and those who were born in Ireland. A question I would ask at this stage: are these migrants too? They are Irish nationals but not born here. 6.5% of the population are UK-born people and yet just under half of this proportion claim Irish nationality. Other, related data might help us to answer these questions.

Table 3: Ethnicity of those usually resident in the Republic of Ireland 2006.
Source: www.cso.ie/census/default.htm (last accessed July 2008).

Usually resident	**Ethnicity**					
	White Irish	*White Irish Traveller*	*Other White*	*Black or Black Irish*	*Asian or Asian Irish*	*Other*
Leinster	86.00	0.50	7.16	1.40	1.71	1.23
Munster	88.92	0.46	6.69	0.71	0.76	0.92
Connacht	88.06	0.98	6.99	0.67	0.72	1.22
Ulster (part of)	91.05	0.29	5.82	0.43	0.54	0.72
State	87.37	0.54	6.93	1.06	1.25	1.11

Finally we see the ethnicity of the population by province and in the State. As problematic as these groupings are (you apparently have to be, for example, Black or Black Irish to be a member of an ethnic minority – irrespective of your nationality), they are the only data available for the tabulation of ethnicities in the State. Just 0.54% of the population of the State are from a Traveller background, with higher proportions in Connacht than anywhere else in Ireland. There is about 7% of the population classified as people in the Other White category which means they are neither White Irish nor White Irish Traveller but White.[2] Is this referring to their ethnicity or nationality? Defining people for tabulation can be problematic but the selection of these categories is particularly problematic.

So what can figures like these tell us about community development and change? The first thing to note is that being in a place, a location in space does not determine one's ethnicity or nationality. Many of us hear people saying things like 'there are too many immigrants in this town' or 'we have more than our fair share' as if the choices that migrants might have in relation to where they live is entirely theirs or perhaps even a matter of policy. People bring their collected knowledge and experience of their families and communities to new places. Their ethnicity /

---

2. Mary Gilmartin, *The Same But Different* (Dublin: *The Irish Times*, 2006).

nationality may only then become problematised when there is a host community that perceives their arrival as a threat. All categories create outsiders, those excluded and those marginalised from decision-making and -taking. It is in these spaces of marginalisation and exclusion where, I believe, the most change can take place. Those who are comfortable in a high status position do not question the basis for their own authority and have little interest in change.

This is where Irish identity takes on a less homogeneous character, one which does not depend on being white, Catholic or born on the island. An assumed homogeneity of 'being Irish' is a story we tell ourselves to overcome the complexity and contradictions that the arrival of migrants can bring about. The narrative of 'the land of saints and scholars' is an example of this in that it relies on a pre-Plantation image of an Ireland unsullied by people coming from elsewhere. I suspect that its strength as an image of ourselves lies more in a defensiveness than an inclusivity. It is as if the faith that the saints possessed, as well as the knowledge that the scholars amassed is under threat, not to be shared with others.

Data on the proportions of the resident population who professed a religion from Census 2006 show that over 92% stated that they were Catholic. 3.2% stated that they were Church of Ireland and smaller proportions from the world's other main religions. These data should not be a source of comfort or indeed censure, where high proportions of the population express a Catholic faith with minor others making up 'the rest'. These are not data to observe carefully over the years for the slightest variation of each part of the population and bemoaning the fact that parishes are not as active as they used to be. This is not about us versus them – Catholics versus the minority religions. What used to be, remains what is for thousands of people living in Ireland – women denied educational opportunities and jobs, the marginalisation of the poetic and the emotional, ambition-denuding unemployment as well as literal and figurative curtain-twitching. The ways in which these can be embedded within parishes and communities are not taken for granted by people unfamiliar with Ireland.

But the point of this paper is not to point a finger at a past that existed or throw any babies out with the bath water. Communities of interest arise in many places across and within this 92% of the professed population. It is not important that one is 6% or another is 20%, across time or between censuses or surveys. What are important are the spaces for engagement within and between communities. I want to talk about one of the ways in which these spaces can develop in the context of a changing Ireland.

In their report *Immigration, Faith and Cohesion* for the Joseph Rowntree Foundation, Jayaweera and Choudhury conclude with eight ways in which their research found hope for the future as well as portents of danger in present-day Britain. While the report was based on research carried out in areas where large numbers of Muslim people live and work alongside Christian people, it has resonances for small areas of interaction in this country too. One of the conclusions they draw is that in spaces of social interaction, daily and weekly contact is most important:

> Although Muslims were more likely than other residents to meet people of similar religious and or ethnic origins in more social spaces outside of the home, there was considerable evidence of *meaningful, informal social interaction across religious and ethnic boundaries in a variety of spaces visited in the course of daily life*, including sports and leisure facilities, residents' associations, and colleges and schools (whether as parents or participants in the education process). Significantly, this social interaction with people from other backgrounds was particularly the case for women with family responsibilities, as well as for those who were working or in education. This challenges a common perception of economically inactive Muslim women, in particular, as isolated from wider society. (emphasis added)[3]

If there is one thing that Irish people know well it is the minute social interaction, the stopping on the street, the casual greeting on the road, the knowing nod of the head as we go about our daily business. Much of this interaction takes place in the full knowledge that 'we' are knowing of each other, a pooled sense of identity and of a common space and purpose. This is precisely why it happens in smaller towns more often than it does in larger towns and city suburbs. People pass through

---

3. Hiranthi Jayaweera and Tufyal Choudhury, *Immigration, faith and cohesion: Evidence from local areas with significant Muslim populations* (York: Joseph Rowntree Foundation, 2008) 123-124.

large towns and suburbs, on the way to somewhere else, on holidays, to work, to seek out the ultimate leisure and that authentically 'Irish experience' on the west coast. What is seen in the report by the Rowntree Foundation also is the sense in which the migrant belongs to both one place and another place, a place unknown to the receiving communities and perhaps the object of imaginative wanderings of one kind or another. There is little conflict in belonging to one place and also another: being Polish and being in Ireland, for example.

> Most migrants ... felt there was little conflict in belonging to both their countries of origin and to Britain. As one Muslim woman said, 'I got my life here but I got my memories there'; and a Polish man: 'You don't have to make a choice between the two.' Recent migrants, as expected, had the strongest sense of attachment to their country of origin and to people from that country ('transnational identification'), a majority saying that the most important people in their lives were not in Britain. For established Muslims born outside the UK, the position was reversed, 60 per cent saying that the people most important to them were in Britain. Information and visits to their country of origin remained important to them, but with very limited evidence of financial, business or political involvement abroad.[4]

Other studies based in Ireland have also charted this sense of being in one place and belonging to another. In their 2006 study of Ratoath in County Meath, Peillon, Corcoran and Gray talk of the town being a new suburb with many people living there with no sense of shared history of the town or the locality.[5] The parish cannot be assumed to be a unifying representational structure, and in a broader sense this lack of a shared understanding has significant consequences for local governance and the fostering of that much overused term: social capital. It is as if in not being able to recognise new people who move into the area (people who grew up Catholic, are white and like both English soccer and Irish stout), 'the community' reverts back to nothing at all with little account taken of the very real political

4. Jayaweera and Choudhury, *Immigration, faith and cohesion: Evidence from local areas with significant Muslim populations*, 126.
5. Michel Peillon, Mary Corcoran and Jane Gray, *Civic Engagement and the Governance of Irish Suburbs* (Dublin: The Policy Institute, 2006) 60-77.

concerns of these expanded suburbs of Dublin. In the absence of anything formal to foster participation, social capital is deemed to be lacking, as if it emerges only when conditions are right. So when locals seek a new school or object to the siting of an incinerator, this is deemed not to be the 'right kind of social capital'.

If there was any evidence that to be part of a community you do not have to be in a place for any length of time, it is this: experiences of migration are lived in a place of instability, of passing through. Migration means not always knowing the head nods and the local greetings, the idle banter between the handing over of money and the receipt of change. It is in these spaces that parishes and communities now live: in the very instability of a sense of community; of being in neither one place nor the other; being neither fully in a city nor in its suburbs. This, I believe, is as true for people who grew up here as for those who have only recently arrived. Binge drinking, road accidents and dietary ill-health are but three ways in which this instability is made manifest in Ireland today.[6]

This instability causes a problem for those who believe that communities are fields, sets of roads, bounded by history and a shared understanding of faith in a place. It is in the instability brought about by change that some find real difficulties with new arrivals. Friends of mine resident here for 10 years but from South Africa and Australia experience this in the question, often repeated year after year: 'And why did you come to Ireland?' meaning of course 'When are you going home?' As has been written by Poznański about Polish Catholics:

> Most Poles live on a temporary basis in Ireland. Poles move, change and exchange, appear and disappear constantly.[7]

And so Poznański goes on to ask most forcefully and eloquently, if Poles can actually join an Irish parish, a structure where lay activity is predominant and which requires stability of housing and a longer term commitment. Were Irish parishes to remain communities of place and not enter into a dialogue with other groups about communities of shared interest and practice then the future is indeed very grim for increasing lay in-

6. Kieran Keohane and Carmen Kuhling, *Collision Culture: transformations in everyday life in Ireland* (Dublin: The Liffey Press, 2004) 100-107.
7. Jacek Poznański, 'Polish Catholics and the Hopes of the Irish Church,' *The Furrow* LIX (2008) 297-302.

volvement. Poznański and others chart the decline in weekly practice, if this be a sufficient measure of Christian values, amongst Polish migrants in Ireland. The devotion of some Polish young people may provide an inspiration to an older Irish generation but is this what the church in Ireland is seeking to return to? In a time when the parish's embodiment of its existence in its priest is shortening, and in a place where shared knowledge of things as simple as driving directions and as complex as faith are contested, there must be a reimagining of what a parish is in a time of immeasurable instability. I agree with Poznański and others when he states that integration does not mean assimilation. All attempts to co-opt migrating populations into an orthodox vision of what being a Catholic is, having a faith and seeking grace and justice, will fail. We know this as a migrating people; the memory of migration is still very vivid in the collective imagination. We have to know how to read it in our physical and intellectual landscapes.

Lest you think that I have moved from the formally statistical to the lyrical, I want to present a very practical way in which to think about communities of interest where agreement is not always reached, where the instability that comes with some of our lives can be accommodated and where the positive aspects of transitory spaces can be harnessed.

According to the political philosopher Iris Young, proponents of democracy do not adequately address the problem of inclusive participation.[8] By assuming a homogeneous public, they fail to consider institutional arrangements for including people not culturally identified with dominant norms of reason and respectability. Young urges that public policy should undermine group-based oppression by affirming rather than suppressing social group difference. By affirming the differences between groups, there is more learning for both those seen as different and those for whom the difference is a problem. Affirming differences between groups also obviates the need for debates where 'me winning' means 'you losing'. This particular zero-sum game is very prevalent in discussions of resource allocation and power distribution in Ireland, for example, government policy on minimising poverty for single parents without con-

---

8. Iris Marion Young, 'Justice and Politics of Difference,' *Gender and Planning: a reader*, ed. S. S. Fainstein and L. J. Servon (New Jersey: Rutgers University, 2005) 86-103.

ceding something to all other family types. Basing her vision of
the good society on the differentiated, culturally plural network,
Young argues for a principle of group representation in democratic publics and for group-differentiated policies. This brings
with it some crucial lessons in what can be called non-geograph-
ically circumscribed interests. Earlier I have mentioned the
threat perceived by some of the outsider and how change can
occur in spaces of marginalisation, in the very places of dissent
and disagreement. Young provides us with some valuable tools
to think about people in human groups who share perhaps very
little but who feel for one reason or another that traditional
forms of organisation have failed them.

The example I want to present is that of the online technolo-
gies collectively known as social networking sites. These are col-
lectivities of people, using the things we find around ourselves
every day, to create and recreate communities of interest. They
are the enabling places where people seek meaning and interest
in each other and our surroundings. This is not something that
happens in teenagers' bedrooms or in internet cafes in our towns
and cities. It is happening on the streets and homes of Cork and
Limerick and Derry and Longford and Thurles. I say *we* and *our*
because I am a part of some of these shared online spaces known
as social networking sites. For example, one of my interests is
photography. I like to take photographs of new urban spaces and
people in towns and cities. I share these with other people and I
also write an online narrative to this and other processes.

These online spaces have been in the press lately because of
so-called cyber-bullying and suicide tributes amongst young
people. I am not going to call this a virtual community because
this does the communities a grave disservice and does not assist
in understanding what I have to say about these communities of
interest. Because a computer is used does not mean that all that
is talked about are binary programming and social profiling.
Underlying this practical way of being a member of these communities, is the sense that people still want to meet face to face.
The computer is a tool that enables people to meet and there is
still the desire to commune for specific events. We may have little
else in common between us but we find each other because of
one thing or two things in our lives. Computers are all very well
but people want to meet up, look each other in the eye and chat
and compare experiences.

None of the images I have presented to you have a geograph-ically-bounded space: it is the city, the town and on the web it-self. All of the activities in these images have been facilitated through online social networking sites. They involve some mi-grants and some people born in Ireland.

Now I am not trying to compare a personally transformative experience that the breaking of bread can be with the seeming triviality of urban graffiti. However, I would finally ask you to examine the following characteristics of these communities of interest. In thinking about migration and the challenges I presented earlier about community development and parish change, we might seek to think about the unity involved in these activities, the shared experience and be aware that what is unfamiliar to us can often present moments of great change.

I ask you to engage with these communities of interest. There is a search for authenticity in these activities which does not depend on physical location: this authenticity sees the good in people who share your interests. In re-imagining what a parish community is, let us not assume that we are a homogeneous public, all else lying outside norms of respectability and reason. We are living in unstable times, brought about sometimes by events outside of our control, although we are not always good at recognising what it is that is valuable to us. The migrant moves here and she is seeking work, stability and happiness. She can be vulnerable and constantly aware that moving on again might be the best way to manage this vulnerability. For now, people from other cultural and religious experiences reside in our communities and our parishes. As residents they have an interest in what goes on around them but are not always interested in telling us their story. They are not citizens, although this will become more common as time goes on. There are important stories to tell and to hear. We too have to communicate with the migrant as 'the other'. We should listen but we must also share our own stories. Otherwise it is a futile exercise in the consumption of some exotic culture and way of life. We must be assured of our own stories and not tell stories that we get more out of ourselves than the other does. In opening up a more constructive dia-logue, community building can occur not just around a physical space but around a common idea where not everyone agrees on in all its elements.

CHAPTER FIVE

Parish Life: Facing a Challenging Future

Donal Murray

The first thing the Code of Canon Law says about the parish is that it is a definite community of the Christian faithful.[1] It goes on to say that this community is stably established and that its pastoral care is entrusted by the bishop to a parish priest. The future, not to speak of the present, challenges our picture of the parish in all of these aspects.

In our situation in Ireland today, the parish may not feel particularly stable. Declining priestly vocations will necessitate increasingly painful changes in the number of Masses; priests will no longer be readily available even for things that have been taken for granted – like funerals, anniversary Masses and parish functions; the prospect of cancelling Sunday Masses at short notice because no priest can be found to cover for a man who has taken ill is not far off. Many parishes can foresee the day when they will not have a parish priest resident among them. Many parishes see what used to be a vibrant community being emptied of its facilities and its social life – schools, post offices and so on as well as religious services. Many people wonder whether the idea of a parish is viable at all in the urbanised, secularised, pressurised lifestyle of our time where people may have little attachment to the place in which they live. I want to reflect on the challenge which the future poses to the modern parish in becoming a community which is geared to respond to the world of today.

The Parish is a Community

The Canon Law's description of the parish as a community is not what one might have expected in a legal document. The pri-

---

1. Code of Canon Law 515§1: A parish is a certain community of the Christian faithful stably established within a particular church, whose pastoral care, under the authority of the diocesan bishop, is entrusted to a parish priest as its proper pastor.

mary focus is not on the territory or the buildings or the duties and rights of the parish priest but on all the people who make up the community.

But that has become problematic. Many of the factors that characterised the community in the past have been transformed and weakened. In the smaller, more rural, communities which were the norm in the past, people knew their neighbours and were involved with one another's lives. Perhaps they knew too much about one another's lives.

It was not necessary to bring to their attention the fact that a new baby was being baptised or that the young people of the parish were receiving First Communion or Confirmation. Nowadays many people in a big parish are hardly aware that such events are taking place – events that are meant to be high-lights in the life of the community. We have 'Do this in Memory' both so that the first communicants may realise that the whole parish community is concerned to share their First Eucharist with them and so that the community may realise that this is their role. We are developing Confirmation preparation pro-grammes to meet the same need. The revival of the RCIA is now beginning to be a feature of life in the parish and diocese; this highlights the fact that Christian initiation is about a whole com-munity receiving a new member into communion.

The sense of belonging to the parish community has dimin-ished. In the past it could be taken for granted; now it is not so visible; it is something that has to be worked at. Even in rural parishes, large numbers of the parishioners may be commuting to work in the surrounding towns; many of them may have come to the area because housing is cheaper than it would be in the city or suburbs. They may not feel a strong sense of belonging.

These changes are fundamentally sociological and not spec-ific to the church. We live in a new kind of world where belong-ing and active participation, at least in the sense in which they were understood in the past, are a problem for almost all institu-tions and organisations. At the same time, paradoxically, there appears to be a growing problem of loneliness in society, even, perhaps especially, in crowded cities. The church is not alone in suffering from this mixture of detachment from structures or in-stitutions, on the one hand, and an unsatisfied need for belong-ing, on the other.

Today the challenge is for a parish to find ways or fostering its own identity in a new context. Of course it was always the case that the identity of a parish was everyone's responsibility and was not created simply by the parish priest. It arose out of the efforts of the whole community to provide itself with churches and schools and the involvement of parishioners in all sorts of activities from the Altar Society to the Scouts to the people who organised the annual Fete or the Card Club or amateur dramatics and, of course, the GAA and other sporting activities.

But all of that took place in a community conscious of itself as a community. Today the challenge takes on a new urgency. This is a world in which people often do not really belong to any particular place, but work in one location, live in another and feel that the place where they are really at home is somewhere else.

We should not idealise the sense of community that existed in the past. It was real, but it had its flaws. It existed alongside an understanding of faith that was often rather individual. People attended Mass together, often praying devoutly but individually, seeing the Mass as something the priest was doing while they said their prayers. There was often no clear sense that they were part of a prayer being offered to the Father by the community united in the Holy Spirit, joined with Christ in his Paschal Mystery, with all the church on earth and with all the angels and saints.

So the first challenge of the future is for the parish to become what it fundamentally is: a community which knows its own identity. Pope John Paul put the challenge like this:

> (The parish) must rediscover its vocation, which is to be a fraternal and welcoming family home, where those who have been baptised and confirmed become aware of forming the People of God. In that home, the bread of good doctrine and the Eucharistic Bread are broken for them in abundance, in the setting of the one act of worship; from that home they are sent out day by day to their apostolic mission in all the centres of activity of the life of the world.[2]

That text is thirty years old. The document was published in October 1979, just after the Pope returned to Rome from his pastoral visit to Ireland and the United States. Like the address he gave in Limerick, it is as true today as when it was first spoken.

---

2. John Paul II, *Catechesi Tradendae*, (1979) 67.

Rediscovering the Vocation

The challenge that faces parish life today can be summed up in that one phrase, 'to become aware of forming the People of God'. The parish is not just an association which we join for a particular limited purpose; it is a family home and, like any family, it is a setting in which we learn who we are and a setting to which we belong with our whole lives. Like any family it is made up of people who, apart from the husband and wife, have not chosen one another. It is not an exclusive group of likeable, always compatible people. In the Sunday Eucharist we share our faith with that family and recognise one another in the Body of Christ.

One of the most important lessons in growing up in a family is learning that the family does not exist simply for my own benefit. We have to learn that the care and support we receive should be reciprocated. Perhaps a baby thinks to him or herself: 'This is very satisfactory; if I cry loudly enough they all come running!' As we grow and mature we learn to hear the often silent cries of other people in the family and to ask more what we can do for them than what they can do for us.

I remember reading an article by an African bishop many years ago. He expressed deep gratitude and admiration for all that the missionaries had done in his country. But he pointed out that the zeal and effectiveness of missionaries could all too easily create the impression that the church is an outside agency that does things for us – wonderful things, constructive things. It provides education, health care, religious services and so on. But then he said that the church would never really take root in Africa until it became clear to his people that the church is not just what other people do; it is what they themselves are called to do for one another and for the world.

And so the parish is a community which sends out its members day by day. Both sides of this statement are important. The members are sent out beyond the community, but it is the *community* which sends out its members with the good news to be proclaimed to the world.

In Ireland we are experiencing something akin to what the African bishop pointed to. If people are to become aware of forming the People of God they have to stop thinking of the church as an institution outside themselves from which they receive services and guidance. It means seeing the church as a community in which each person has an essential role. That is easily said, but making it real involves a change of mindset.

The magnificent work of religious congregations in Ireland through the years in health care, in education, in pastoral work now poses a critical challenge to the rest of the church. Are we ready to recognise that these admirable works are not and never were just the responsibility of the religious alone? They are the responsibility of the whole Christian community. In particular, we need urgently to recognise that the work of Catholic education at every level is a matter for all of us.[3]

The message to which Christians bear witness is not just about God's love for me as an isolated individual. God has willed to make human beings holy and to save them 'not as individuals without any bond between them, but rather to make them into a people who might acknowledge him and serve him in holiness'.[4] Only a community aware of itself as forming the People of God can bear effective witness to this truth.

What we have to offer the world is a way of life, the way of life of God's People. We are pointing not to ourselves but to a community gathered around Christ, a community which is Christ's Body. And we recognise that this community gathered to celebrate the Eucharist is the fullest expression of who we are and is the source of our strength and our mission. The Eucharist is the summit and source of the life of the whole church and of each parish. That is why we need to put all our prayer and effort into encouraging vocations to the priesthood without which the availability of priests will continue to diminish dramatically.

The decline in vocations to the ordained priesthood and religious life raises very serious questions about the future shape of the parish and of the diocese. If, God forbid, the present decline were to continue, twenty years would see an astonishing change. In other words, if we do not turn a corner within the next dozen years we will be moving steadily towards the kind of situation in which our priests are currently working in Peru – just two priests in a parish with about half the population of the diocese of Limerick. The change will happen a lot more quickly if we fail to understand the pressures that are on priests and the unreasonable expectations that are placed on them, often by good people who don't realise how great the pressures are.

---

3. Irish Catholic Bishops' Conference, *Vision 08*, Pentecost 2008.
4. Vatican II, *Lumen Gentium*, 9.

The responsibility that falls on the church, on every parish and on every member of it, is to be 'a sign and instrument both of a very closely knit union with God and of the unity of the whole human race'.[5] A positive fruit of the decline in vocations is that it has become clearer and clearer – the reality is utterly inescapable – that if Christian faith is to survive in Ireland we all have to be involved in sharing the Good News with others and with a new generation.

Of course, this was always the case. Through years of persecution and hardship it was the faith of parents and teachers and other lay faithful that kept the flame of faith alive. But we need a reminder of that in the circumstances of our time. Too often the reaction to reports of falling Mass attendance, or to declining vocations, or to a certain invisibility of belief in social and political life, or to a drift away from the church by young people is to say 'the bishops must be worried' or 'what are the priests doing about it?' The challenge is not just to the clergy, it is to every member of the church. Until we all recognise that, we will be missing the real nature of the parish and of the church; and we will be failing to recognise and respond to the challenge we face.

There are many categories of people who have drifted away or who feel alienated. Pope John Paul said what was needed over thirty years ago: '(The parish) must rediscover its vocation, which is to be a fraternal and welcoming family home.' It must become a setting where people can see that they have a place and a role, where their gifts are needed.

Do we for instance think not just of how 'we' can persuade 'them' to come back to Mass and not enough in terms of how 'they' could become part of the 'us' which cannot function fully without the gifts that the Holy Spirit has given them. How many people who rarely go to Mass would respond to an invitation to come some Sunday, perhaps for a special parish occasion and might find their way back to regular practice? I wonder how many have ever received such an invitation.

At Confirmation I tell young people that their gifts are for the whole community and that we are delighted to know that they will be playing their part. We tell them that we will support and encourage them in every way. But is it true? Will they find a welcoming family home ready to appreciate their gifts, to listen to their ideas, to encourage their contribution of their vitality to the life of their parish?

---

5. *Lumen Gentium,*1.

In the past, we assumed that young people would find their place in the community without any particular effort. It would follow naturally as they became adult participants in the overlapping activities that made up the local community. Now sporting bodies and other voluntary groups make serious efforts, often with only limited success, to attract a new generation and help them to realise that they are needed, and that no organisation can survive without an intake of fresh blood from time to time. But what exactly do we do as a community of faith to help them realise that they are needed and that, without their generation, the church as we have known it in Ireland will not survive?

I wonder too how many new arrivals in Ireland feel that their local community is not only accepting of their presence but positively and actively welcoming. Could it be that a young person from Eastern or Central Europe could attend a Sunday Mass in one of our churches without hearing a welcoming word from anyone, still less being invited, at least occasionally, to share a cup of tea with some of the other parishioners? Do we really appreciate how people from other lands can bring a new richness, new approaches and new vitality to the life of our community?

To All the Life of the World

But why do we need new members and new vitality? One important answer is that the parish does not exist simply for its own sake or for the sake of its individual members, or even for the sake of those within it who are sick or in need or adrift. It has a bigger mission than that. It is not a refuge where we hide from the world and its problems. It is not the wagons drawn in a circle to keep the world at bay. It is a base from which we go out to change not only the parish but the world, to play our part in the Holy Spirit's renewal of the face of the earth (Ps 104:30): 'From that home they are sent out day by day to their apostolic mission in all the centres of activity of the life of the world'. We are to be a sign and instrument for the world – a world that seems less ready to hear the wonder of the gospel than the one in which many of us grew up.

Probably for the first time in history, religion is in many ways at the margins of Irish society. The challenge of addressing a secularised world is a daunting task. It means trying to find ways of bringing the gospel to a culture no longer penetrated by the transcendent, a culture in which the things of God seem to have little place, a culture which often seems to feel no hunger for what has been called 'the God who is not missed', a culture, as Pope John Paul put it on another occasion, which is marked by the silence or absence of God.[6]

One clear sign of that secularisation is the notion, which affects believers too, that religion has its place. It has relevance in the church, or when we encounter difficulties, when we pray. In other areas we live with little conscious reference to God. God, as Pope John Paul once put it, does not appear above the horizon of our lives.[7] But we must be clear. A god who is not the God of all creation and of every second and every inch and every aspect of creation would not be God at all.

Obviously, how that faith in God's presence is to be expressed and what it means in many of these areas is something on which we have to reflect. The first thing to be said, however, is that the challenge needs to be correctly read and realistically responded to. During his visit to Ireland Pope John Paul also said that:

> Every generation, with its own mentality and characteristics, is like a new continent to be won for Christ. The church must constantly look for new ways that will enable her to understand more profoundly and to carry out with renewed vigour the mission received from her Founder.[8]

In other words, each new period in history brings new situations and challenges that have not yet been touched by the gospel. That is particularly true of the century in which we live. Because of the pace of change that we are experiencing, our time presents many areas which have never previously been lived in or reflected on by Christians and which are, therefore, a sort of mission territory, not yet evangelised. In order to hear the Good News addressing this new world, there is a vital need for what Pope John Paul in *Evangelium Vitae* called 'a contemplative outlook' which sees life as a gift and sees in all things the reflection of the Creator and in every person the Creator's living image.[9]

It is a world, globalised as never before; a world of inform-

6. John Paul II, *Master in the Faith*, 4th Centenary of the Death of St John of the Cross (1999).
7. cf John Paul II, Address to Pontifical Council for Culture, 5 March 1988.
8. John Paul II, Homily in Knock, 30 September 1979.
9. John Paul II, *Evangelium Vitae* (1995) 83.

ation technology; a world whose environment is threatened by our lifestyle; a world of incredibly destructive weapons; a world where huge inequalities are obvious; a world of increasing multicultural and interreligious contact – and often unfortunately not just contact but conflict. These, and many other areas, require experience and expertise if one is to deal realistically with them, to speak sensibly about them or even to formulate clearly the issues that need to be addressed and reflected upon.

It is a world as uncertain as any in history. It would be a brave person who could be sure whether we are heading to a world of unimagined affluence and technological advance or a world blighted by energy and resource shortages and disastrous climate change. It would be a brave person who would predict where the balance of power will lie in our world a couple of decades from now. It is a world whose characteristic musical theme might be whistling in the dark!

These issues are not just areas of our world; they are areas of our lives and of ourselves. Even we Christians lead large portions of our own lives in areas which have never been lived in or reflected on in the light of the gospel. We live in the mission territory of a very new generation. There is no use leaving it to the next generation to make sense of this world; we have to begin the process of reflection; we have to raise the questions about how to live as a follower of Christ in this new world.

Concerned Christians who are well informed and deeply involved in areas like medicine and medical research, or politics or economics, or environmental issues, or the European Union, sometimes ask why priests and bishops do not speak about the issues that arise in these areas, without any apparent awareness that it is they themselves who are best placed to speak about these spheres.

Our world will become increasingly secularised, unless Christians who have the relevant expertise and experience bring their faith to bear on it. And, of course, everyone has experience and expertise that are relevant, because everyone has a unique individual perspective, history and network of relationships. Each person has his or her place in the new continent and his or her possibilities for evangelising it. If believers do not bring the gospel into their own situations, nobody else can. The parish is the family home from which believers go into all of these areas where they are the ones who have to apply their faith to problems that the rest of us simply do not understand as they do.

A rounded pastoral approach to secularisation will mean recognising that people, whether lay or clerical, who believe that the challenge can be met exclusively, or even principally, by clergy, are badly misreading the situation. They are looking in a direction that cannot provide an adequate response. Of course the clergy have a crucial role to play, but the world cannot be evangelised unless all the variety and range of gifts that the Spirit gives to the church are brought into action.

As we face the complex world of today, we can hardly expect to make any impact if we fail to value and to use the gifts of the community. If we think it is a task for someone else, for the bishop, the priest, the religious, we are ignoring what St Paul said about the body of Christ: '… there are many parts, yet one body. The eye cannot say to the hand, "I have no need of you," nor again the head to the feet, "I have no need of you".' (1 Cor 12: 20, 21).

It is a task for all the members of the church. A priority for the life of the parish is to challenge, encourage and support parishioners in bringing their gifts to bear on the profound human questions that arise from living in our kind of world – on the questions about human dignity and on the possibilities and threats to the growth of the human family, on how it is possible to hope in the face of those threats and on the Christian response to the issues of the world in which we live. These questions have never arisen in the same way before. We have, of course, our tradition of faith, but we have no tradition of how it is to be lived in Ireland and in the wider world of the twenty-first century.

Pope John Paul once again presented to the Irish Bishops during our *ad limina* visit in 1999 the ideas he expressed in Limerick now almost thirty years ago:

> The new evangelisation which can make the next century a springtime of the gospel will depend very much on the lay faithful being fully aware of their baptismal vocation and of their responsibility for the gospel of Jesus Christ. *Today it is often the laity who must be in the forefront in seeking to apply the church's teaching* to the ethical, moral and social questions which arise in their communities or at the national level. The specific mission of lay men and women is *the evangelisation of the family, of culture, and of social and political life*.[10]

---

10. John Paul II, Address to the Irish Bishops, 26 June 1999 (Emphasis in the original).

Failure to see that the task is for everyone will result in a decline of Christian faith and an opening of the way to ever growing secularism, or, more likely – because secularism is nothing like as satisfying a worldview as it may seem at first sight – to other religious expressions, some of them quite superficial and superstitious.

Education for Mission
This is the reason why the parish needs to become aware of itself – it is a community with a mission both to its own members and to the wider world. This is why it needs to gather and encourage and use all the gifts at its disposal. It also needs to mobilise itself in order to respond to the challenges of today and tomorrow. Pope John Paul is very clear on the basic need to ensure that the parish should prepare its members for the task ahead by educating, catechising them in the faith that they are to bring to bear on the whole of their lives:

> ... every big parish or every group of parishes with small numbers has the serious duty to train people completely dedicated to providing catechetical leadership (priests, men and women religious, and lay people), to provide the equipment needed for catechesis under all aspects, to increase and adapt the places for catechesis to the extent that it is possible and useful to do so, and to be watchful about the quality of the religious formation of the various groups and their integration into the ecclesial community.[11]

Some good work has been done in responding to the challenges set by this document, not least by this college through the NOSTRA programme, through the work of the Diocesan Pastoral Centre and the Dominican Biblical Centre. We have made some progress in grouping parishes to reflect and learn and act together. But I think we have to say, 'much done, more to do'.

In particular we need to address 'education for mission'. In other words, what we need above all is an education which prepares people to understand and to respond to the task of bringing their faith to bear on the whole of their lives. This has a number of dimensions but, very clearly, the first task in a world which is marked by the silence or absence of God is to learn the truth of the God who is everywhere and always at the heart of our lives.

---

11. *Catechesi Tradendae*, 67.

Sometimes the challenge we face is posed in ways that distort what the church is. So we hear challenges like, 'If a business had lost 25% of its customers in fifteen years it would be heading for bankruptcy; a company whose returns were in such sharp decline would be rebranding itself as a matter of urgency; if an enterprise was unable to recruit new senior staff, it would be in crisis.'

Of course declining statistics do pose a challenge for us. Of course they prompt us to ask whether we could be doing things better. Of course we need to be asking ourselves whether we are speaking the message in a way that can actually touch the hunger in people's hearts today. I do not want in any way to diminish the challenge of bringing the gospel into the world of the twenty-first century. But that challenge is not, in the first instance, about improving an institution; it is about enabling a community, and all of its members, to live more fully. That is why statistics may be misleading.

We have to resist the idea that the message of the gospel can be adapted in response to the findings of market research. We have to be sceptical of the idea that the success of our preaching of the gospel can be measured in terms of the number of people who attend church regularly. Financial and statistical returns are not the final criterion for measuring the vitality of the church.

No marketing manager would speak to his customers in the way Jesus did: when many of them turned back and would no longer follow him, he seemed to make things worse by saying to the remaining few, 'Do you also wish to go away?' (Jn 6:66f). This would be seen as very poor management technique and a disastrous approach to public relations; it ignores market research!

Not the least of the problems about the image of the 'institutional church' is that unless one has a deeper vision, renewal can get lost. 'Renewing the institution' may well need to be done, but only in order to help advance the vocation and mission of Christians to grow in Christ. If that purpose is not kept in view then what is left is only fiddling with structures.

At several points the document, *Novo Millennio Ineunte*, puts it bluntly. What comes first is holiness:

First of all, I have no hesitation in saying that all pastoral initiatives must be set in relation to holiness.

It is fatal to forget that 'without Christ we can do nothing' (cf Jn 15:5). It is prayer which roots us in this truth ... When this principle is not respected, is it any wonder that pastoral plans come to nothing and leave us with a disheartening sense of frustration?

Let us have no illusions: unless we follow this spiritual path, external structures of communion will serve very little purpose. They would become mechanisms without a soul, 'masks' of communion rather than its means of expression and growth.[12]

It is much easier and more attractive to move straight into action. The uncomfortable truth may be that the best advice is: 'Don't just do something, stand there' or better still, 'Don't just do something, kneel there.' Nothing but frustration will come from trying to renew the parish without nourishing people's sense of being in communion with one another in the life of God, and their realisation that, in the end, this is God's work. 'Unless the Lord builds the house, those who build it labour in vain' (Ps 127:1).

So the primary goal of the parish is to help people to hear the Word of God speaking to them, to help them to pray: 'When we pray properly we undergo a process of inner purification which opens us up to God and thus to our fellow human beings as well.'[13] This prayer and holiness are the foundations of our looking beyond ourselves and our own families and communities.

But that leads us into the second aspect of education for mission. It is not individuals who emerge from their prayer and reflection who go out and change the world; it is a community, a part of the People of God, that is sent out. If they become more aware of 'who they are', they also become more aware that they are engaged together in the same mission. They will need to tease out together what that means – what the implications of being a follower of Christ are in their families, in their community, in their work, in their social and political responsibilities, in relation to the environment, in relation to the developing world.

In some of these areas there will not be a single, specific answer; there may be room for legitimate disagreement. The making of political and moral judgements is not the same kind of thing as making a judgement about mathematical truth or about the result of a scientific experiment:

12. John Paul II, *Novo Millennio Ineunte,*(2001) 30, 38, 43.
13. Benedict XVI, *Spe Salvi,* (2007) 33.

Often enough the Christian view of things will itself suggest some specific solution in certain circumstances. Yet it happens rather frequently, and legitimately so, that with equal sincerity some of the faithful will disagree with others on a given matter ... Hence it is necessary for people to remember that no one is allowed in the aforementioned situations to appropriate the church's authority for his opinion.[14]

What is important, however, is that we come to those issues with an understanding that there is no such thing as a purely secular decision if by that we mean a decision that has no connection with our relationship with God.

It is clear that the Christian community to which we belong is a context in which we should be reflecting and praying together on the issues that will shape the future of our society. That reflection is necessary first of all so that the parish can have some sense of the task it faces, not just in keeping the plant and the church services going. It is a matter not just of maintaining the things that the parish provides for its parishioners but rather of responding to the mission of the People of God in the new continent of the twenty-first century.

Building on the foundation of prayer of which I spoke earlier, we need to find ways of undertaking reflection on practical questions. We face an endless list of issues – such as how our parish can be a place where young parishioners feel welcomed, encouraged and respected; how we prepare the parish to be a living community of faith ten years from now; how we can grow in prayer and in knowledge of our faith; how we can welcome immigrants; how we can fulfil our responsibility for the environment; how we can show our care for our brothers and sisters – in other words the brothers and sisters of Christ – in the developing world and closer to home. Obviously not everybody can do everything. That kind of reflection would need to take place among small groups of people interested in particular topics. I don't envisage the parish priest, even if there is one resident in the community, sitting in on all of these reflections. 'Today it is often the laity who must be in the forefront in seeking to apply the church's teaching to the ethical, moral and social questions which arise in their communities or at the national level.

It may seem unrealistic, but we need to ask ourselves a ques-

14. Vatican II, *Gaudium et Spes*, 43.

tion: If there are no spaces in our parish community where we can address together the issue of how to be a Christian in the various contexts in which we live and can try to respond to the challenges of the world around us, what kind of Christian community can we be? And how can we hope to meet the challenges of living and sharing the faith in the twenty first century? We are all busy and tired – and maybe that is a clear symptom of the problem. But following Christ is not something that is done for us; it is something we are called to do ourselves. We need to ask ourselves what it takes to be a follower of Christ today, with our whole heart and soul and might (Deut 6:5; Mt 22:37 / /).

The issues that we need to address together are not just about reaching out beyond ourselves; they also include matters within the parish. The obvious examples are youth ministry – that is ministry by youth as well as for youth – support for families, bereavement groups, baptism preparation and so on. Part of the enrichment of parish life will be not only to undertake new challenges for the new century but also to value and to enhance all the many things that are already part of the life of the parish but are often not appreciated as such. I mentioned some of these earlier, the GAA and other sporting activities, associations and clubs. It is particularly important that we recognise that the life of families – their struggles and their joys, their anxieties and their celebrations – are a vital part of the life of every parish as are all the efforts of every parishioner to live their faith. God is present in every aspect of life.

In the past, when everybody knew everybody, all of these activities were seen as part of the richness of the life which the community celebrated in the Eucharist. As life changed and became compartmentalised we were tempted to see the parish almost exclusively in terms of what happened in the church. The hurling or football team also had a parish base , but the connection between it and the church often remained fairly vague until prayers were needed coming up to a big match.

It is not too fanciful to say that this narrowing of what counts as parish is itself a kind of secularisation – a symptom of the idea that some parts of our lives are not part of our following of Christ. In many admirable ways Parish Pastoral Councils have begun to address these issues and have begun to reverse that trend.

I hope and pray that this will continue to develop, not just within the parishes but in the relationship between parishes. Just as an isolated Christian is a strange anomaly, so would a parish which did not look beyond itself. The future of parish life and its efforts to live and witness to the gospel in 'new ways that will enable her to understand more profoundly and to carry out with renewed vigour the mission received from her Founder, is going to be more and more bound up with its relationship to the parishes around it and with the wider church of the diocese and beyond – but that is a reflection for another day.

CHAPTER SIX

Clustering Parishes:
Reflections on the Practice and Theology

Eugene Duffy

1. Introduction

In recent years most Irish dioceses have begun to think about how best to plan and manage their pastoral activities as the country experiences a profound change in its social and religious landscape. The issues that confront the church in Ireland are by no means unique and have already been faced in many other parts of the Western world over several decades.[1] Here it is proposed to look at the issue in practical pastoral terms and then to provide a theological rationale that underpins the process. A working definition with commentary will be offered as a starting point. Then various models will be explored, some of which will be more immediately applicable in the Irish context than others. A rationale for clustering will be examined and some concrete suggestions offered as to what pastoral activities might benefit from this arrangement. Finally, but very importantly, a theological underpinning will be proposed, which it is hoped will show that this contemporary challenge for renewal and development is entirely consistent with a sound conciliar theology, especially the ecclesiology of Vatican II.

It may well be argued that the clustering of parishes is simply delaying the application of more radical solutions to the current challenges in the Irish ecclesial landscape. There are other issues such as the removal of the demand of mandatory celibacy for the diocesan clergy, the ordination of women and much better structures of leadership at parish and diocesan levels which merit serious attention. However, in the immediate future these are not likely to be addressed at the magisterial level, the only level that can legitimate such change. In the meantime, it is necessary and appropriate to work with what is both possible and legitimate, but this should not preclude the other options being

---

1. See, for example, H. Witte, 'Clustering Parishes: Insights from the Dutch Experience' in this volume; also, K. Schuth, *Priestly Ministry in Multiple Parishes* (Collegeville, MN: The Liturgical Press, 2006).

discussed and debated at all levels in the church. The Spirit has been given to all with a view to discerning what is true and best for the community.

2. A Definition of Clustering

It may be helpful to begin with a definition of a cluster and then explore some of its implications for current practice. Later, models for clustering will be considered. A cluster is a group of parishes committed to the long term relationship of collaboration to plan and provide for the spiritual, sacramental and pastoral needs of their respective communities. It involves the sharing of personnel, resources, programmes and facilities so that the needs of the constituent parishes or communities can be addressed without straining the resources of individual parishes. It contributes to the strengthening rather than diminishment of the life and ministry of each individual parish or community.

The size of a cluster can vary greatly from diocese to diocese as the number participating parishes or communities will be determined by a variety of factors. These will include: the availability of ordained priests; the population of the communities being clustered and their financial viability; the proximity of the parishes and their accessibility to one another; the size of the church buildings, the availability of office space, meeting rooms and other facilities; the location of schools; cultural factors, such as language or sporting affiliations. If a cluster is too small, it may lack the dynamism and stimulus to challenge the participants to be creative and courageous in facing the pastoral challenges that confront them. On the other hand, if the cluster is too large, it often lacks any sense of coherence, belonging or responsibility that is necessary if participants are to have a sense of identity and its ministers a unity of purpose.

In the Irish context, it is very common for parishes, especially in rural areas, to have at least two venues or more for Sunday liturgy. The communities that gather in each of these local churches or chapels often have a deep sense of identity and belonging that has been built up over generations. These half-parishes, as they are sometimes called, are in fact profound expressions of church and community, which in other parts of the world might be termed 'basic Christian communities'. Often they have their own resident priest and a pastoral council, operating as parishes in everything but name. Therefore, in the context of the clustering of parishes, these 'half-parishes' need to be considered in a way that is respectful of their history and supportive of the sense of community they have acquired, sometimes over nearly two centuries. This does not suggest, however, that they should not be challenged to look beyond their own boundaries to work with and support neighbouring faith communities.

A cluster, like any individual parish, is concerned that the spiritual, sacramental and pastoral needs of its members will be properly addressed. A parish is not primarily a territorial entity nor is it simply a canonical structure. It is a living community of people, more akin to a family than an administrative unit. The focus in a cluster must be on how the needs of the people that comprise it can be met, not on how priests can be more effectively deployed. Irish parishes over the past 150 years have become accustomed to having a resident priest and have implicitly accepted such a presence as part of what it is to be parish. Now the focus needs to be on the local community and the question asked: how can we as a local or diocesan church support local communities of Christians in living out their vocations as authentic disciples of Christ in today's circumstances? Any community needs a lot of help and encouragement to do that, including catechesis, sacramental preparation and various programmes of spiritual renewal. They need pastoral care, for example, home visitation, care for the sick and housebound, chaplaincy support for schools, hospitals, nursing homes and industrial campuses, outreach to marginalised groups such as travellers, immigrants, homeless people or those with handicaps. None of these areas of pastoral activity requires an ordained minister. Until relatively recently in Ireland, many of these pastoral responsibilities were undertaken by religious women and men, as well as by the clergy. Since these are areas of responsibility that any baptised person can assume there is a challenge to local communities to see how they can begin to respond to these areas of pastoral need and put the personnel and resources in place to do so. The changed religious landscape now allows all of the baptised to give expression to their basic vocation as it was presented in the various decrees of the Second Vatican Council. The decline that has occurred in priesthood and religious life has opened up a new space so that each baptised person can share a greater responsibility for the overall mission and well-being of the church. This can only be seen as a positive development in the life of the church and may well be a corrective action on the part of the Spirit. None of this means that there is not an important role for the unique witness of religious men and women and the service of ordained ministers.

The singular witness, generosity and exclusive dedication of vowed religious people will always act as a leaven within the church, encouraging all its members to renew their commitments to live their own unique vocations to the full. The ordained ministry is an essential element of the church's life, providing an authoritative proclamation of the Word of God and a gathering of its hearers to celebrate it in the sacraments. This essential ministry must be made as generously available as possible to each Christian community so that it can be nourished by the Word and with the Body and Blood of Christ.

3. Models of Clustering

Currently there is no agreed structure for a cluster with the result that the organisation and activities of these new groupings vary considerably from diocese to diocese. Here six models will be outlined, thus highlighting the possibilities that are available for those exploring the potential of clustering arrangements.[2]

i) *Separate Parishes Co-ordinated by Parish Priests and Councils:* In this arrangement each parish retains its own parish priest, curate (if it has one or more), other ministers, parish pastoral council and finance council. The co-operative activities of the cluster are facilitated by a co-ordinating council or cluster pastoral council. Liturgical services, programmes and resources are shared among the participating parishes and these are co-ordinated through the collaboration of the clergy and the members of the co-ordinating council. A channel of communication and feedback is maintained also with the parish pastoral councils of each of the parishes.

In this model Mass times can be co-ordinated across the participating parishes to ensure that an adequate service is maintained if a priest has to be absent from his parish. Other liturgies such as penance services, ecumenical services, special commemorative services and other such events can be organised and celebrated at one venue in the cluster area.

---

2. The diocese of Green Bay, Wisconsin provides in part the template for these models. See its website: http://www.gbdioc.org/pdf/pastServMulti ParishClusterModel.pdf

Adult faith formation, liturgical formation, youth and family ministries and other programmes can be similarly organised by the co-ordinating council. This makes for a better use of personnel and resources, especially where local communities are not populous and cannot be expected to provide a wide range of facilities on their own.

ii) *Separate Parishes with a Priest Moderator and other Priests*: In this model one priest in the cluster acts as moderator and each of the parishes or communities retains its own resident priest but none of them holds the canonical office of Parish Priest. In practice it may operate in a fashion similar to the previous model but the moderator has a role of *primus inter pares* and is the person responsible in law for the ministry of the grouping of parishes. However, it is expected that he work for a consensus in all decisions affecting the pastoral well-being of the parishes. A weakness of the model is that sometimes the priests involved in it may sense a loosening of the bonds which they normally have with their parish of residence. This is a model which holds a certain appeal for large urban communities where there is still a sufficient availability of priests to have a presence in individual parishes.

iii) *Separate Parishes and One Pastor:* In this model one priest provides leadership, liturgical services and pastoral care for all the communities in the cluster. Meanwhile each individual parish retains its own internal leadership structure through its parish pastoral council, finance council and other personnel who are actively involved in the leadership and pastoral care of the faith community.

This model may appeal to some small adjoining rural parishes. In many instances it is possible for a priest to preside at a Sunday liturgy in two or three communities without being unnecessarily overburdened. Equally, small communities can easily be supported by a non-resident pastor in calling forth and facilitating the variety of ministerial and leadership gifts already present in the communities. As is the case for all parishes in a clustering arrangement, their association with other parishes will help to compensate for any of the deficiencies in their own.

iv) *Separate Parishes with one Priest Parish and Several Pastoral Leaders:* In this model there is one priest available to the cluster and each of the participating communities is assigned its own pastoral leader, who may be employed full-time. This person could be a deacon, a member of a religious community of men or women or any baptised person. Thus each parish or community may be under lay leadership, retaining its own parish pastoral council, finance council and other lay ministers. However, the priest appointed by the bishop has a duty of oversight, as provided for in Can 517§2.

In this model the priest's sacramental role is obviously increased and his pastoral activity is seriously curtailed. His role as servant leader can come more into focus but the other ministries of leadership and pastoral action are also given much greater scope and greater visibility in the respective communities. The co-ordinating council for the cluster, too, will inevitably play a greater role than in the first model and so will the pastoral councils in the individual communities.

v) *Merged Parishes with one Parish Priest:* In this model all the pastoral councils, parish committees, finances, sacramental records, etc, are merged together to create a new canonical parish. Everything is now centralised in the one place, except the places of worship. This is a very radical step, but one which may be necessitated in some instances where parish populations, material resources and the availability of ordained ministers dictate the move. In fact, many parishioners fear that this is the inevitable direction in which the clustering agenda is moving.

vi) *Close existing parishes and Build a New Parish:* This model is a step further than the previous model and obviously more radical. It means that the existing parish buildings, churches, halls and residences are closed and sold to finance the building and equipping of a new parish complex. This will only be necessary in relatively rare situations, especially in an Irish context, given the attachment there is to traditional parish churches and properties. The new parish will then have one parish priest, pastoral and finance councils, an appropriate team of lay ministers and other resources to meet the pastoral needs of the newly created parish community.

These models are indicative of the range of options available for those involved in the task of clustering parishes. Whatever option is chosen, it has to be recognised that the move from the familiar arrangements in a parish to one where greater sharing of personnel and resources is called for will always be difficult for all concerned. Therefore, it is a transition that calls for great sensitivity on the part of those planning for the future pastoral resources of a diocese or pastoral area. It calls for prayerful discernment, open dialogue, attentiveness to various local circumstances, histories and sensibilities so that all the genuine concerns can be heard and addressed as sensitively as possible. Otherwise, the end product may be a series of grieving and divided communities who are unable to witness to the communion of life to which the disciples of Jesus are called.

4. Rationale for Clustering

The issue of clustering has come to the fore in recent times as the numbers of ordained ministers and religious decline dramatically in the Western world. Not only are they declining numerically, but their age profile is increasing significantly as well. The result is that greater demands are being made on a group of people whose energy is in decline and who cannot possibly respond adequately to all the demands being made upon them. If the demands being made upon them continue to increase then they will not be able to endure the strain; exhaustion will precipitate an even bigger crisis. Therefore, if the present trend is allowed to develop the church will experience ever greater problems, the quality of parish ministry will be weakened and pastoral resources will not be in any way adequate to meet the demands that are made upon them.

The situation in Ireland at present is not as drastic as in many other parts of the world. It still has one of the best ratios of priests per head of Catholic population anywhere in the world. However, this actually strengthens the case for addressing the inevitable problems now because failing to do so may well allow future circumstances to dictate responses that may be less helpful. It is better to plan well for the future than to have to react in panic when the crisis moves beyond manageable proportions. Sometimes the fear of falling into some kind of semi-Pelagianism seems to deter church leaders from facing the realities that confront them and in their own bewilderment they convince themselves that the Holy Spirit will take care of the situation even while they remain inert. Such a theological vision or spiritual outlook is not that of the church which has always been willing to plan for the building up of God's kingdom, while totally cognisant of the fact that it is ultimately God's achievement.

While current demographics of those in ministry may be forcing change, the new situation can also be seen as a blessing in disguise. It presents a radically new opportunity for a renewal and regeneration of the church in Ireland. Among the priests themselves, it creates a new sense of a diocesan presbyterium, challenging them to work in a more fraternal and collaborative fashion, rediscovering rich sources of personal, spiritual and professional enrichment. It spells the end of the era of clerical individualism when a parish priest might view his parish as kind of personal fiefdom over which he alone presided. Not only is the pastor challenged to work more collaboratively with his neighbouring priests, he is also challenged to seek out more actively those capable of ministry in his own parish, to recognise their gifts and call them into the service of the community.

In a situation where priests and other members of a pastoral leadership group begin to work together new energies are released and a potential emerges that could never be possible when a priest or even a single parish pastoral council works alone. Now new ideas can surface. Broader perspectives on the pastoral needs and more creative responses become possible. Given that a number of parishes are working collaboratively, there is a bigger pool of talent on which to draw. All of this provides a fresh opportunity to engage with the mission of the church in a more enthusiastic and spirited fashion.

The clustering of parishes facilitates a better stewardship of the resources in a pastoral area. Many of the services that an individual parish may have struggled to provide can now be done collectively. A group of parishes working together may, for example, be well positioned to engage a youth minister or a director of music or liturgy, whose services would be paid for by the participating group of parishes. Similarly, programmes in adult faith formation, training for ministries, liturgical formation and other educational services could be provided more effectively and efficiently if groups of parishes work in a spirit of partnership. Not only will it cost less, but those who participate in such activities will have a wider cohort of peers with whom they can confer and from whom they will draw support in living out of their own particular ecclesial vocations.

Administrative burdens can be shared and many of the routine expenses involved in the running of a parish could be much more efficiently handled if parishes worked in closer co-operation. Most rural parishes in Ireland were structured to accommodate people when transport to and from places of worship was by foot and the era of telecommunications had not yet dawned. Sufficient attention has not been paid to these factors in contemporary planning and redistribution of resources. In this context, too, it may be worth considering the living arrangements of the priests serving parish clusters. There are many social, pastoral and financial advantages to having central accommodation units from which priests travel out to their communities. Such an arrangement would address the isolation that many of them feel living independently of any real peer support. It would also mean that older priests would not be isolated from their familiar surroundings as they moved into retirement.

The sharing of personnel and resources that clustering involves requires a certain humility on the part of the communities and individuals concerned. All have to recognise that very few parishes have all the skills and talents that are required to meet their pastoral needs, but every parish has a range of gifted people. So, if these needs are to be adequately met there has to be generosity in sharing resources with other communities, and perhaps even more challengingly, there is the need for receptivity to the gifts that can be offered by another community. It is often easier to be a generous giver than a humble recipient. One of the great advantages for the church in Ireland at the moment is the very significant number of people who have taken courses in theology and specialised areas of pastoral ministry and who are willing to put their skills at the disposal of their communities. Indeed it is sometimes overlooked now that there are more people today taking courses in theology in the country than when the seminaries were fully of students preparing for the priesthood. Not only is there a great reserve of talented people with the knowledge, skill and competence to serve local communities but, they also have the right and responsibility to exercise their proper roles in the life of the church.

The goal of any clustering arrangement must be to ensure that each local Christian community is as well resourced as possible to live out its mission to the full. The focus has to be on the needs of the communities in the first instance not on the needs of the clergy or their distribution. Provision must be made for the proclamation of the Word of God and the celebration of the sacraments, especially the Sunday Eucharist. Then, all other pastoral needs have to be considered and the personnel put in place to respond to them. If the cluster is working well, there is no reason to fear that this will not happen as the pooled re-sources in terms of imagination and creativity, personnel and finances will be much greater than has heretofore been exploited. Thus the clustering of parishes offers an exciting opportunity for a genuine movement of renewal in the church at this mo-ment. However, this is not something that can be easily legislated. It will require leadership and encouragement simultaneously at the diocesan and local levels. It will require genuine discern-ment and openness of heart on the part of all those who are affected by the process.

5. Theological Foundations

Any worthwhile pastoral initiative must have a solid theological foundation and this is true for the process of parish clustering. It will be considered here under five headings: an appropriate image of God; an ecclesiology of communion; an inclusive theol-ogy of the priesthood; a spirituality of collaboration; a renewed vision of parish.

i) Images of God

Most people of an older generation were formed on an image of God that suggested a remote monarch who was omniscient and omnipotent, who presided in judgement over the affairs of the world and its people. It somehow conveyed the idea that God was dispassionate, totally rational and uncontaminated by the emotion that seemed to mar human interactions. Recent decades have seen a much more biblical approach to imaging God and this has led to a greater appreciation of the Triune God. Leonardo Boff remarked once that 'Sticking only with faith in one sole God, without thinking of the Blessed Trinity as the union of Father, Son and Holy Spirit, is dangerous for society, for political life and for the church ... It can lead to totalitarian-ism, authoritarianism, paternalism and machismo.[3] This evalu-ation has been sadly borne out by some researchers who have noticed among those guilty of sexual abuse that they have been

---

3. Holy Trinity, Perfect Community, (Maryknoll, New York: Orbis, 2000), 7

conditioned by images of God that were authoritarian and dom-
ineering. It is a salutary reminder that our images of God do
influence our ways of relating and interacting with others. It is
particularly significant in the context of a call to work more collaboratively with other individuals and groups in clustering
arrangements.

Inevitably any language about God is inadequate and ana-
logical. However, the New Testament gives us the least inadequate language to describe God when it says: God is love. Love
is a dynamic between persons in a relationship. It suggests mutuality, reciprocity, vulnerability, goodness, truth and integrity.
The Christian doctrine of the Trinity is an attempt to capture
something of these characteristics as they pertain to God. The
doctrine of the Trinity is a systematic and intellectual attempt to
give a coherent statement of how God is best understood in the
light of the human experience of God's interaction with the
world and its people. Above all else, it is a working out of how
God has related to the world in the person of Jesus of Nazareth,
God's Word among us. Reflection on the life, death and resurrection of Jesus leads one to see that he is the Son of the Father,
that he embodies in his works and words the compassion of
God for humankind and that his mission is kept alive and active
through the power of the Holy Spirit. There is, then, a dynamism of love at the heart of the ministry of Jesus: he reveals
the extent of the Divine love, that is prepared to empty itself in
compassion for humankind, willing to embrace even death in
the desire to manifest that love as concretely as possible. This divine love is revealed in the full integrity of a human life, without
any trappings of what might pass as a show of divine power.
Rather, the divine love is given a fully human expression and in
turn shows what the human person is capable of when fully responsive to God's initiative. The Spirit that animated Jesus in his
life is then given to his disciples after his resurrection so that the
divine love can continue to be experienced and expressed by
them until his return in glory.

In recent decades this image of the Triune God has been pop-
ularised by the use of the Rublev icon of hospitality. It depicts
three angels seated around a table, with an open space facing
the viewer. Their pose suggests equality, gentleness, joy and
hospitality towards those who may eventually occupy that open
space before them. It is as if they are sharing a banquet around

the table and are awaiting more guests to join them. One could imagine the Son being sent out with the invitation to come to the banquet. Such a thought is suggested by the meals which Jesus so regularly shared or spoke about in his ministry, an image of the Messianic times already familiar to the Jewish people. He communicates something of the reality of what this banquet is like in his public life and when he returns to his place in glory, this invitation is kept alive by the action of the Spirit. However, the banquet will only be complete when the persons of the Trinity are joined by the whole human family, whose presence they so obviously desire. Such an image of God is true to the bible and at the same time consistent with the great Christian doctrine about God. It is, even in this pictorial representation, so much richer and inviting than those familiar images of God as a lonely old man seated on a cloud above the world, with the finger of one hand raised in admonition and the tablets of stone inscribed with the commandments in the other hand.

The image of the Triune God acts as a model for all those involved in ministry. It is particularly apt for those being called to work in greater collaboration with other ministers and other communities. It is a reminder of the life of communion to which all are called, mirroring in the process the very communion of life that is at the heart of the Trinity. It challenges all systems of dominance, individualism and isolationism. So, if the older image of God was reflected in the rather monarchical approach to church structures, a consideration of the Trinity demands a much more relational and participative approach to ministry and governance. The church, even in its most local manifestation, is called to mirror the life and love of the Triune God. The rich relational dynamics demanded by parish clustering is well placed to effect this witness.

ii) An Ecclesiology of Communion

Just as the image of God has been revised in recent decades, so too has the image of the church. Since Vatican II the church is presented more as a communion of communities than as a universal, monolithic, static institution. It is the outcome of the activity of the Triune God: the creation of the Father, the embodiment of the Son's own mission, animated and empowered by the life-giving Spirit. The images used to describe the inner life of the church also reinforce this understanding. They are taken from the life of

the shepherd or the cultivation of the land, from the art of building or from family life and marriage,[4] suggesting growth, development, imagination, creativity and a network of close interpersonal relationships. Vatican II, then, speaks of a communion of
life which is grounded in the heart of the Trinity and which
finds genuine expression in the concrete life of the Christian
community. The church is to be the sign and instrument through
which the Spirit effects the union of all people with God and of
all people with one another.

This communion of life at the heart of the church is experienced in very concrete ways at the most local level. Whenever a
community assembles to celebrate the Eucharist it is already
sharing in the Banquet of Life prepared by the Triune God. It is
an assembly of people who are continually striving to grow in
communion of life among themselves, through their common
worship and their efforts to support and encourage one another
in various social and material ways beyond the eucharistic gathering. Not only is there a communion of life expressed by those
present at the celebration, but the gathered community is reminded of the fact that they are also in communion with all
those other communities that comprise their diocese under the
leadership of the bishop and even beyond this to include all
those communities who are united under the leadership of the
pope. The ordained ministry in the church is a visible agent of
ecclesial communion, ensuring that each local celebration of the
Eucharist is a bonding of those present with one another under
the presidency of their presbyter who is in communion with his
bishop, who in turn guarantees unity with the pope and the
other members of the episcopal college, in other words with the
universal church. This is a sacramental foundation for collaborative relationships in the church.

The very nature of the church then demands that people
work collaboratively, in a genuine spirit of partnership that reflects the dynamic of love and mutuality that characterises the
Triune God. No minister can serve his or her community as if he
or she were an isolated individual. The minister, lay or ordained, is always in relationship with others. This is as true for
the pope as it is for the pastoral assistant in the most remote
parish. In fact, when Vatican II spoke about the collegiality of
bishops it was simply giving concrete expression to this ecclesi-

---

4. *Lumen gentium,* 6.

ology of communion. The same quality of collegial relationships belongs to all who minister in the church. Just as the bishops are called to co-operate with one another under the leadership of the pope, so are the priests of a diocese called to co-operate with one another under the leadership of their bishop. Similarly, all those who serve in the ministry of the church are called to work collegially with one another and under the guidance of their pastors. Again, this is played out in a very concrete way in a cluster of parishes. The collaborative nature of the ministry required by this arrangement means that priests and all who are engaged in ministry must work in greater collaboration with one another in their own communities and with all those who minister within the related communities.

An ecclesiology of communion can remain an abstraction unless it is practised at the most local level of ecclesial life. It is not something that applies only to the ministry of the church; it applies to communities as well. Each community is in relationship with all other Christian communities, in a sacramental way through the Eucharist, but this needs to be expressed in a very concrete way if the eucharistic reality is to bear full fruit. Communities are called to share their resources with one another, to support one another so that all are built up to be more credibly the sign and reality of Christ's presence in the world. This is precisely what happens in a cluster situation.

This development then presents a graced opportunity for renewal in the church in Ireland as the familiar ministerial profile undergoes remarkable change. There is now a real opportunity beginning to emerge for more of the faithful to assume a greater sense of responsibility for the life and well-being of the Christian community. There are sufficient numbers of well-educated and dedicated people to exercise roles of pastoral care and leadership in local communities. Current socio-political realities, too, have created the expectation that people should have a greater say in the decision-making processes that affect their lives. An ecclesiology of communion is well suited to respond to this contemporary mind-set and it provides a very sound theological underpinning for the ministerial activity within clusters.

iii) An Inclusive Theology of the Priesthood

If previous generations laboured with an image of God as one who was aloof and isolated, this was mirrored in the popular perception of the ordained priest. Vatican II helped to retrieve a richer understanding of the ordained ministry by situating it in relationship to the entire community of disciples and also by accenting again the collegial nature of the diocesan priesthood. Brief reflections on each of these themes are in order as they bear on our discussion of clustering parishes.

A number of key decisions at the council determined a new and richer approach to membership of the church. First of all, baptism was presented as the foundational sacrament in the life of the church. It brings one into communion with the Triune God; it brings one into relationship with all the other members of the church; it gives one a mission to be an ambassador of Christ to the world. This community of people who are called together by baptism are a priestly people. It is this priestly people who together offer the sacrifice of praise and thanksgiving to God by the witness and conduct of their lives and who bring this sacrificial offering to the altar to be offered in the Eucharistic celebration. This foundational liturgical principle was amplified in a second important decision in the area of ecclesiology, namely, to treat of the whole people of God before speaking of the hierarchical structure of the church. In this perspective the ordained ministry in the church is at the service of the entire community, ensuring that it is structured and equipped to fulfil its mission as the community of disciples, witnessing to and effecting the presence of the risen Christ in the world. Therefore, any planning in the church must focus on the needs of the community in the first instance, not on the needs of the ordained ministers. This should be a guiding principle for any decisions about the clustering of parishes, namely, how can each community be best enabled to be the priestly people of God?

The Decree on the Ministry and Life of Priests, *Presbyterorum ordinis*, situates the ordained ministry in the context of the whole people of God, all of whom are called to offer their lives in a sacrifice of praise to God. The ordained minister enables this offering to be made, in the first instance, through the preaching of the Word. This dimension of the priestly service is given prominence, because it is foundational to the celebration of all the sacraments. It evokes and supports the faith of the Christian community so that it can more deliberately offer a worthy sacrifice to God. 'Priests should carefully study liturgical knowledge and art, to the end that through their service of the liturgy the

Christian communities entrusted to them may ever give more perfect praise to God, the Father, and Son, and Holy Spirit.'[5] The focus is on enabling communities to grow in faith, to be more conscious of their vocation to know, love and serve God in their daily lives and especially in common worship, above all in the celebration of the Eucharist. The goal is to ensure that all God's people are equipped to realise their true vocation and that each local community becomes a genuinely priestly community.

This conciliar perspective, then, situates the ordained priest within the local community as a servant leader. He is no longer the isolated figure whose main function is the celebration of the Eucharist, in which others participate passively. Rather, he is now understood as the one who ensures that the gathered community is one that can fulfil its mission to the greatest possible extent both in the Eucharist and in the witness it offers to Christ in every circumstance of life, individual and corporate. It does not diminish the sacramental role of the ordained minister but connects his ministry more explicitly to the everyday lives of people. In the words of *Presbyterorum ordinis*, priests are to 'discern with a sense of faith the manifold gifts, both exalted and ordinary, that the laity have, acknowledge them gladly and foster them with care ... Furthermore, priests are set in the midst of the laity to lead them all to a loving unity.'[6] In other words they are the leaders of the Christian community, facilitating its unity, which finds the high point of its expression in the eucharistic gathering.

Another characteristic of the ordained ministry that is developed in the conciliar documents is the collegial nature of the ministry. This flows naturally from an ecclesiology of communion that underpins so much of the conciliar thinking. The communion of life at the heart of the church is manifest in the eucharistic celebration, as already outlined. In an explicit way this sacrament witnesses to the bonds of communion that exist among the ministers of the church, as well as among all the baptised. The eucharistic prayers of the Roman Rite name this explicitly in the intercessions: 'Strengthen in faith and love your pilgrim church on earth, your servant pope N., our bishop N., and all the bishops, with the clergy and entire people your Son has gained for

5. *Presbyterorum ordinis*, 5 (all translations from Norman Tanner, ed, *Decrees of the Ecumenical Councils*, Vol II, London: Sheed & Ward, 1990).
6. Ibid, 9.

you".[7] The ordained ministry in the church is a visible agent of communion, as was already highlighted.

Collegiality was a notable feature of the early church and it became so again in the ecclesiology of Vatican II. While it was expounded primarily in respect of the episcopate, it also has implications for the way in which all authority and leadership are exercised in the church.[8] It is a term, then, which can be applied analogously to the presbyterium and its bishop in a diocese. The very first document issued by the Second Vatican Council makes this quite clear. It states:

> They should all be convinced that the church is displayed with special clarity when the holy people of God, all of them, are actively and fully sharing in the same liturgical celebrations – especially when it is the same Eucharist – sharing one prayer at one altar, at which the bishop is presiding, surrounded by his presbyterate and his ministers.[9]

Lumen gentium also points in the same direction when it says that: 'The individual bishops, however, are the visible principle and foundation of unity in their own particular churches, formed in the likeness of the universal church; in and from these particular churches there exists the one and unique Catholic Church.'[10] The implication is that the local church is not a mere sub-division or branch of the universal church but is that church in its local manifestation, a situation where one might expect to find the basic characteristics of the universal church mirrored with a local expression.[11] Certainly, since Vatican II, one of the characteristics of the church which we have come to expect is that of collegiality. At an early stage in his pontificate, Pope John Paul II spoke of collegiality as 'the adequate development of organisms, some of which will be entirely new, others updated, to ensure a better union of minds, intentions and initiatives in

7. Eucharistic Prayer III.
8. Although the noun 'collegiality' is not used in the documents of Vatican II, episcopal governance is described as 'collegial' (fifteen times) and the hierarchy is described as a *collegium* (thirty-seven times). See Michael Fahy in Richard McBrien, ed, *The Harpercollins Encyclopedia of Catholicism* (New York: HarperCollins, 1995) s.v. 'collegiality'.
9. *Sacrosanctum Concilium*, #41,
10. *LG* #23.
11. See Joseph A. Komonchak, 'The Local Church and the Church Catholic: The Contemporary Theological Problematic', *The Jurist* 52 (1992), 416-447.

the work of building up the Body of Christ, which is the church.'[12] Recent literature speaks of 'effective' and 'affective' collegiality. The former refers to the supreme power in strictly collegiate acts by the whole college of bishops in union with the pope. This is the dimension of collegiality with which the council primarily concerned itself. Affective collegiality is a less juridical term and refers to the spirit of mutual concern, charity and co-operation that exists among the bishops as a body. It describes the kind of relationships that are meant to exist among those who share responsibility for the mission and ministry of the church. This affective collegiality is rooted in the gifts of the Spirit and necessarily precedes any codification in law or well-defined structures.

The Dogmatic Constitution, *Lumen gentium*, speaks clearly of the collegial nature of the priestly ministry of the priests of a diocese united with the bishop. It says:

> As prudent co-operators of the episcopal order and its in-strument and help, priests are called to the service of the People of God and constitute along with their bishop, one presbyterium though destined to different duties ... Under the authority of the bishop, priests sanctify and govern the portion of the Lord's flock entrusted to them, in their own locality they make visible the universal church and they pro-vide powerful help towards the building up the whole body of Christ (cf Eph. 4:12).[13]

Among themselves 'priests are bound together in a close frat-ernity, which should be seen spontaneously and freely in mutual help both spiritual and material, both pastoral and personal, in reunions and in the fellowship of life, work and charity'.[14] Priests are also called 'to unite their efforts and combine their resources under the leadership of their bishops'. *Christus Dominus* states, 'Moreover, all diocesan priests should be united among them-selves and fired with enthusiasm for the spiritual welfare of the whole diocese.'[15]

---

12. *Insegnamenti di Giovanni Paolo II*, I (Vatican City: Libreria Editrice Vaticana, 1978), 15, quoted in Charles M. Murphy, 'Collegiality: An Essay in Better Understanding', *Theological Studies* 46 (1983), 41.
13. *LG*, 28.
14. Ibid.
15. *CD*, 28.

So, whether one takes a purely theological starting point or a more practical approach to the ordained ministry, the conciliar teaching is very clear that it is a genuinely fraternal and collegial ministry. Yet, it is a teaching that has not been as fully received as one might have hoped, but its appropriaton is crucial to the success of the clustering project. While the perspective of the magisterial documents is that of the diocese, most priests in their parishes think much more locally. The practice of fraternity and collegiality will begin in their immediate pastoral area or cluster. It is in this concrete situation that they will most easily and conveniently begin to co-operate with one another, sharing the burdens of the ministry with one another and assisting one another in very concrete ways. Such a collegial spirit will mean that each priest will be open to offering the benefit of his own resources, personal and material, to neighbouring presbyters and their communities and he will be equally open to accepting what those other neighbouring communities have to offer him and the community(ies) where he ministers. It is within this theological framework, then, that the practical considerations that were discussed earlier can be properly anchored. Once again, parishes that are clustered require a collegial style of ministry from all those involved and the theological rationale for this has already been well developed in the conciliar documents. Therefore the success of all clustering initiatives will be enormously dependent on an ecclesiology of communion and a collegial understanding of ministry.

iv) A Spirituality of Collaboration

The ecclesiology of communion guides the spirituality of all those who are engaged in the ministry of the church, not just those in the ordained ministry. All ministers are called to act in a collaborative fashion because by its very nature the church is a community graced with a variety of complimentary gifts so that it may grow in unity and charity (1 Cor 12). As Richard Gaillardetz comments on this Pauline theology of community, it 'is dynamic and organic. It conceives of Christian community as constituted by a shared life in Christ begun in baptism and nurtured in the Eucharist'.[16] To be a member of the church is to be part of an interdependent community of people, where the bonds are both

---

16. *Ecclesiology for a Global Church: A People Called and Sent*, (Maryknoll, New York: Orbis Books, 2008), 22.

spiritual and concrete. St John speaks eloquently of the how one's love of God has to be expressed in the quality of interpersonal human relationships in the community. He says that there is little point in speaking of one's love for God unless one is showing signs of that love in the way one relates to those with whom one lives and works (1 Jn 4:20-21). The New Testament is probably much more helpful in providing a spirituality for ministry than providing clear guidelines for its structuring. In this respect, too, it is more concerned with a spirituality for communal living and ministering than in providing a spirituality for the individual. Again, Gaillardetz remarks, 'The Christian life is always conceived as a life of shared belonging and discipleship. ... this shared belonging was articulated in a rich variety of metaphors each of which suggested a spiritually grounded in solidarity among believers (e.g., 'the body of Christ', 'a priestly people', 'a flock', 'a fraternity') ... Where formal structures of ministry were considered at all, they were conceived relationally as a call to public service rather than as an opportunity for the discrete exercise of power.'[17] It is quite clear, then, that in the New Testament the call to holiness is not a private affair but a call to be in relationship with God through a pattern of loving, respectful relationships with all those in the community.

As the Christian community settled into the Mediterranean world in the early centuries of its existence, it had to develop and define its structures to carry out its mission. Gradually, because of various historical developments over several centuries the ordering of the community's life accentuated the ranking of the various orders within the church and in the process devalued the foundational significance of baptism for the spiritual life of all its members. The result was that holiness, too, became graded according to the rank that one held in the hierarchy of order. It also became individualised or privatised, as if holiness were primarily or exclusively how one related to God.

Vatican II did much to restore something of the original perspective on holiness and spirituality. In *Lumen gentium*, Chapter 5, the council deals with the universal call to holiness and in Chapter 6 it deals with the religious life, suggesting a parallel with it how it earlier considered the whole People of God before its treatment of the hierarchy. We have to begin with the foundational call to discipleship before talking of any other specific

---

17. Ibid., 32.

vocations within the community. That first vocation is a call into fellowship with the community of the disciples of Jesus, where one is called and empowered to imitate his compassionate expression of divine love for all people, especially those in the greatest need. The second vocation to religious life is not one that implies or guarantees a greater holiness but invites those who accept it to witness in a particularly public way to the demands of their baptismal calling. Those who enter religious communities offer themselves not just to God but to the whole community as witnesses to the divine desire for all people to grow in the joy of fellowship with the Triune God and with one another. Similarly, the ordained ministry is not about a higher level of holiness, but is a service to the community, reminding it of Christ's initiative towards it, ensuring that it hears God's word addressed to it and that it is helped to respond to that word in the most comprehensive way possible. While the ordained priesthood is essential to the very being of the church, 'it aims at promoting the exercise of the common priesthood of the entire people of God'.[18] The differentiation of roles and ministries in the church, then, is never about superiority or inferiority, it always with a view to service. In the words of *Pastores gregis*: 'Every sort of differentiation in and between the faithful based on the variety of their charisms, functions and ministries is ordered to the service of the other members of the People of God.'[19]

A spirituality that is rooted in baptism is one that takes the centrality of *kenosis* seriously, that is, it realises that it is in self-surrender and self-giving that we really rise to new life with Christ. We recognise our own poverty and helplessness and grow in appreciation of the fact that all we have comes from God and not from our own resources. Not only do we depend on God, but we depend on other human persons, too, for all that enables us to flourish and reach our full potential and destiny. God's gifts are at work in them not just for their personal well-being but for the benefit of others as well. This means that not only are we challenged to show great generosity in the service and love that we show for one another, we are equally chal-

---

18. John Paul II, *Pastores dabo vobis*, Post-Synodal Apostolic Exhortation (London: CTS, 1992), #16
19. John Paul II, *Pastores gregis*, Post-Synodal Apostolic Exhortation (London: CTS, 2003), no 44.

lenged to be humbly receptive to what others can offer us in our poverty and weakness.

All of these considerations bear on the demands that the clustering of parishes will bring to individuals and communities. Unless this kind of spirituality begins to percolate through to all who are involved in the process no amount of new structures or arrangements will enable the full benefits of the opportunity to be experienced. A spirituality of collaboration is the only antidote to the inevitable temptations to competitiveness, careerism, distrust and jealousy that beset individuals and communities who try to work together. Priests who have traditionally tended to see their ministry in individualistic or personal terms are invited now to see what they can learn and receive from other members of the presbyterium and other ministers as well as what they can offer in return. All who are involved in the process of clustering are invited to relinquish some of the possessiveness or pride that they may have had in their own area or community and be willing to accept the gifts of their neighbours or to offer some of their own resources to enable a less richly endowed community to thrive and flourish. Pride can be taken in seeing that all those on whom we border are beginning to grow in stature as communities of the disciples of Jesus.

v) A Renewed Vision of Parish

Parish identity and parish loyalty have become deeply rooted dimensions of Irish life, so much so that 'parish' is often uses as a synonym for local community. It is interesting to note, however, that this very central expression of ecclesial life is one that has not been at all well researched by theologians or historians.

The word parish has its origins in a Greek word, *paroikia*, which had two different meanings in the early church. It could mean those who lived close by one another, or it could mean those who were sojourners in an alien land, diaspora communities amidst pagan neighbours. It was only gradually, over centuries, that it came to mean a congregation led by a presbyter or a cluster of congregations led by an *episkopos*. In fact up to the 13th century, parish and diocese were interchangeable terms. Even when dispersed these communities had a sense of connection with one another; they extended hospitality to visitors; sent messages and received news from one another with a sense of solidarity and responsibility towards each other. In this way they retained a sense of catholicity and communion among themselves.

During the medieval period, major churches in local areas or clusters were distinguished from lesser ones by being designated as baptismal churches, where records of sacramental activity were kept. The presbyter or priest in charge of the major church was the dean and the subordinate churches and their local communities made up the deanery. The deanery in reality was a cluster of parishes in a distinct region of the diocese headed by the dean who assisted the bishop in the administration of the congregation in the area. Other developments at a later stage of the Middle Ages led to a weakening of the sense of partnership among the neighbouring parishes, and this was further compounded by priests adopting a sense of ownership with respect to their parishes. The factors that contributed to this development included the fact that proprietary churches became very common in Europe in the early Middle Ages where the landowner owned the church, the residence and all the church buildings and he appointed the priest to his duties on his territory. This in turn contributed to the presbyter becoming more independent of the bishop and the benefice system developed whereby the priest earned his living from the services that he provided to the parish so that the parish was seen more in terms of providing a living than providing pastoral care. Indeed up to 1983 the parish was both a spiritual reality and a temporal reality – a benefice. This background is significant in that it is part of the residual common memory that often inhibits freedom of pastoral action across parish boundaries.

Contemporary approaches to parish focus less on territorial and economic factors than was the case until relatively recently. Pope John Paul II summarised the present thinking when he said: 'The parish is not principally a structure, a territory, or a building, but rather, "the family of God, a fellowship afire with a unifying spirit", "a familial and welcoming home", "the community of the faithful".'[20] Once again the focus is on community and relationships rather than canonical considerations, which often only make sense to the clergy and very little to the regular parishioner. The Pope developed the vision for parish further when he said: 'We believe simply that ... the parish has an indispensable mission of great contemporary importance: to create

---

20. *Christifideles laici*, 26.

the basic community of the Christian people; to initiate and gather the people in the accustomed expression of liturgical life; to conserve and renew the faith of the people of today; to serve as the school for teaching the salvific message of Christ; to put solidarity in practice and work the humble charity of good and brotherly works.'[21] In the context of the process of clustering this vision is important. The emphasis is on building Christian communities, not safeguarding territory or securing economically viable areas to support a priest. Therefore, it seems to be important that existing communities be supported in their living of their Christian vocation and that they are not manhandled into arrangements that diminish their sense of community simply to satisfy some other strategy that overlooks the priority of communion as both a social and spiritual reality. If the parish is to be considered as a place where people can explore their most fundamental questions and address the deepest longings of their hearts in the light of the gospel, then there has to be a sense of belonging and closeness for this vision to be realised.

Clustering parishes, then, is a delicate and sensitive pastoral agenda. It is not a rationalisation process that one might find in business or industry. It is rather an attempt to ensure that local communities are in the best possible relationship with one another in their efforts to be genuine communities of the disciples of Jesus Christ. The process is profoundly relational and grounded in the reality of the church as a communion of communities. This is not a purely human achievement but is also the work of God's Holy Spirit whose gifts are generously given to lead all the disciples of Jesus into a deeper fellowship and unity with one another and with the Triune God.

---

21. Ibid.

CHAPTER SEVEN

Clustering Parishes:
Insights from the Dutch Experience

Henk Witte

Many Irish dioceses are currently looking at ways to reorganise or cluster their parishes, with a view to ensuring adequate pastoral services into the future. Similar processes have been on the agenda of the Dutch dioceses and deaneries for more than twenty years. Sometimes we have been able to do this successfully. On other occasions we made mistakes, not only in the process of clustering itself, but also in the theological suppositions underlying the decisions we made. For example, decisions concerning the position and task of ordained and lay ministries or the way in which the nature of the church and its mission were perceived. I want to share some insights with you from this Dutch experience of clustering parishes. I hope you will be able to benefit from some of our insights.[1]

I will be taking the future of the parish as the main question around which we may share some of our experiences. This question can be dealt with from a number of perspectives. I intend to discuss this along three lines of thought.

1. The way in which parishes in the Netherlands are involved in organisation processes with a view to safeguarding their future.
2. How do they perceive their many tasks? After all, one can consider their agenda as a strategy to safeguard their future.
3. Finally, one could debate whether the parish system has any future at all.

---

1. According to the Flemish sociologist Staf Hellemans, who works in the Netherlands, the Dutch society in its entirety is characterised by organisational flexibility. He considers 'the organisational fury' in the Catholic Church in the Netherlands as its reflection among the faithful. See Staf Hellemans, 'De katholieke kerk in Nederland 1960-2020: Van volkskerk naar keuzekerk,' in Staf Hellemans, Willem Putman & Jozef Wissink (eds), *Een kerk met toekomst? De katholieke kerk in Nederland 1960-2020* (Zoetermeer: Meinema, 2003) 9-39, 21.

I intend to address each of these questions in turn, but would like to start with a concise introduction to the Catholic Church in the Netherlands.

1. The Catholic Church in the Netherlands

The Roman Catholic Church in the Netherlands is made up of seven dioceses. In 2006, 26.6 percent of the Dutch population, about 4.3 million inhabitants, was officially registered as being Roman Catholic. Of these, approximately 8 or 9 percent actively participate in church life. The differences between the dioceses themselves are striking. The situation of the diocese of Groningen-Leeuwarden, for instance, is that of a Diaspora Church: 6.2 percent of the population is Catholic. On the other hand, more than 75 percent of the inhabitants of the diocese of Roermond are registered as being Catholic. However, participation in church life in the northern diocese is remarkably higher than in the southern dioceses. The religious market is pluralistic above the river Rhine. There used to be a Catholic monopoly in the South. In the past, religious pluralism in the Netherlands used to divide into a fifty-fifty segmentation between Catholicism and Protestantism, these together forming a large Christian majority. At present, Christianity has been reduced to a minority as a result of the process of secularisation and the increase of immigrants from other backgrounds. Almost half of the Dutch population now considers itself to be without any significant religious conviction. This demographic development is one of the reasons why, about 15 years ago, the Dutch bishops decided to promote a policy of becoming a more missionary church.[2]

The recent history of the Catholic Church in the Netherlands must be understood against the background of a century-and-a-half long struggle for social and cultural emancipation on the part of Dutch Catholics within a nation dominated by Protestants. This struggle for emancipation necessarily called for a strong corporate identity. It shaped a closed Catholic subculture, eager to obey Roman directives, in which the collective dominated over the individual. In the aftermath of the Second World War,

---

2. The turning point was the report they made in the framework of their visit *Ad limina apostolorum* in 1994. cf Nederlandse Bisschoppenconferentie, 'De R.-K. Kerk in Nederland anno 1992: Rapport, opgemaakt bij gelegenheid van het Ad Liminabezoek van 7 tot en met 14 januari 1993,' *Kerkelijke documentatie* 21 (1993) 21.

the urge for collective emancipation died away. The prospect of individual emancipation of the faithful – a precursor to individualisation and secularisation – emerged as the renewal resulting from the Second Vatican Council became known. The desire for individual emancipation and enthusiasm for church renewal both intensified and strengthened each other. They turned the Catholic Church in the Netherlands into a symbol of renewal. In the opinion of some bishops and the Roman authorities, this renewal was accompanied by tendencies which needed to be both withstood and corrected. As a result a paralysing polarisation developed, lasting about 30 years, during which time the dioceses and several of their parishes grew apart from each other.

Statistics can demonstrate the need for clustering parishes. Firstly, I would like to show you some figures relating to church life between 1960 and 2006.

Table 1: Participation in Church life[3]

	1960	2006
Baptisms	104,102	30,705[4]
First communions	98,019	37,665
Ecclesiastical marriages	35,644	6,455
Funerals	33,292	33,435
Attending weekend services	66%	7.4%

These figures show the decrease in the number of baptisms, first communions, ecclesiastical marriages, and attendance at the Eucharist or Word-and-Communion services on Saturday or Sunday over a period of 46 years, less than two thirds of a lifetime. However, the number of funerals remained the same. This would suggest that the Catholic Church in the Netherlands has become a community of the elderly. Everything else is decreasing, except the average age of the faithful, which is on the rise. This has obvious implications for the agenda of a parish. The number of funerals implies that an active priest would, on aver-

---

3. Alice M. Garritsen (ed), *Pius Jaarboek: Almanak Katholiek Nederland 2008* (Houten: Bohn Stafleu van Loghum, 2008) 487-501, specifically 488-490; Theo Schepens, Leo Spruit & Joris Kregting, *De Rooms-Katholieke Kerk in Nederland, 1960-2000: Een statistisch trendrapport*, Memorandum 326 (Nijmegen/Tilburg: KASKI, 2002) 21-37.

4. This is 16.6% of all newborn children. The Catholic Church in the Netherlands counted 520 adult baptisms in 2006; besides, 690 Christians, baptised in another church, joined the Catholic Church in the same year.

age, conduct 35 funeral services a year, each involving about 15 hours of work. This is based on the supposition that the priest is not appointed to a parish in which the elderly are in the majority and also that a Requiem Mass and not another service will be celebrated. Over the course of time, we have come to appreciate the missionary impact of a funeral service, for it is precisely on such occasions that the church is given the opportunity to reach those who would not otherwise attend a church service.

It is also remarkable to note the number of priests, deacons and lay pastoral workers, in dioceses active, in relation to the number of parishes.

Table 2: Active ministers and pastoral care units[5]

	1975	2006
Active priests	4156	948
Active deacons		240
Lay pastoral workers[6]	143	775
Pastoral care units	1797	1425

The statistics speak for themselves. In forty years the percentage of Catholics regularly participating in church life has dropped from 66% to less than 8%. The number of pastoral care units was, in the same period, reduced by a mere 20%, this is partly explained by a slight increase in pastoral care units in the early 70s due to the expansion of new residential building estates at that time.

However, a pastoral care unit is not simply a parish with a church building plus priest, deacon or pastoral worker as a professional with, at the very least, a part-time appointment. The term pastoral care unit includes all claims made on the time and energy of the available manpower. For example, the more pastoral care units there are, the more time spent in meetings. The way in which church life is organised is no longer on a par with levels of participation by the faithful or with staffing and running costs. 'We cannot afford an organisation which is too large for our needs', the Dutch bishops wrote in their *Ad Limina* report of 2004.[7] That a drastic restructuring of the Catholic Church in the Netherlands is necessary, is no longer a point of discussion.

5. Garritsen (ed), *Pius Jaarboek*, 39-51.
6. The number of women among the lay pastoral workers was 9% in 1975, and 46.3% in 2006.
7. Nederlandse Bisschoppenconferentie, 'De Rooms-Katholieke Kerk in

2. Clustering parishes: tensions between restructuring and vision

Realistically speaking, almost every Dutch parish has had to face restructuring at some point. Such processes clearly demand some degree of vision about the nature of the church, its mission and its local presence. This would, perhaps, seem to be self-evident but unfortunately this is not the case. There are obvious tensions existing between the need for re-organisation on the one hand and the need to formulate a vision for the future of both parish and church on the other. The road leading to reorganisation and the development of vision is a treacherous one. And caught in the middle of all these tensions we find the parish itself as the embodiment of the community of faith.

Theologically speaking, a parish is the smallest unit in the ecclesiastic landscape in which the church may claim really to be church. The question is, whether it is successful in substantiating this. Is the parish still able to carry out its essential tasks, its 'core-business'? These essential tasks can be divided into four main categories: building and maintaining a community of faith, celebrating the liturgy, proclaiming the gospel and attending to the pastoral, spiritual and material requirements of the needy. Normally speaking, the liturgy is celebrated within a parish. However, one could question whether the liturgy is presented in its full shape when, as is so often the case, the Eucharist is not celebrated on Sunday. Community building is often strongly orientated towards the inside of the parish and reduced to a search for volunteers to man work groups or to resolving conflicts. However, what about catechesis and proclaiming the gospel, especially outside the context of the liturgy? What about charity and pastoral care? If these are not sufficiently looked after, one can only wonder if, in fact, the parish can still be called church in a theological sense.

The over-sized organisation of the Dutch Catholic Church also had and has effects in the area of ministry. Every parish necessarily requires a pastorally trained professional who works under a mandate from the bishop and carries the primary responsibility for it. This can be a priest, a deacon or a pastoral worker, male or female. As a result, these three ministries, ordained or not, strongly resemble each other in the actual carry-

Nederland aan het begin van een nieuw millennium: Rapport ten dienste van het Ad Liminabezoek van de Nederlandse bisschoppen van 7-13 maart 2004,' *Kerkelijke Documentatie* 32 (2004) 24.

ing out of the task. Opportunities for each ministry to develop its own particular profile, the one complementary to the others, have so far been disregarded.

2.1. Scale enlargement and scale reduction

Originally, scale enlargement seemed to hold the key to re-solving the organisational problems of the Dutch dioceses. However, we have since come to realise that scale enlargement must necessarily go hand in hand with scale reduction, or as a recent document setting out the policy of the diocese of Breda says, with 'scale refinement'.[8] However, building a community of faith still demands a physical coming together, and cannot be reduced to a virtual reality.

The policy of the diocese of Breda can be regarded as exemplary for Dutch dioceses as a whole. The term 'parish' now refers to a larger network of co-operation between what were previously independent parishes. Often one of the church buildings is designated as the main church. Within the parish, in this new sense of the word, communities of faith of all shapes and sizes come together. These can comprise the original parish communities, parts of the former or entirely new communities. At the same time, they are all connected with the larger community of the parish. They are attuned to the policy and leadership of the parish and yet take responsibility in a self supporting way for the experience and expression of their faith. Theologically speaking, it is not necessary for them to carry the entire range of essential functions of the church as this is covered by the mandate of the parish as a whole. It is enough that they take care of one or more of the missionary areas covered by the parish as a whole, or at least a part of these. Within the parish new-style, each group of professionals is now able to emphasise the distinctive features of their own ministry and tasks. This means that both priest and deacon are now in a better position to define their own individual ministry in the same way that the position and tasks of the pastoral worker also become clearer.

In managerial and organisational terms, it is an important but clearly difficult task to determine what is to be dealt with on the larger scale and what on the smaller. Where, for example, should the First Communion be celebrated and where should

---

8. Bisdom van Breda, *In de duizend gezichten van Uw volk: Diocesane beleidsnota 2007* (Breda, 2007) 11, 23-24.

the preparatory religious instruction take place? Where should funeral services be held? Where should marriage services or anniversaries be celebrated? In my view, the main criterion for making these decisions is the location at which the Sunday Eucharist is held. In general, this will be the main parish church. The Sunday Eucharist is the very heart of the faith community because, after all, it is in the Eucharist that the death and resurrection of Jesus Christ are commemorated. It is the origin and source of our faith and of our identity as church. However, the question is whether the Eucharist can successfully be taken as a starting point when thinking about the way in which the parish and parish life are to be arranged.

2.2. The tension between vision and organisation

It is not necessarily true that, in reorganisation processes, parishes intending and planning to work together will share a mutual perception of the parish and its mission. From a management point of view, however, this is absolutely necessary. After all, organisation and management are the means to an end but not ends in themselves. And yet, before they even get started, many parties involved in these processes are convinced that it will be impossible for them to reach a mutual vision. There are, they suppose, just too many points on which they differ in order to be able to reach consensus. Sometimes these differences are due to local developments. In other cases, there are theologically different perceptions. This is particularly true of the way the parties involved perceive the nature and mission of the faith community, as well as the role and responsibilities of both ordained ministers and lay ministers, irrespective of whether these are deployed on a professional or voluntary basis. Whilst polarisation is certainly now less of an issue on the level of the Dutch ecclesiastical province and of the Bishops' Conference, it remains a frequent point of debate on diocesan and parish levels. Due to the not entirely unjustified expectation that one is doomed to disagreement, the premature conclusion is drawn that it would be impossible to reach a mutual vision. Efforts are therefore confined to the reorganisation itself. In point of fact, this is simply delaying the matter. As a result, numerous decisions relating to the organisation of church life are often theologically speaking not thought through and run the risk of a necessary revision in the future.

Disagreements on how the church and its ministry are seen are not necessarily due to prejudice or a lack of vision on the part of those involved. They are also indicative of tensions within the church as a whole and result from the way in which the Second Vatican Council approached the question of church renewal. The council used a strategy of juxtaposition between the then common perception of the church and renewing insights. The generally accepted concept of church was the result of resistance to the Reformation, whilst more revitalising insights were gained by going back to scripture and the oldest traditions of the church. The council placed these elements side by side, resulting in polarisation between different groups of the faithful and their perceptions in the post-council period. Different groups laid their own emphases and both sides tried to convince the other that they were right. This resulted in a distinctive style of communication, characterised by an endless number of 'yes, buts ...'. Each group invested in its own point of view and dismissed that of the opposition, unable to even consider a different point of view.

Is there a solution to such a stalemate? Two points could be useful here. Firstly, both sides should be made aware of the way in which they communicate with each other. Once patterns of communication have been made clear, change may be invited. Secondly, both parties could, together, draw upon authoritative sources such as the documents of the Second Vatican Council and other texts which sustain the way in which the church sees herself. Joint study of these sources can lead the way from conflict to fellowship.

2.3. Restrictive factors

Flawed vision aside, there are other factors which could prevent successful reorganisation between parishes. I would like to discuss three of them.

Firstly, there is the lack of experience regarding matters reaching above and beyond parish boundaries. 'I'm from St John's', one might say. Whatever happens beyond the borders of one's own parish is not a matter of concern. However, processes of merging and co-operation between parishes now challenge parishioners to regard those who were previously 'them' as now being 'us'. The former 'stranger' has now become 'one of our own'. The original meaning of the Greek *paroikia* supports this, as the term was originally used to define the area surrounding a settlement of houses and families for the benefit of passing strangers. Once understood in this way, the term 'parish' now invites the faithful to consider themselves part of a church which surpasses their own particular situation and experience. In fact, this is implied by the catholicity of the church whilst, in reality, the truth often proves to be quite different. The question is, whether one should accede to the authority of origin, to that of a familiar past, or that of an oncoming mutual future, however uncertain this may be. Strategically speaking, the solution to this problem requires that those working towards the reorganisation of a vital parish community, should have experience of parish affairs beyond their own in order to be able to pass these insights on to their fellow parishioners.

A second factor can be identified in the theologically and legally weak position of an intermediate level between the diocese and the parish. This is illustrated in the way in which a deanery functions. Whilst the church fully expresses her identity and mission on both parish and diocesan levels, this intermediate level cannot be perceived as anything more than a structure of service intended to support the various parishes in being church. A deanery, for instance, does not come together to celebrate the Sunday Eucharist. It supports the wellbeing of the church (*bene esse*), for instance by encouraging inter-parish cooperation, but is not in itself an expression of the church's identity (*esse*). This level of inter-parish collaboration will have a limited say, as it relies not only on the willingness of all parties to co-operate voluntarily with each other but is also dependent on a sympathetic dean and a sympathetic staff. One constantly sees how deans and their staff spend their time and energy generating and nurturing agreeable and co-operative relationships between parishes. At the same time, they must be prepared for a parish to pull out at any moment if, for example, it has a reasonably fit pastor who could be expected to carry on working for at least another ten years. After all, in terms of canon law, the position of the parish is stronger than that of the deanery. The only way parishes can prevent mergers being inflicted on them by 'the diocese' is to work together towards a situation which envisages and encourages co-operation on a grass-roots level.

A third factor relates to the professional worker in the parish whether priest, deacon or pastoral worker. Their heart, at least within the Dutch situation, often lies in liturgy and pastoral care and matters such as policy and organisation are regarded as necessary evils. Normally speaking, the older generation has not been trained to deal with such affairs. Many are used to working alone and find it difficult to co-operate with or adapt to others. As a result, situations arise in which conflicts or differences of opinion are more easily regarded as a personal affair rather than as a matter of business.

3. What determines the parish agenda?

Pope John Paul II gave an interesting piece of advice to the Dutch bishops during their *Ad Limina* visit in March of 2004: 'In order to accommodate the missionary needs of the Dutch church, you have courageously started to adapt its internal organisation, in particular by re-organising the services of the Netherlands Conference of Roman Catholic Bishops and by re-grouping the parishes within your diocese in order to achieve more coherent units. Make sure that this aggiornamento is not simply a question of formal restructuring, but see it also as an opportunity to rediscover the essential role of the parish and in the particular the missionary role played by the faithful within it, so that all may better be able to work towards spreading the gospel.'[9] These words contain a number of striking points. Firstly, the pope sees a direct connection between the restructuring and the missionary character of the church. Restructuring is not a goal in itself, but is the means to an end. It presents an opportunity for a rediscovery and renewed awareness of the parish's role in proclaiming the gospel within all walks of life. Secondly, it is remarkable that the pope himself did not use the word 'pastoral' in order to define the church's mission, even though we often use this ourselves. He did, however, invite us to consider the parish's policy, tasks and agenda from a missionary perspective and, in so doing, to take into account target groups and their religious needs which would otherwise go unnoticed. His words suggest that a missionary approach will influence our perception of what a parish is and what it has to do. In other words, as a religious community, we would be able to reach a better understanding of who we are and why we exist.

---

9. Johannes Paulus II, "Toespraak tot de bisschoppen van Nederland bij gelegenheid van het bezoek 'Ad Limina Apostolorum'," *Kerkelijke Documentatie* 32 (2004) 64.

The words of Pope John Paul II raise the question: what, in fact, determines a parish's agenda? The annual cycle of Sundays and holy days is foremost, since these go on, regardless of whatever else happens. Celebrations such as the First Holy Communion and Confirmation are related to these feast days. The parish agenda is also determined by events such as birth, marriage and death, all of which may be anticipated but not planned for. Further activities may be found in the fields of catechesis, charity and pastoral care, all depending on the extent to which time, manpower and expertise are available. Finally, activities of a more structural or conditional nature require the attention of a parish council, for example, the appointment of a new priest or pastoral worker, the maintenance and upkeep of the church building, conflicts within the parish, collaboration with other parishes or legal affairs. It is the responsibility of the parish pastoral council to ensure that all these activities, each recurring time and time and again, are all dealt with and, one would hope, dealt with properly. The question is, which denominator is to unite the various parish activities and what are the implications of this choice for the parish's options in the future?

3.1. A pastoral agenda

An obvious item on a parish's agenda is pastoral care. Whether parish activities are related to liturgy, charity or catechesis, to proclaiming the gospel or simply making these things possible, they can all be regarded as forms of pastoral care or as supporting pastoral activities. In fact, the whole parish agenda could be characterised as being one large pastoral agenda.

However, this is a questionable choice. Does the adjective 'pastoral' cover the parish's mission as a whole? Is pastoral care – often in the form of individual care which emphasises proximity and presence – not too intensive and expensive, possibly even elitist, in times of limited manpower and money? Does it generate new parishioners? Does it arouse latent believers to active faith? Does a pastoral agenda sufficiently take into account the religious and spiritual needs in the area surrounding the parish?

Beneath all this lies a more fundamental question regarding the organisational nature of the parish. Is the parish primarily a service-orientated organisation, such as one would almost exclusively see in category-related forms of pastoral care such as, for example, hospital chaplaincy? Or is it an organisation oriented primarily towards membership? Or is it a little of each?[10] And, deriving from this, the question arises as to which group the parish should target. To what extent should loyal parishioners be cared for? And how much time and attention should be given to those who, whilst sympathetic, are further removed from the parish, only presenting themselves when they feel a need for a blessing? How much time and energy should be invested in active key members of the parish? How much attention is paid to outsiders? Is what the parish has to offer determined by the diversity of these target groups? Or does it offer a uniform assortment of services to all groups, irrespective of their own particular needs?[11]

The Second Vatican Council identifies three roles, assignments or areas of work (*munera*) within Christ's ministry. He is prophet, priest and king or shepherd. The council also applies this classification to those who share in Christ's ministry, the faithful and ordained ministers alike.[12] The prophetic task is that of proclamation of the gospel. The priestly task is to administer the sacraments whilst that of the king or shepherd is to guide the community of faith and the individual faithful.

Throughout the history of theology, the ministry has been characterised by one of these roles in particular. This was certainly true of the priestly role within the Roman Catholic Church prior to the Second Vatican Council. As a result, the practical exercise of pastoral care was firmly anchored within the administration of the sacraments. For example, a boy attending confession could expect to be asked if he wanted to become an acolyte or if he perhaps had a vocation to the priesthood. Advice was also given on matters concerning sexuality and family planning. The churches of the Reformation combined the various aspects

10. See Kees de Groot, 'Religieuze organisaties in meervoud: Mogelijkheden voor 'de kerk' in de huidige Nederlandse samenleving,' *Praktische Theologie* 28 (2001) 5-24.

11. In Erfurt cathedral – in the strongly secularised former East-Germany, where Catholics are in the minority – regular services are held for those who have no affiliation to a church. Examples are: monthly services for those who are dealing with personal loss, St Valentine's Day services celebrating friendship and services for non-believers on Christmas Eve.

12. See the *Dogmatic Constitution on the Church* of the Second Vatican Council, Nos. 10-12 (the faithful), 24-27 (bishops), 28 (priests), 29 (deacons) and 34-36 (lay faithful).

of ministry under the denominator of proclaiming the gospel. This is reflected in the way in which a minister was regarded as a preacher or 'servant of the divine Word'. In the years following the Second Vatican Council, the term 'pastor' grew to characterise the ministry as a whole. Whoever worked in the church as a professional with an appointment by the bishop, irrespective of ordination, was considered a 'pastor' and wanted to be addressed as such.

One could ask which elements, within the historical context of the church, could account for such choices. In the past, the title given to ministers was clearly influenced by the conflict between Rome and the Reformation. But why have 'the pastor' and 'pastoral care' played such a central role in the last forty years? To my mind, this is partly due to increased attention towards the faithful as individuals.[13] Another factor is that, in the same period, processes of secularisation and individualisation were taking place. Both processes imply at least the possibility of a partial breaking away from the church on the part of the faithful. Pastoral care, therefore, has become the means by which the church is able, to some degree at least, to remain in contact with them. However, pastoral care has also turned into a field of conflicts about what still corresponds to church life and what does not.

3.2. A missionary agenda

In their *Ad Limina* report of 1993, the Dutch bishops drew attention to the need for a more missionary agenda. At the time, they declared that 'the primary missionary role of the church now lies within the Netherlands'. Their appeal was met with scepticism. The bishops foresaw that evangelisation would be associated with a fear of propaganda and indoctrination.[14] At present, their point of view receives both respect and support. The previously quoted words of Pope John Paul II emphasise the need now to consider the parish's agenda in missionary terms. It has become increasingly clear that bearing witness is an inherent part of our faith. Every believer knows that testifying to the gospel is not a question of imposition but of selfless-

---

13. This is set out in chapter 1 of the Second Vatican Council's Pastoral Constitution on the Church in the Modern World.
14. cf footnote 2.

ness. 'A Christian knows when it is time to speak of God and when it is better to say nothing and to let love alone speak.'[15]

Initially, Catholic Holland wondered, rather uneasily, what missionary work within one's own country could actually entail. After all, her experience in this field was based on work abroad. However, over the course of time, material became available, thus enabling parishes to become more aware of their missionary assignment. An example of this may be found in a brochure issued by the diocese of Rotterdam which encourages parishes to become aware of their strengths and weaknesses in the missionary field and explains how to strengthen the latter.[16]

3.3. A spiritual agenda

A parish's assignment may also be defined by the concept 'spirituality'. Does a parish's agenda contain a certain spiritual quality? In the first instance, the term 'spirituality' comprises a number of very varied activities. From a Christian perspective, however, spirituality is about the relationship between God's Spirit and his people. Are parish activities a hindrance or a help towards God's Spirit descending on the hearts of the faithful? Are they a hindrance or a help when searching for ways of expressing how the Spirit is at work within their lives? Do they lead towards familiarity with the mystery of God or do they lead in the opposite direction?

The question is, to what extent the parish agenda – whether pastoral, missionary or spiritual or a combination of these – is able to increase awareness of the parish as being the embodiment of the local community of faith. The church is not about 'the church'. It is about God and about people. It is about how God and people come together; about God coming into contact with people and people coming into contact with God in a fundamental and meaningful way. The church is a means to this end. It is both sign and instrument of God's search for men and

---

15. Pope Benedict XVI, *Deus caritas est*, Encyclical, no 33, *Origins* 35, (2006) 553.
16. Dienst Missionaire Kerk van het Bisdom Rotterdam, *Goed Nieuws voor alle mensen: Om het missionair vuur van de parochies aan te wakkeren*, (Rotterdam, 2007). Regrettably, the brochure limits the missionary impulse to the parish and does not consider it from an inter-parish level which would be desirable in an urban or semi-urban environment. cf also the episcopal letter *Getuigen van de hoop die in ons leeft! Bisschoppelijke brief over missie*, published as quire in *rkkerk.nl* 4 (2006) 297-320.

women and of their desire to come into contact with the mystery that God is. Both movements come together in the figure of Jesus Christ. He is God's means of searching for us and it is he who leads us to God. The church is the sign and instrument of Christ, these being terms expressing its sacramental identity. Theologically speaking, this implies some serious soul-searching on the part of the parish. Are its agendas and activities, its policies and priorities, the organisation and dedication of volunteers, and the way in which target groups and surroundings are arranged all to be considered and re-evaluated from this perspective?

4. The future of the parish system as ecclesiastical structure

In the Code of Canon Law the parish is described as 'a certain community of the Christian faithful stably constituted in a particular church, whose pastoral care is entrusted to a pastor (*parochus*) as its proper pastor (*pastor*) under the authority of the diocesan bishop'.[17] This definition emphasises the character of the parish as a community and places its geographical boundaries in a secondary perspective. Mention is certainly made of the territorial aspect, but this is in relation to the diocese as particular or local church. This definition illustrates how the church is not necessarily dependant on a strict demarcation of boundaries in order to be able to realise a 'community of the Christian faithful'.

In the early church, the 'church' as such was an urban phenomenon.[18] The bishop was at the centre of church life. He acted as a *pater familias*. How church life was further organised, depended on the understanding of the missionary and pastoral assignment of the church. However, the actual establishment of a community was firmly anchored in the diocesan centre itself whenever the Word needed to be preached, sacraments needed to be administered or when the livelihood of the ordained ministers was involved.

In the early Middle Ages church life gradually moved to the country, often calling for reorganisation in the form of decentralisation. Local branches of the church were created, using

---

17. Canon 515 § 1.
18. For the following see Bernardus A. M. Luttikhuis, *Een grensgeval: Oorsprong en functie van het territoriale beginsel in het gereformeerde kerkrecht* (Gorinchem, 1992) 12-37.

clergymen to provide pastoral care to the faithful within a certain area. Whilst not bishops themselves, these ministers were entrusted with competencies such as the authority to baptise which, in the old church, had been the exclusive right of the bishop. As a result of this, the faithful experienced the bishop as having become more distant and his influence diminished. In order to assure parishes of income, tithing was developed, relying on agriculture as the main source of income. Tithing requires the precise demarcation of boundaries, as seen in Charlemagne's *Capitulum* 10 of the *Capitula Ecclesiastica*, dated between 810 and 813: 'Every church must have a boundary of tithe-paying estates'.[19] Here lie the origins, at least on the European continent, of the well-known territorially based parish system. Over the course of church history, this system has been taken as both the means of organising the church and of enabling her to fulfil her mission. When, for example in the 12th century, city development increased and the urban version of parish development along territorial lines proved unable to provide adequate pastoral care, new religious orders such as the Franciscans or Dominicans were more than able to satisfy pastoral demands.[20] In such cases, another principle of organisation, often of a spiritual nature, complemented the principle of territorial organisation of the parish, sometimes even competing with it. However, the central question remains the church's missionary and pastoral assignment. The most important thing is that the assignment is carried out. How this is done, is a secondary concern.

One may conclude that the parish system plays a supporting role. Where this is no longer effective, it may be reorganised or reinforced with complementary structures. In our own time, these may be found in new ecclesiastical movements in which spiritual affinity is the common denominator. In the same complementary perspective, institution or category related pastoral care may now be seen as an exercise of the church's pastoral and missionary assignments, now focused on specific situations in life such as illness, old age, youth, study, prison or the armed forces. However the church chooses to organise herself, the central question will always be how God and humankind may come together, both now and in the future.

---

19. After Luttikhuis, *Een grensgeval*, 26.
20. See Luttikhuis, *Een grensgeval*, 35-36.

CHAPTER EIGHT

Parish Pastoral Councils:
From a Theological Vision to a Lived Reality

Myriam Wiljens

While addressing the members of the seventh diocesan pastoral council in his diocese the Bishop of Rottenburg-Stuttgart in Germany, Gebhard Fürst, reflected on his understanding of the participation of the laity and the special contribution they had made to his own work through the pastoral councils.[1] The bishop recalled that the pastoral council finds its origin in Vatican II: first, he said, the council made clear that dialogue with the world and contemporary culture is necessary. The bishop explains that this is to be understood in light of the programmatic opening sentence of the Pastoral Constitution on the Church in the World, *Gaudium et Spes*, which urges Christians to be true Christians: 'The joys and hopes and the sorrows and anxieties of people today, especially of those who are poor and afflicted, are also the joys and hopes, sorrows and anxieties of the disciples of Christ' (*GS* 1).[2] Vatican II thus urged the church to enter into dialogue with the world and thus address the issues of our times. Then the bishop adds, however, that the pastoral councils find their origin as well in Vatican II's rediscovery of the position of the laity in the church: the council affirmed that the laity – as all other members of the faithful – participate in the three-fold ministry of Christ and that they together with the priests, deacons and religious compose the people of God. Before the differentiation with the hierarchy is made, the council affirmed the equality in dignity and action of all faithful (*LG* 32). Subsequently, Bishop Fürst remarked that counsel and advice are necessary for making and taking decisions: not only bishops giving counsel to the faithful, but also the faithful providing

---

1. Report on the reflections of the bishop in 'Der Rat der Laien,' *Salzkörner*, 28th February 2007, 9-10.
2. English translations of all conciliar texts are taken from Norman P. Tanner, *Decrees of Ecumenical Councils* (London: Sheed & Ward, Washington DC: Georgetown University Press, 1990).

advice and counsel to the leadership of a diocese. Bishop Fürst furthermore stressed that the experience of participation in decision making and in carrying through a decision that was once made, increases identification of the faithful with the church as such. He finished his speech by sharing that as a bishop he would let himself be inspired by a model of leadership such as that found in the first letter of Paul to the Corinthians (12:1-13) and in Romans (12:4-8),[3] where Paul speaks about the many different gifts present in the whole body that can only unfold when they are used in a complementary way. Bishop Fürst stressed that such an understanding does not reduce the competency of decision-making and responsibility of the bishop; on the contrary it increases the quality of the decision and its acceptance. He emphasised that if correctly understood the authority of the bishop does not suffer either, but is in fact strengthened. When all knowledge and experience in secular and in faith matters are pooled, the processes of counsel and co-operation are optimised, and so also is the ministry of the bishop enhanced. It is vital for the church that the best possible decisions are made and the best pastoral concepts and proposal are developed.

The thoughts of the Bishop of Rottenburg-Stuttgart reveal a very positive experience and are worthy of further reflection. The bishop made them with regard to diocesan pastoral councils, but his reflections could be easily applied to parish councils as well. Both the diocesan and parish council are modalities (institutions) enabling the diocese and the parish to make use of the wisdom and experience of all the faithful. With Vatican II the church rediscovered the role of the laity; this rediscovery took place on the level of theology and not just on a practical level in the sense that it would be timely to ask the laity to get more involved. Neither was it simply the outcome of a growing societal expectation for better developed structures to ensure more democratic decision-making in the church. It is important to note that this rediscovery took place on the theological level, which implies that it touches the church in its inner being.

3. Romans 12, 4-8 reads: 'Just as each of our bodies has several parts and each part has a separate function, so all of us, in union with Christ, form one body, and as part of it we belong to each other. Our gifts differ according to the grace given us. If your gift is prophecy, then use it as your faith suggests, if administration, then use it for administration; if teaching, then use it for teaching. Let the preachers deliver sermons, the almsgivers give freely, the officials be diligent, and those who do works of mercy do them cheerfully.'

The council thus provided a renewed perspective and doctrinal understanding of the laity and their role in the church. But is it enough to express in a document a renewed understanding of the laity? What must be done for this understanding to shape the life of the actual community? In order for a vision to become a lived reality it might be helpful to have structures and institutions that assist the community to appropriate the vision. Thus structures must be found and set up enabling the community to make use of what the faithful may contribute. The diocesan and parish pastoral council are such institutions. Other institutions based on the same theological vision are the diocesan synod, the diocesan and parish finance council and, to some extent, the parish visitation conducted by the bishop. All of these institutions have as their purpose to listen, exchange ideas and make responsible decisions in and for the community while benefiting from the richness and experience present among all the faithful of that community.

Hence there is a vision and there needs to be a structure to implement the vision. Why this emphasis on the connection and differentiation between a vision and an institution? The differentiation allows for identifying what can be changed and what is more substantial. The theological vision is more likely to remain, but structures might change and could, indeed, be adapted to changing and available resources such as personnel, finances, civil law, culture, etc. Actually, in recent times the declining number of priests forces the church to reconsider its parish structures.[4] Thus over the course of time, the church changes its structures to adapt to new needs and resources.[5] The differenti-

---

4. In many parts of the Western world there was a disproportionately high ratio of priests to parishioners at the beginning of the 20th century which led to the building of many new churches and the establishment of new parishes. Thus many parishes had two or more resident priests. The declining number of priests first led to one priest per parish and is currently leading to one priest for several parishes. At the same time never in history has there been such a highly educated laity in the parishes, some with professional training as theologians. This development requires further reflection: the theological connection between a priest, parish priest and parish as well as the connection between a parish and its sacramental celebrations. It would seem that the circumstances 'force' the church to reflect theologically on the institution of 'parish' anew. For such a reflection new paradigms might be necessary.

5. The church even adapted to new situations with regard to such central

ation between the vision and the structures also allows for a plurality at the same time: what might be good and fitting for one place, might not be suitable or even achievable for another.[6] To differentiate between a vision and structures will allow for a natural process of evaluating the structures: are they indeed the best we have, considering the resources available or should the existing structure be adapted or even be replaced by something else?[7] The differentiation between the vision and the structure will also help people to accept a new or adapted structure, because they can see that the intentions remain the same.[8] Of course not all change is just on the mere structural level. The institutions of diocesan and parish pastoral councils are the result of a rediscovered theological vision.

This study will first reflect further on the theological achievements of Vatican II. Subsequently it will be possible to attend to the structure that was chosen to assist the community in appropriating the new vision. The final section will focus on the composition of and by the parish pastoral council.

---

institutions as the sacrament of reconciliation. Not only does the name of the sacrament change so as to emphasise one or the other aspect (sacrament of reconciliation, of penance, of forgiveness, etc) but its structure also changes from, for example, public penance to private penance. Although there are dramatic changes over the course of time, nevertheless some basic theological elements such as contrition by the penitent, the forgiveness of God, the mediation of a priest, and penance remain.

6. The Church provides one general structure for a diocese. Yet, the dioceses of Reykjavik, Mexico City and Gibraltar are very different with regard to the number of faithful, parishes, available priests and the size of the territory. The structures envisioned by the universal law must be given shape in light of the existing conditions.

7. A classical article on decision making is Robert T. Kennedy, 'Shared Responsibility in Ecclesial Decision Making,' *Studia canonica* 14 (1980) 10-20. See also the excellent article by John Beal, 'Consultation in Church Governance: Taking Care of Business by Taking Care after Business,' *CLSA Proceedings* 68 (2006) 25-54.

8. In recent times several priests from different dioceses have commented that the presbyteral council is 'of no use', because they feel that the consultation taking place through this medium is just *pro forma* and not a true consultation. They feel that the bishop has already decided what he wants before he consults the council. It would be necessary to diagnose the source of this problem: does the bishop not appreciate the advice and insights of his priests?

The Archbishop of Liverpool showed quite a different appreciation of his presbyteral council. He had planned to dedicate a church exclusively to the

1. The Theological Vision of Vatican II

What was the theological vision that the Vatican II developed or rediscovered with regard to the faithful in parish life? When the bishops arrived in Rome, in 1962, for the first session of Vatican II, they brought with them a (canonical) understanding of the diocese and parish. On the one hand, they focused on the bishop and the parish priest as officeholders and, on the other hand, on the property held by a diocese and parish. Overstretching it a bit, one could say that the diocese was the bishop and the parish was the parish priest. Around them were gathered the faithful. The image of shepherd and sheep fitted the picture well. 'Father knew it all' and the faithful would just listen and obey. Within the realm of teaching this became very clear: Christ, the founder and head of the church, communicates revelation to Peter and the other apostles, who in turn hand it on to the Pope, bishops and priests. They subsequently teach it to the laity as obedient receivers. In this model the activity of the laity consists in being obedient to what the authority teaches and decides.[9] This understanding reflects a christological model of the church.

Vatican II, however, teaches something else: it affirms that God's Word is addressed to the whole people of God (the hierarchy included). It emerges within the whole people of God through a complex set of relations between all the baptised, theologians, bishops – individually and collegially – and priests. This is affirmed in the way the council understands how tradition grows and develops, namely through all the baptised and not only through the bishops. The council thus spoke of the

---

1962 Rite in Liverpool city centre. The proposal was to suppress the parish and transfer the parish and its territory to the Metropolitan Cathedral. According to c. 515 §2 the bishop can suppress or alter a parish only after having heard the presbyteral council. The presbyteral council objected to the proposal. The bishop subsequently cancelled his plans. The law would have allowed the bishop to go ahead even against the opinion of the presbyteral council, because he did not need their permission. Yet, the bishop listened to his advisors. (Reported in The Tablet July 26, 2008, 42.)

9. For an excellent description of the conciliar change from a christomonistic to a trinitarian ecclesiology see Hermann Josef Pottmeyer, 'Der Heilige Geist und die Kirche: Von einer christomonistischen zu einer trinitarischen Ekklesiologie,' Tutzinger Studien 2 (1981) 45-55. Pottmeyer points out: 'Im christomonistischen Modell steht das Amt einseitig der Gemeinde gegenüber. Es kommt zu einem Dualismus von Amt und Gemeinde, weil der aller verbindende Geist fehlt, der die communio bewirkt' (47).

sensus fidelium and the *sensus fidei*. A major reason for this new understanding was the rediscovery of the participation of all baptised in the threefold ministry of Christ, namely in the prophetic, the priestly and the royal office of Christ. Another reason for the change lies with the affirmation that all baptised possess the Spirit of Christ (*LG* 14).[10]

A consequence of the doctrine that all baptised participate in the threefold ministry of Christ is the council's affirmation that there exists among all the Christian faithful an equality with regard to dignity and action by which all build up the body of Christ according to their own condition and function (*LG* 32). This implies that all the baptised not only have a right but also an obligation to participate in the building of the body of Christ. Each member of the body has to make his or her talents available to the community in building the kingdom of God. The community has the obligation to see that the resources available are harnessed and well used. Due to the office they hold, the diocesan bishop and the parish priest have a particular responsibility in this regard. The council states of the laity: 'In accordance with the knowledge, competence or authority that they possess, they have the right and at times the duty to make known their opinion on matters which concern the good of the church' (*LG* 37). The council adds that institutions should be set up for this and this should 'be done with respect for the truth, with courage and with prudence, and in a spirit of reverence and love towards those who by reason of their sacred office represent Christ' (*LG* 37). Then the other side of the coin follows: the faithful should 'be prompt to accept in a spirit of Christian obedience those decisions that the sacred pastors make as teachers and governors of the church and as representatives of Christ' (*LG* 37). This is, finally, followed by a call to the pastors: 'The sacred pastors are to acknowledge and promote the dignity and the responsibility of the laity in the church; they should willingly

10. In 2007 I spoke at a Leuven Encounters in Systematic Theology (LEST) conference about the doctrine of Vatican II regarding the *sensus fidelium* and its 'translation' into canonical institutions in the post conciliar time. A shortened version of this text is already published: '*Sensus fidelium* – Authority: Protecting and Promoting the Ecclesiology of Vatican II with the Assistance of Institutions?' in Victor George D'Souza (ed), *In the Service of Truth and Justice: Festschrift in Honour of Prof Augustine Mendonca*, (Bangalore, St Peter's Pontifical Institute: 2008) 425-448.

make use of their prudent counsel; they should confidently en-
trust to them offices in the service of the church and leave them
freedom and space to act' (LG 37). The council describes this 'interaction' as a familiar relationship from which all will benefit
(LG 37).[11]

In recent times it has become more common to speak of a co-
responsibility of all faithful. In 2006 Cardinal Rodrigez from
Honduras, while addressing the Canon Law Society of America,
made the strong statement, that 'the whole Church', and each of
our particular churches is not fully constituted (established) if
an adult and co-responsible laity does not exist in conjunction
with the bishops, priests and religious.'[12] The Cardinal made
this remark in light of the participation of all baptised in the
threefold ministry of Christ and the so-called *communio* ecclesiology.

Indeed it is not only the awareness that each baptised person
participates in the threefold ministry of Christ, but it is also the
doctrine of Vatican II to see the baptised not primarily as individuals but as a community; yes, as the people of God.[13] Only

11. The same line of thought can be found in the Decree on the Ministry
and Life of Priests, *Presbyterorum ordinis*, 9. It states that priests are disciples of the Lord and 'reborn like everyone else in the baptismal font,
they are brothers among brothers and sisters, members of the one and
the same body of Christ which all are bidden to foster.' The priests
should work with others being aware that they are there to serve them.
Priests should acknowledge and promote the standing of the laity, listen to them, 'recognising their experience and competence in various
fields of human activity, so as to join with them in reading the signs of
the times.'
12. Oscar André Cardinal Rodriguez, 'Consultation in the Life of the
Church: In Service of communio, *CLSA Proceedings* 68 (2006) 9.
13. It is not just a community but a faith community. This implies a certain interaction of all members of that community who not only as individuals have received the Spirit but as a community, which in turn
enjoys the assurance that it cannot err in faith (LG 12). Following the
council the church spoke about a so-called theology of the People of
God which according to Hermann Josef Pottmeyer means: 'Theologie
des Volkes bezeichnet eine Rede von Gott und der von ihm bewegten
Heilsgeschichte, in der die Erfahrungen, die das Volk im Alltag und
Gemeinde mit Gott und der Wirksamkeit seiner Verheißungen macht,
bezeugt und im Licht des Evangeliums gedeutet und die Weisungen
des Evangeliums für ein Leben aus dem Glauben und ein zeitgerechtes
Glaubenszeugnis bedacht werden.' The theology of the people of God

subsequently is a differentiation between ordained and laity introduced.

Before further reflecting on the *communio* ecclesiology, it is important to recall another major change in the council: originally the draft for what was going to be the Dogmatic Constitution on the Church, *Lumen gentium*, had different chapters on the hierarchy, laity and religious respectively. The bishops requested, however, that these three chapters be preceded by a chapter on the People of God which would deal with what all hold in common. The differentiation between the hierarchy, laity and religious would only make sense in light of the overall mission of the church to which all are called. It is important to note not only the content of this chapter, but also the decision of the council to insert this chapter before the differentiation. The council wanted to emphasise the communality. This then is an important criterion for an interpretation of the law today: it is necessary to start with what is held in common. That must govern not only the reading of conciliar texts, but also the way people in the church interact and apply the canonical norms.[14]

---

cannot be found so much in academic books, but more in witnessing literature, in the life of people, in the customs they develop, etc. It has a more narrative character. cf Hermann Josef Pottmeyer, 'Theologie des Volkes: Ihr Begriff und ihre Bedingungen,' Adolf Exeler, Norbert Mette (eds), *Theologie des Volkes* (Mainz: Grünewald, 1978) 143-145.

14. There has been little reflection by scholars so far on the application of the law in light of Vatican II. Hermeneutical studies on Vatican II reveal: 1) how complex the interpretation of the council is; 2) that the final documents must be read in light of the changes made; 3) read in the context of other documents that were issued at the council; 4) read in light of the reception of the documents. The hermeneutics of Vatican II have become a debated issue, but canon lawyers appear to take little or no notice of the debate. That has immense consequences because the interpretation and even more so the application of the law contributes very significantly to the reception of the council. See for some further reflections Myriam Wijlens, 'Die Konzilshermeneutik und das Kirchenrecht,' Dominikus Meier, e.a. (eds), *Rezeption des Zweiten Vatikanischen Konzils in Theologie und Kirchenrecht heute, Festschrift für Klaus Lüdicke zur Vollendung seines 65. Lebensjahres*, Beihefte zum MKCIC, Nr 55 (Essen: Ludgerus, 2008) 711-729 and Idem, '"The Newness of the Council constitutes the Newness of the Code" (John Paul II): The Role of Vatican II in the Application of the Law,' *CLSA Proceedings* 70 (2008).

In his reflections on the church in the third millennium, Pope John Paul II phrased this beautifully when he urges the people to take on a spirituality of communion, which 'indicates above all the heart's contemplation of the Mystery of the Trinity dwelling in us, and whose light we must also be able to see shining on the face of the brothers and sisters around us. A spirituality of communion also means an ability to think of our brothers and sisters in faith within the profound unity of the Mystical Body, and therefore as "those who are part of me" … It means to make room for our brothers and sisters bearing "each other's burdens" (Gal 6:2) …'[15] For a canon lawyer this call for a spirituality of communion implies not only seeing this as a guiding, indeed a pre-eminent principle for interpreting and applying the law, but it is also an invitation to (re-)phrase questions concerning situations that demand an application of the law from within the *communio* perspective.[16] Phrasing the questions from this perspective and not from the perspective of competition, power, authority, etc, will also assist the hierarchy to be of service, not just to the people, but primarily a service to the Lord himself and then to the people of God.[17] In this way the spirituality of communion will become what John Paul II calls, the soul to the external structures of communion: 'Unless we follow this spiritual path, external structures of communion will serve very little purpose. They would become mechanisms without a soul, 'masks' of communion rather than its means of expression and growth.'[18]

In order that the spirituality of communion become a lived reality, structures for participation must be set up. The parish pastoral council provides for such participation. It is a translation of theological concepts into juridical structures.

15. John Paul II, Apostolic Letter, *Novo Millennio Ineunte* No 43, *AAS* 93 (2001), 266-309. English translation taken from the Vatican website.
16. Any application of the law starts with the question that it must address. It is important to realise that the question often already implies a certain theological perspective. It is important to identify whether this perspective is in congruence with Vatican II doctrine or if it is necessary to rephrase the question in light of Vatican II. For further reflections on this see the literature mentioned in footnote 14 above.
17. cf Myriam Wijlens, 'The Doctrine of the People of God and Hierarchical Authority as Service in the Latin Church Legislation on the Local Church,' *The Jurist* 68 (2008) 328-349.
18. Johannes Paul II, *Novo Millennio Ineunte*, No 43.

Before attending to the structures of participation it is necessary to emphasise that due to these theological notions the diocese is seen first and foremost as a community in which the faithful are gathered by the bishop in the Holy Spirit through the gospel and the Eucharist (cf CD 11). The parish can be understood in a similar way.[19] Both diocese and parish are not defined exclusively by territory and thus as administrative sections of a larger corporation, but they are understood as a community of people gathered around the gospel and the Eucharist; all the faithful participate in this in their own way. Pope John Paul II wrote: 'The parish is not principally a structure, a territory, or a building, but rather, 'the family of God, a fellowship afire with a unifying spirit," "a familial and welcoming home," the "community of the faithful." Plainly and simply, the parish is founded on a theological reality, because it is a Eucharistic community. This means that the parish is a community properly suited for celebrating the Eucharist, the living source for its up-building and the sacramental bond of its being in full communion with the whole church. Such suitableness is rooted in the fact that the parish is a community of faith and an organic community, that is, constituted by the ordained ministers and other Christians, in which the pastor – who represents the diocesan bishop – is the hierarchical bond with the entire particular church.'[20]

2. Giving Structure to the Vision: the Parish Pastoral Council

Among the structures for participation by all the faithful in the life of the parish is the parish pastoral council. Vatican II hinted only at parish pastoral councils and mentioned them in conjunction with the diocesan pastoral council in the Decree on the Laity:

> As far as possible, in dioceses there should be councils supporting the apostolic work of the church, whether in the field of evangelisation and sanctification or in charitable, social

---

19. cf SC 42, LG 26, CD 30, AA 10, AG 37.
20. John Paul II, Post-Synodal Apostolic Exhortation, *Christifideles laici*, *AAS* 81 (1989), 393-521. (English translation taken from the Vatican Website.) Guidelines for the revision of the Code determined that territory should not be the principal criterion any longer. In line with this new understanding the diocese and parish are not any longer seen as juridic persons composed of an aggregate of things (such as temporal goods), but primarily as a juridic person composed of people (c. 116 § 1).

and other fields, involving the co-operation of clergy and religious with laypeople. These councils will be able to serve the mutual co-ordination of associations and initiatives among laypeople, while preserving the special character and autonomy of each. Such councils should also exist, where possible, in parochial, interparochial and interdiocesan situations as also at the national and international levels' (*AA* 26).

The *Code of Canon Law* foresees the possibility of having a parish pastoral council, but unlike the parish finance council, the parish pastoral council is according to the Code not obligatory; the diocesan bishop may decide after having heard the presbyteral council whether he considers the parish pastoral council to be opportune or not. The 2004 Directory for the Pastoral Ministry of Bishops, *Apostolorum successores*, seems to take a somewhat different approach: it appears to leave the establishment of parish pastoral councils less a matter of free choice to the bishop. It calls their existence desirable 'unless the small number of parishioners suggests otherwise'.[21] In a way the perspective has changed: whereas the Code said that the bishop has to judge whether it is opportune to have a parish pastoral council, the Directory seem to say that they ought to exist unless there is reason not to have them. The Directory affirms furthermore that the diocesan bishop should hear the presbyteral council, but not with regard to the question whether the parish pastoral council should exist, but if he should make it mandatory for all parishes or for the larger ones.[22] It is exactly here that the reflections of-

21. Congregation for Bishops, Directory for the Pastoral Ministry of Bishops, *Apostolorum successores* (Vatican: Libreria Vaticana, 2004) No 210.
22. Directory for Bishops, No 210. The Code does not differentiate between small and larger parishes. It states simply that when the bishop has concluded that it is opportune to have a parish pastoral council, it must be erected in each parish (c. 536). The Code does not prescribe that the bishop must decide that the parish pastoral council is either opportune for every parish or for none of them. He might well conclude that they are opportune for some kind of parishes, but not for others. They might for example be opportune for larger inner city ones, but not for small rural ones. Once the bishop has decided that they are opportune for a certain kind of parish, then they must be established in each parish within that category. C. 536 holds two moments of action: first, the bishop deciding whether the parish pastoral council is opportune or not for (certain kinds of) parishes in his diocese; second, the parish priest being obliged to have the parish pastoral council when the bishop has decided

fered in the first part of this study apply: when these norms are read in light of the communion spirituality, the bishop will not need to act solely on the basis of a legal prescription, but he will feel the need to have parish pastoral councils, because they provide a means for the parish – not just for the parish priest – to make use of the gifts the parishioners can offer to parish life. Hence, the bishop will urge that the parish have a parish pastoral council.

Once the parish pastoral council is established, the parish priest will consult with it on important pastoral matters, assuming that he will also appreciate the theological reasons for the engagement of the parishioners. From the drafting process of the canons on the parish pastoral council one could well conclude that the parish pastoral council is an advisory board to the parish priest. However, in light of a *communio* ecclesiology, where there is an understanding of all bringing and offering their talents, gifts and vocation to the community, and in light of the new understanding of what a parish is, namely, 'a communion of persons so that it can be a true community of faith, of grace and of worship, presided over by the parish priest,'[23] the parish pastoral council could be seen as advisory to the community of which the pastor is the leader. Could the parish pastoral council be seen as a means for the whole parish to reflect on issues and, under the guidance of the parish priest, to arrive at decisions? Ultimately the parish priest has to make the decision as he is also the one who must preside over the parish pastoral council,[24] but that in itself does not make the parish pastoral council an advisory body to the parish priest alone.

---

that it is opportune for his (kind of) parish. The canon thus does not leave discretion to the parish priest to have a parish pastoral council. For a different opinion see Heribert Hallermann, *Direktorium für den Hirtendienst der Bischöfe: Übersetzung und Kommentar* (Paderborn: Schöningh, 2006) No 269.

23. Directory for Bishops, No 211.

24. C 536 §1. The 1997   Instruction by several Roman Dicasteries on 'Certain Questions Regarding the Collaboration of the Non-Ordained faithful in the Sacred Ministry of Priests' (Vatican: Editrice Vaticana, 1997) states in Art 5: § 3: 'It is for the Parish Priest to preside at parochial councils. They are to be considered invalid, and hence null and void, any deliberations entered into, (or decisions taken), by a parochial council which has not been presided over by the parish priest or which has assembled contrary to his wishes.'

These reflections point to another sensitive point: the mere consultative character of the parish pastoral council. Canon 536 §2 determines that the parish pastoral council enjoys a consultative vote only. This was a debated issue during the revision of the Code. Some wanted it to have a decisive vote, others wanted to state that it has a consultative vote and again others that it has only (*tantum*) a consultative vote. The secretary of the Code Commission did not accept a proposal to drop the adverb *tantum* because it would diminish the importance of such councils. He re-affirmed the council's consultative character and the pastor's pre-eminent parish leadership role.[25] It must be acknowledged that the word *tantum* leaves a negative connotation and it is not well received by the majority of the people who are used to being involved in decision-making even when they do not take the final decision.[26] It should be noted that the church in any case does not have a tradition of arriving at a decision by majority vote. The tradition of the church has always been to talk long enough to be able to arrive at a decision that reflects more or less a consensus of all involved.[27] Such a procedure requires time and patience, lots of patience. It requires an openness for and capacity to dialogue: dialogue not in the sense that

25. *Communicationes* 14 (1982) 226.
26. John Beal has rightly pointed out that ordinary people – who make up ordinary faithful – work in companies or institutions – he mentions Microsoft, General Electric, the Army or even a baseball team – that are not democratic institutions, but they have built in levels of consultation and of accountability. The church could learn something here (John Beal, 'Consultation in Church Governance,' 28). People who are involved in decision-making are more eager to execute the decision and carry it through when difficulties arise. They have made the choice made by another their own because they were involved in the decision-making process. That has major repercussions for the success rate in the implementation of decisions made. In fact, Bishop Fürst, to whom I referred in the opening of this study, mentioned this in his speech while addressing his diocesan pastoral council.
27. Hans Hattenhauer explains how with Christianity consensus obtained a different quality *vis-à-vis* the principle of majority. As the New Testament already shows, consensus was, from early times on, seen as an expression of the working of the Holy Spirit. In Acts 15:5 where with consensus on the issue of the submission of the non-Jewish Christians to the Jewish law is decided. It is not a majority vote that decides the issue, but a time-consuming and painstaking procedure in which God and the faithful participate, leading to a consensus. It did not imply that

one tries to convince another of one's own opinion, but that people together seek the truth and the best avenue that lies ahead of them.[28]

What does it mean to have a consultative vote? Anyone involved in making decisions knows that the most important part is not necessarily the power to take the ultimate decision, but the possibility of being involved in the decision-making itself. Formulating the question, collecting the data, judging and evaluating the data are of pre-eminent importance. The legislator prescribes that as a rule the one who consults follows the advice given unless there is a reason that is overriding in his judgement.[29] Normally a parish priest should follow the counsel he obtains. Of course if the parish priest himself is not led by a spirituality of *communio*, but is more interested in his own power, maybe because he is afraid of the knowledge and experience of the laity, then there is little that can be done. The law does not prevent him from not listening. At times canon lawyers are called upon to provide advice as to whether a parish priest can decide this or that without consulting any one or neglecting the advice given. It is tempting for a canon lawyer to respond on a legal level, but the answer mostly lies with clarifying the underlying theological notions that both sides take. Then mediation with the intention of engaging both parties in dialogue is what is required. In light of the different vocations and positions within the community it must be clear that the parish pastoral council 'can neither be considered as "a rubber stamp" to blindly say "yes" to all that the pastor decides, nor can it be likened to a democratic assembly to resolve every problem of the parish by

all spoke with the same authority, but all participated. From here the principle developed '*quod omnes tangit, ab omnibus debet approbari*' (*Liber sextus* 5, 12, 29). See Hans Hattenhauer, 'Zur Geschichte von Konsens- und Mehrheitsprinzip,' in *Mehrheitsprinzip, Konsens und Verfassung*, eds Hans Hattenhauer, Werner Kalterfleiter (Heidelberg: C. F. Müller Juristischer Verlag, 1986) 1-22.

28. See in this regard the interesting reflections offered by Bradford Hinze, *Practices of Dialogue in the Roman Catholic Church: Aims and Obstacles, Lessons and Laments* (New York: Continuum, 2006).

29. C. 127 §2, nr 2 reads: 'If counsel is required, the act of a superior who does not hear those persons is invalid; although not obliged to accept their opinion even if unanimous, a superior is nonetheless not to act contrary to that opinion, especially if unanimous, without a reason which is overriding in the superior's judgement.'

'popular vote'. In the final analysis, what is important is not *who* has the power to decide, but *how* a decision is taken.'[30]

3. The composition and work of the parish pastoral council

After these more general reflections it is necessary to devote some time to the composition of the parish pastoral council.

Membership in general. Canon law determines that the parish pastoral council is composed of 'the Christian faithful along with those who share in the pastoral care of the parish in virtue of their office' (c. 536). There are thus two categories: persons from the parish community and persons who are engaged in pastoral ministry *ex officio*.

The first group is thus composed of ordinary faithful. Although canon law does not determine directly what the qualifications of the members must be, by analogy to diocesan pastoral councils (c. 512) it is safe to say that they should be in full communion with the Catholic Church, outstanding in firm faith and high in moral standards and prudence. To be in full communion means to be Roman Catholic. From a legal perspective it is somewhat difficult to state what 'firm faith' means and what it means to be 'high in moral standards and prudence'. The Code also does not state who may judge this. It could well be argued that these qualities are to be presumed of every member of the faithful unless the contrary is proven. (The same is presumed for clergy, including bishops!). With regard to the laity the questions may arise at times concerning remarried divorced people.[31] A general blunt statement can certainly not be made here as each situation might differ and ask for a differentiated response. Pope John Paul II wrote in 1979: 'Pastors must know that, for the sake of truth, they are obliged to exercise careful discernment of situations. There is in fact a difference between those who have sincerely tried to save their first marriage and have been unjustly abandoned, and those who through their own grave fault have destroyed a canonically valid marriage. Finally, there are those who have entered into a second union for the sake of the children's upbringing, and who are sometimes subjectively certain in

---

30. Sebastien Karambai, *Structures of Decision-Making in the Local Church* (Bangalore: Theological Publications, 1994) 217.
31. It should be noted that civilly divorced persons enjoy full rights in the church. Problems and questions arise only when people are civilly remarried.

conscience that their previous and irreparably destroyed marriage had never been valid.'[32] A differentiated decision with regard to membership of the parish pastoral council is thus needed.

Belonging by territory or choice. In recent years many people do not automatically practise their faith in the parish to which they canonically belong. They see themselves as 'belonging' to that parish that they have come to appreciate. The principle of territory, which determines to what parish someone belongs canonically, does not always coincide with the actual belonging.[33] As an accommodation to this situation several bishops in different dioceses have decided that those who feel that they belong to a certain parish which is not their territorial parish can be on the parish pastoral council, provided they declare that they only belong to one parish when they exercise voting rights with regard to the parish pastoral council.[34] Some parish priests do not like this solution. This applies in particular to those priests whose parishioners walk off to other parishes. They see the parishioners as 'their' people and fail to see that they are there to serve the parishioners. Canonically, the parish priest is more obliged to the parishioners than the parishioners to the parish priest.[35] It is important to remember that the principle of territoriality is secondary even in canon law. Migrant and student parishes testify to this. It is the community that matters. Moreover,

---

32. John Paul II, Apostolic Exhortation *Familiaris consortio* AAS 74 (1982) 81-191, No 84. English translation taken from the Vatican Website.

33. According to c. 102 §1 someone becomes a parishioner by residence within the territory of a certain parish which is joined with the intention of remaining there permanently unless called away or has been protracted for five complete years.

34. This is not unlike citizens of one country who decide to participate in the electing for the European Union in another country. These citizens must declare that they use their right to participate in the election in only one country.

35. An example: Due to his office the parish priest is obliged to offer preparation for receiving sacraments, but the parishioners are not obliged to receive his offer. They do not have a duty but only a right *vis-à-vis* the parish priest. Thus parents may well decide that their children receive catechesis for First Communion somewhere else (e.g. in the context of an ecclesial movement such as the Focolare, or Opus Dei). The parents may even prepare the children themselves. The children would have to be prepared and the priest admitting them to First Communion may test whether they are rightly disposed (v.g. c. 843).

canon lawyers must be creative in responding to the challenges
that arise from mobility.

Representation. The parish pastoral council should be composed of a good representation of the people who belong to the
parish. The reason for this is easily explained: in an ideal situation the parish as a community gathers as a whole to discuss a
certain issue. This, however, would be impractical; hence a good
representation is necessary. The representation should take into
consideration age, gender, social position, cultural background
(especially in parishes where there are immigrants), canonical
status etc. It is a misconception to believe that the parish pastoral
council is composed solely of laity; it is not a lay council and
thus religious could also be part of it. The people chosen are not
chosen for their social position or educational qualifications but
for their diverse charisms and status in life. Of course a person
could bring different aspects at the same time: be a married person, mother of young children, nurse and thus engaged with the
sick in a parish. Even though each person brings his or her own
talents, nevertheless, the members of the parish pastoral council
should remember that they have a responsibility for the whole
parish and may not just consider and defend their own interests.

Manner of Appointment. With regard to the manner of appointment it is important to note that canon law does not prescribe – or to phrase it differently 'leaves it open' – how people
become a member of the parish pastoral council: it could be by
election or appointment. It could also be by a mixture of both. It
is left to the bishop to decide on this. In some dioceses people
are encouraged in general to volunteer their names for membership. In other dioceses parishioners and/or the parish priest ask
some people to submit their names for election. Ultimately the
whole parish, that is, every one over the age of 16 has an active
and passive right to vote. In other dioceses there is no election of
individuals, but the parish pastoral council is composed of a
representation of different groups in the parish: the commission
for liturgy, the first communion catechists, the youth group, the
group attending to the sick and dying, etc. These groups then
name a delegate to the parish pastoral council. Another model
could be to have a mixture of some elected members and some
chosen by the pastor.

'There are advantages and risks involved in both nomination
and election. Election is a good method to identify different

charisms and talents of which the parishioners would be better aware than the pastor. Besides, it enhances responsibility among the members and builds confidence within the community.'[36] Cultural factors might play a decisive role in this.[37] Canon law does not prohibit the parish priest himself from selecting and appointing all members, but this does not seem to be a good model as it risks having only people who think alike becoming members of the parish pastoral council.

The number of members. Canon law does not determine at all how many people there should be on the parish pastoral council. It is left to the bishop to provide for this in the statutes. It would be wise to have a size of group that indeed reflects the parishioners and yet it should not be so large that a fruitful discussion is not possible any more. Religious institutes might offer here a sound model: the constitutions often determine only a minimum and maximum number for chapters and consultative institutions so as to be able to adapt to local possibilities and needs.[38] The council in residence determines how many should be in the succeeding one. The acting parish council could determine how many people should make up the parish pastoral council succeeding it.[39]

The ex officio members. Ex officio members are those who are involved in the pastoral care of the parish. They would be the other priests working in the parish, as well as the deacons and catechists. Neither teachers of religion in a school nor all the men belonging to a religious institute, unless they have an assignment in the parish, would be *ex officio* members. It is important to keep a balance of *ex officio* and other members, even if they be chosen or appointed by the parish priest. Often statutes determine that the number of elected members must outnumber the appointed ones.

---

36. Sebastien Karambai, *Structures of Decision-Making*, 220.

37. An interesting cultural factor can be found in India where the caste system might play a role. cf Sebastien Karambai, *Structures of Decision-Making*, 220.

38. Religious institutes have both a long practice of composing institutions in which a good representation is called for and of adapting to local circumstances as some of their communities might be very small and others rather large.

39. A similar provision is made for the college of consultors. The bishop decides how many members should be on the college. cf c. 502 §1.

President of the parish pastoral council. Canon law determines that the parish priest must preside. This does not imply that he must also chair the meeting. To preside does not mean that he necessarily alone has the right to determine the agenda. Again, the statutes by the bishop could provide for others to get something on the agenda or to ask for a convocation of a meeting as well. Related to this is also the frequency of meetings. The bishop could prescribe a minimum number of meetings per year. If any of these things must be forced on the presiding priest, there is need to talk with him about his own understanding of his role and the role of the faithful in the parish he is called to serve.

The task of the parish pastoral council. Finally it is necessary to reflect briefly on the task of the parish pastoral council. The Bishop of Rottenburg-Stuttgart mentioned that with Vatican II the church declared that the joy and sorrow, the concerns of the people are also the concerns of the Christian. This is an important aspect of what a parish community is to be about: to proclaim the Word *ad extra* and *ad intra*, to celebrate the faith and to testify to the faith by looking after the needy.

The purpose of the parish pastoral council is to assist the community to fulfil its mission under the leadership of the parish priest. Its task then lies with the three areas of proclamation, celebration and living the faith (caritas: living the works of mercy).

In order that no confusion might arise, it is necessary also to point out what the parish pastoral council cannot do. Firstly, the parish pastoral council is not a legislative body: the bishop is the sole legislator for the diocese. The pastor does not hold legislative power either; yet the parish council might assist in drawing up a policy on how things are being done.[40] This could be done with regard to times for weddings and funerals, arrangements for cemeteries, etc. The parish pastoral council could assist in setting up the liturgical schedule and thus determining how and

---

40. Policies do not enjoy the force of legislation! Hence care must be taken that they are not implicitly diminishing the rights of people, for example, with regard to the sacraments. See in this regard an interesting decision by the Holy See against a policy of a bishop to administer the sacrament of confirmation only at a certain age and not before that. A child who although prepared and rightly disposed had not reached the age established in the policy was refused the sacrament. The parents of the child appealed the decision by the bishop and won their case. Vgl. *Congregatio pro cultu divino et disciplina sacramentorum, Litterae Congregationis prot. N. 2607/98/L. Communicationes* (2000) 12-14.

when, e.g., first communion, confirmation and anointing of the sick are celebrated. Secondly, the parish pastoral council has no competence with regard to matters of faith in the sense that it cannot change the doctrine of the church; however, it could well deepen its own understanding of faith issues in order to provide better advice. Thirdly, it is not competent to handle financial issues. This is the task of the finance council and finance officer (c. 537). Fourthly, the parish pastoral council does not enjoy judicial power and it is not a judicial place where, for example, matters of remarried divorced people are discussed or resolved.

Concluding reflection

At the beginning of this study reference was made to the address of the Bishop of Rottenburg-Stuttgart according to which he considered himself and the diocese entrusted to his care to be blessed because through the medium of a diocesan pastoral council they had been able to benefit from the charisms and experience of the people in his diocese. This study reveals that the parish pastoral council can be a blessing for the parish and the parish priest as well: it can assist the community to make use of the resources available in the parish. This study revealed that the theological vision of Vatican II on the role of all the faithful in the mission of the church can be well expressed through the institution of the parish pastoral council. A successful expression of the vision depends on a spirit of communion and a related willingness to respect and listen to each other on the part of all the participants. Ultimately such respect is rooted in an awareness and appreciation of the working of the Holy Spirit in each and every person according to his or her position in the community. With this comes a warning. No canonical structure can provide for the Spirit: it is possible to have the institutions in place, to even gather the people, but if there is no willingness to listen, to really enter into dialogue and ponder what is the best way forward for this community, if there is no appreciation of the gifts of all that are present in the community, then the parish pastoral council will be a waste of time and lead to immense frustration on the side of the faithful. I, therefore, wish the parishes in Ireland just that: the courage to break down the reservations about involvement of laity in the parish life and to travel new unknown roads while being assured that the Holy Spirit will guide them.

CHAPTER NINE

The Priest and Clustering: Law and Practice

Patrick Connolly

Introduction

Christians have always felt somewhat ambivalent about the proper role of law in a life of faith, and in the church law is auxillary in that its role ultimately is to assist people in the reception of God's saving mysteries. Nonetheless, a viable community needs not only goodwill and fraternal love, but also requires rules for the orderly conduct of its affairs, to delineate the functions of its leaders, and to govern relationships among its members. Without structures, vision lacks reality. So for as long as the church has existed, it has had some form of canon law in which it attempts to express its own self-understanding. This ecclesiological self-understanding can adapt itself to changed circumstances, leading to a change in canonical structures. Historically, parishes and indeed parish priests were seen as fairly independent of each other in a canonical sense, relating more directly to the bishop and the diocese than to each other. This is in contrast with the current thinking behind parish clustering. However, that is not to say that clusters of parishes have no canonical precedents or current canonical analogues.

Under the old canon law of the 1917 Code, the bishop had to divide the diocese into regions or districts which were called 'deaneries' or 'vicariates forane'. The 1983 *Code of Canon Law* makes this sort of division optional for the bishop: c. 374 §2 says that to foster pastoral care through common action, several neighbouring parishes can be joined into special groupings. The only example the canon gives of such a grouping of parishes is the vicariate forane, often still called the deanery in many places. The priest in charge of a deanery or vicariate forane is the vicar forane. He is to visit parishes in accordance with the arrangement made by the bishop, co-ordinate and promote common pastoral action, see that the clergy fulfil their duties and that the liturgy is celebrated properly, ensure that parish registers are kept correctly and church properties are properly maintained, help clergy in difficulty, make sure care is provided for sick clergy and ensure that priests' funerals are worthily celebrated. The office of vicar forane is not attached to a particular parish and any suitable priest can be appointed, though it was (and sometimes still is) often customary to designate a parish in the deanery whose parish priest was automatically the vicar forane.

Practically speaking, deaneries often simply acted as area gatherings for the clergy of neighbouring parishes, and in some places the actual role of vicar forane was and is more nominal than real, with the tasks mentioned in the Code not being pursued too vigourously. This is perhaps not that surprising, because while the vicar forane acts as the bishop's agent in carrying out a number of responsibilities, including supervisory ones, ultimately the vicar's authority is pastoral, rather than legal or governmental in the strict sense, unless this is provided for in diocesan particular law. The Code says nothing about the relationship of the vicar forane with the laity or with the various forms of apostolate which involve all the members of the Christian community.

Therefore, the concept of deaneries or vicariates forane in the Code fundamentally revolves around the clergy, and presupposes the traditional independence of parishes. Thus it seems an inadequate vehicle for the developing concept of 'clusters of parishes'. It is important to note that while c. 374 §2 gives vicariates forane as an example of groupings of parishes, it doesn't restrict such groupings to these vicariates or deaneries. In other words, the bishop can establish other sorts of groupings of parishes. Also, the bishop can create a region or district in the diocese and place an episcopal vicar in charge (c. 476). Hence while the term 'clustering' receives no explicit mention in the Code, it doesn't exclude future developments about how parishes could be grouped together.

The Code is a document written for the universal church and the phenomena of clustering parishes is relatively new. Thus current canon law says nothing explicitly about the concept of 'clustering' *per se*, nor how priests are to relate to this idea, though, as we shall see, there are parts of canon law which do indirectly impinge on these new developments. Indeed, leaving aside the law currently in force, even in the scholarly literature of canon law, there is hardly anything written about parish clustering as a concept in itself. From the point of view of clustering and parish governance issues, we are entering new territory about which there has been little canonical study in the formal academic sense.

This is not really surprising. Historically, in the church the experience of priesthood in relation to parish life has been very diverse, ranging for instance from feudal times, where the parish priest was almost a cultic serf, to the post-Tridentine model in which the laity were considered mere passive subjects of the activity of the parish priest – the model which dominated church life till after the Second Vatican Council. Indeed, the history of presbyteral ordination rites and prayers demonstrates different emphases in the role of the priest at different times.

The theme 'Priest and Clustering' is wide-ranging, so for our purposes, we will restrict our reflections to some thoughts on how the traditional role of parish priest may relate to these new developments whereby parishes are clustered together.

1. Appointment to and Stability in the Office of Parish Priest in the Context of Clustering

One cannot be validly appointed as a parish priest (*parochus*) unless one is in fact an ordained presbyter (C 521 §1). The Code sees each parish being entrusted by the bishop to a parish priest as it proper pastor. Even for a parish entrusted to a religious congregation, one priest must be named as parish priest or as the moderator mentioned in c. 517 §1.[1] The general canonical principle is 'one parish – one parish priest', and so the Code emphasises the importance of the office of parish priest. He is a holder of an ecclesiastical office in the church and thus he has both extensive responsibilities and also certain rights (e.g. he cannot be removed from office except for cause, and a formal canonical process is required for his removal). The church has through experience learnt that it is necessary for a parish priest to have the benefit of what is called 'stability' – a certain right of tenure or security in office. This is not just a comfort zone for the parish priest: it is also the parish's right to stability and continuity in the pastoral care it receives. Genuine pastoral care means that people need time to get to know their parish priest and he

---

1. See A. Palmieri, 'Parishes Entrusted to the Care of Religious: Starting Afresh from Christ', *Proceedings of the Canon Law Society of America* 64 (2002) 222-224.

needs time to learn their particular needs and circumstances. A rapid turnover of parish priests is hardly good for either parishioners or for the priests concerned.

The tenure rights of parish priests have been considerably reduced as a consequence of the Second Vatican Council's wish that the concept of 'irremovable and removable parish priests' be abolished. However, the preference of canon law (as specified in c. 522) is still that a parish priest be appointed for an indeterminate period of time, so that he will have the benefit of stability. The Code regards an indefinite appointment as the usual situation. It allows the bishop to make appointments for a specified period only if the Bishops' Conference with a two-thirds majority has provided by decree for such a term, which also must have been approved by the Holy See (in Ireland, it is six years).[2]

The general canonical principle still remains 'one parish – one parish priest'. So there cannot be more than one parish priest in the same parish (c. 526 §2). But the Code recognises that because of the shortage of priests a priest may be entrusted with the care of a number of neighbouring parishes (c. 526 §1). In other words it is possible for one priest to be parish priest of several independent parishes. Likewise a curate may be assigned to several parishes.

Parochial administrators have the same rights and duties as parish priests, except they do not enjoy stability in office – they serve *ad nutum Episcopi* and can be removed at will, unlike parish priests who can only be removed or transferred against their wishes by the bishop following a canonical process (cc. 1740-1752). Canon law sees that the normal method of provid-

---

2. Irish Bishops' Conference, Revised Decree No 5, promulgated in *Intercom*, September 2005: 'The primary provision of canon 522 that parish priests may be appointed for an indefinite period of time remains in force. Individual diocesan bishops may appoint parish priests to a six-year term of office. The possibility of renewing this term is left to the discretion of the diocesan bishop.' An accompanying commentary by M. Mullaney says a bishop may appoint a parish priest for a longer period, up to nine years. He refers to an unpublished letter from the Holy See which approved the Decree; this letter (whose text is not given) apparently indicated a flexibility in the term of between six and nine years. However, the text of the actual Decree itself is clear that the term is six years and it is the approved promulgated Decree which remains the law.

ing pastoral care for a parish is through a parish priest, while an administrator is seen to be more of a temporary arrangement. Historically, there has been a temptation for bishops to appoint many parochial administrators (e.g. in 19th century USA) because they can be removed or transferred very easily – this was resisted by the Holy See. History teaches us that a balance of rights is necessary in the church: a balance of rights among those of the bishop, the priest and the people.

If a priest has to look after a number of parishes, there are a number of ways in which this can be done. He can be administrator of all the clustered parishes. In the context of parish clustering, some have spoken of this approach as an 'interim juridical solution', but such an approach needs to be treated with caution, because it suffers from the disadvantage mentioned above. A diocese made up of clusters of parishes entrusted to parochial administrators is far from ideal, given the concern about balancing various rights and responsibilities.

The priest can be parish priest of each of the clustered parishes. The parishes do not have to be united or amalgamated. He can be parish priest of one or some of the parishes, and also in line with c. 517 §2 (see below) be the priest endowed with the faculties and powers of a parish priest, sometimes called the 'priest-director', for the other(s).

Another solution is that he can be parish priest of one parish and administrator of the others. It is interesting to note that this is the practice largely found in Spain.[3] It gives the priest a certain stability and security in office, while allowing the bishop flexibility about the other parishes.

2. *Clustering and Situations where there is no Parish Priest*

A. *Entrustment of a number of parishes to a group of priests in solidum, with one priest acting as Moderator (c. 517 §1)*

The pastoral care of a number of clustered parishes can be entrusted to several priests jointly (*in solidum*), but one of the priests must be the moderator of the pastoral care to be exercised and be responsible to the bishop. The priests jointly carry out the pastoral care of the parishes under the direction of the

3. See A. S. Sánchez-Gil, Commentary on c. 526, *Exegetical Commentary on the Code of Canon Law*, ed Á. Marzoa. J. Miras, and R. Rodríguez-Ocaña, English language ed, gen ed E. Caparros, (Montreal: Wilson & Lafleur, Chicago IL: Midwest Theological Forum, 2004), vol II/2, 1312.

moderator. While he holds a particular leadership position in the group, exemplified in that he represents the parishes in juridical affairs (c. 543 §1 3°), nonetheless the moderator is simply a *primus inter pares*.[4] This is a sort of 'team ministry', and some have spoken of 'joint parish priests' or 'co-parish priests'. This latter terminology can be misleading. While for the most part, the priests have the obligations of a parish priest and can exercise the functions and faculties of that office (cc. 542-544), there is actually no *parochus* strictly speaking. No one holds the ecclesiastical office of parish priest in the canonical meaning of the term.

This *in solidum* idea is new in canon law, and has received a mixed reaction from commentators. While recognising that it would provide for some pastoral circumstances, not everyone is convinced that it can lead to better ecclesiastical organisation. If things become difficult in the group of priests, who exactly is in charge and makes the ultimate decisions? Or, to take another example, we could have a cluster of three parishes being served by three priests, each living separately in one of the parishes and acting effectively as its *quasi-parochus*, making one wonder what is the difference in practice is from the traditional model of three parishes, except perhaps as a stepping stone to amalgamation of the parishes. Because the universal law of the Code is silent on the detail of the priests' joint action and co-responsibility, it is probably best if these are specified more concretely in a diocesan statute or ordinance, for example defining the competences of the moderator with greater accuracy, especially to deal with situations where there is no unanimity in the team.

B. Entrustment of a share of in the pastoral care of a parish to a deacon, to somebody is not a priest, or to a community of persons (c. 517 §2)

This entrustment is allowed by the Code when there is a shortage of priests. However, the bishop must appoint a priest with the faculties and powers of a parish priest to direct the pastoral care of the parish. A priest is to direct the care exercised by persons not ordained to the presbyterate, but this priest while enjoying the powers and faculties of a parish priest is not technically the *parochus* of the parish. Canonically, the ecclesiastical office is vacant. No title is given to the priest-supervisor, or

---

4. See the thinking of the Commission for the Revision of the Code in *Communicationes* 14 (1982) 222.

indeed to the deacon or other person(s) who participate(s) in the exercise of parochial pastoral care. In other words, part of the pastoral care of a parish can be given to a non-priest, but a priest must oversee it – he could be, for instance, a neighbouring parish priest or a priest working as a chaplain somewhere else.[5]

It is worth noting that when in 1997 eight departments of the Roman Curia together issued an Instruction on 'Certain Questions Regarding the Collaboration of the Non-Ordained Faithful in the Sacred Ministry of Priests', c. 517 §2 received a lot of attention in the document. It saw this canon as an extraordinary and exceptional form of collaboration, and forbade the use of titles like 'co-ordinator' or 'moderator' or 'pastor' for a person who is not a priest – this person shares in the exercise of pastoral care but does not 'direct', 'co-ordinate', 'moderate' or 'govern' the parish – these are the competencies of a priest according to the Instruction.[6] It doesn't tell us what terminology to use, but certainly is clear on forbidden titles. The Instruction demonstrated a deep Roman unease with developments which in its view undermine the distinctiveness of priestly ministry, and clearly preferred other solutions than that mentioned in c. 517 §2 (e.g. by using retired priests, or entrusting several parishes to one priest or to a *coetus sacerdotum in solidum*). This is related to the ongoing Roman concern about the centrality of priestly ministry to parish life and the danger of reducing the priesthood to a functional existence.[7]

In short, when there is no parish priest, canon law tries to maintain a link between an ongoing constant priestly presence and the parish. The church herself has not yet worked out completely the relationship between priestly and lay ministry. For instance, canon law's hesitancy about *cura animarum* (to use the

5. See G. D. Yanus ('Part 1: The Parish') and T. G. Sullivan ('Part II: The Role of the Parish Administrator'), 'Sacramental Life of Parishes without a Resident Pastor', *Proceedings of the Canon Law Society of America* 66 (2004) 207-241.

6. See Articles 1 §3 and 4 §1 of the Interdicasterial Instruction, *Ecclesiae de mysterio*, On Certain Questions Regarding the Collaboration of the Non-Ordained Faithful in the Sacred Ministry of Priests, 15 August 1997, *Acta Apostolicae Sedis* 89 (1997) 852-877; English translation in *Origins* 27 (1997-1998) 397, 399-409.

7. See, for instance, the Instruction of the Congregation of the Clergy, *The Priest, Pastor and Leader of the Christian Community*, no 26, 4 August 2002, *Origins* 32 (2002-2003) 385-386.

traditional term for pastoral care) by the laity – see c. 150 which says that the holder of an ecclesiastical office 'entailing the full care of souls' must be a priest – has its roots in the equally tentative texts of Vatican II. What the council wished to avoid is often clearer than what it wished to say positively. Frequently, Vatican II was far more concerned with distancing itself from past frameworks than it was in constructing a new, internally coherent, theological framework.

Conclusion

In one sense we have to be patient and struggle with the uncertain, because we are living in the wake of an ecumenical council and a very changed Ireland. Socially, theologically and canonically we are in a state of flux about how priests, parishes and people relate, and that is not too comfortable. It would be much easier if someone could give us the new worked-out canonical model for clustering. However, that is not the way it has worked historically. Practice often comes before theological theory which then expresses itself in canonical structures. Pastoral practice in the church sometimes runs ahead of theological reflection and canonical order. Practical needs arise in the church and people try to respond to them, as we see in the discussion about parish clusters. Law follows life, in the sense that canon law follows on from the lived experience of church life, and often the law takes a while to catch up with that experience. Of course, that is not to say that everything which develops in pastoral practice is necessarily good or desirable in the longer term, which is why so much of canon law seems to be about curbing abuses which existed sometime in the past.

CHAPTER TEN

The Diocesan Priesthood in the 21st Century

Eamonn Fitzgibbon

Introduction

The next twenty years or so will be a time of significant change in the landscape of the local Irish church. The number of priests available to staff our parishes is set to decline considerably. Many dioceses in Ireland have been trying to address the implications of this change; diocesan pastoral centres are now quite common and there are many lay pastoral co-ordinators employed at diocesan level. Much of the work to date has focused on resourcing parish renewal and pastoral development; lay people have been trained for ministry and leadership. I often get the sense that in this regard the Irish church has once more arrived late and breathless as it reluctantly, and of necessity, embraces the ecclesiological vision of Vatican II. In spite of some progress, there is a growing sense that something much more radical is required if we are to continue to have vibrant, faith-filled communities into the future.

In my work as director of a diocesan pastoral centre over ten years and in my current role as one who is charged with developing parish clustering, I recognise a hesitation, reluctance and occasionally resistance among many priests to introducing the required change. The reasons for this are varied and complex. The clergy are an aging body of men with very few young men entering; indeed many of today's vocations are what were traditionally called 'late vocations'. Change is always difficult but when one is trained for a particular style of ministry and when one is accustomed to a particular way of doing things for many years, it is little wonder that many older men say: 'Sure, it'll see me out anyway.' A variety of factors have coincided to drive down clergy morale and this also contributes to a lack of necessary energy and drive to lead change. However, underlying all of this is the theological question. I believe that the operative theology of many priests is not congruent with pastoral development, collaborative ministry or parish clustering. It is extremely important that the theological discussion takes place; at the heart of this is the question of a theology of ministry and more specifically of the priesthood.

In this paper I intend to show that our theology of ministry is developmental and is influenced by the context in which ministry occurs. Priestly identity is conditioned by the culture in which it is lived. Our current reality offers both a challenge and an opportunity. The challenge for today's priest is to avoid becoming a dispenser of sacraments divorced from a real experience of community and separated from other aspects of the role of the priest. The opportunity is to find new ways of being a priest which are sustainable and life-giving. I will argue that parish clustering is much more than a mere administrative or structural solution but is in fact a way of living out the fullness of the Christian vocation. The present reality has forced us to revisit the rich teaching of Vatican II in terms of lay participation and involvement; it is now encouraging us to look again at what Vatican II had to say about priesthood.

Context
Context moulds and influences our very understanding of priesthood and, indeed, adapts our theology of it. To declare that context changes ministry is a recognition that ministry itself is something organic, fluid and dynamic. As Susan Wood says:

> A theology of ministry is always influenced by its cultural and historical context. It is always contextual, which means that a theology of priesthood or of lay ecclesial ministry is never once and for all developed. Such a theology is in dialogue with the theology that preceded it and with the pastoral needs that confront it. It is organic, dynamic, adaptive, characterised by both continuity and change.[1]

The role and identity of the priest has changed through the ages. An acceptance of this fact means we must revisit how we understand and interpret aspects of the theology of priesthood. Still, there are many in the church who insist that priesthood has remained constant and unchanging since the time of Christ. However, church history presents us with a different reality as

---

1. Susan Wood, 'Priesthood: forty Years after Vatican II', in Donald Dietrich, ed, *Priests for the 21st Century*, (New York: Crossroad Publishing Company, 2006), 3.

we discover several descriptions and roles assigned to the *episkopos* and the *presbyteros*, which in turn have produced a change in the theological definition of bishop and priest.[2] Kenan Osborne believes that this theology will develop even further when we come to a deeper understanding of the relationship between ordained and lay ministries:

> Today there are still key Catholics in leadership positions who continue to maintain that episcopal and presbyteral roles have not substantially changed from the time of Jesus down to the present. They claim an immutable and untouchable theological core for this position. Historically, this cannot be demonstrated. Rather, history clearly indicates the changeability of both episcopal and presbyteral offices.[3]

There are a number of aspects of the current context which have a profound impact on priestly ministry.

Shortage of Priests[4]
There is some urgency in Ireland today, to address what could reasonably be termed a crisis in ministry, as a significant decline

---

2. See Kenan B. Osborne, *Priesthood: A History of the Ordained Ministry in the Roman Catholic Church*, (Eugene, OR: Wipf & Stock Publishers, 2003) for an account of the different historical expressions of priesthood.

3. Kenan B. Osborne, 'Envisioning a Theology of Ordained and lay Ministry: Lay/Ordained Ministry – Current Issues of Ambiguity' in Susan K. Wood, ed, *Ordering the Baptismal Priesthood: Theologies of Lay and Ordained Ministry*, (Collegeville: Liturgical Press, 2003) 224.

4. Thomas Mahoney offers the following reflection on Dean Hoge's analysis of the shortage of priests: 'The sociological analysis of the purported priest shortage offered by Dean R. Hoge yields for me new insights and conclusions. Hoge suggests that differing expectations of priesthood and varying experiences with regard to the role of the priest are important determining factors in drawing conclusions about the severity of the priest shortage and its long term effects. Hoge makes the case that there may be no real priest shortage in the United States. Other parts of the world with large and even growing populations of Catholics function with far fewer priests. In these faith communities, more is expected of the laity. In places where a shortage is perceived, even without consideration of women who discern a call to priesthood, there is a ready pool of qualified lay ministers, who are functioning already in important ways within the limits imposed by the church's authoritarian hierarchy' (*Reflection*, in Donald Dietrich, ed, *Priests for the 21st Century*, 191). Dean R. Hoge's analysis, 'Addressing the Priest 'Shortage',' appears in the same volume pp 133-149.

in the number of vocations to the priesthood and religious life make it very clear that traditional structures and ways of ministering are no longer sustainable. Vincent Toomey interprets this as 'a symptom of a much deeper and more serious crisis, that of faith'.[5] Jan Kerkhof goes even further: 'It is more than a crisis of faith, it is a crisis about the meaning of human life.'[6] Vocations to the priesthood and religious life have fallen very sharply and this presents a serious challenge to structures of ministry that are dependent on clergy and religious. Wood says: 'Forty years after Vatican II finds us with a plethora of books on the priesthood, with a widespread acknowledgement that priestly identity today is in crisis, with an indisputable shortage of priests as parishes cluster, with priests who serve multiple parishes.'[7] A tardiness in Ireland around engaging seriously with the requisite change has resulted in priests under significant stress as they try to meet demands and expectations more appropriate to the situation thirty years ago when there were far more 'full-time professionals' available to meet those demands. We rarely see a reduction in the number of Masses celebrated throughout a diocese to correspond with the reduced number of priests available to celebrate those Masses. Priests continue to valiantly expend themselves in traditional pastoral practices such as parish visitation, leading the prayers in the funeral home, visiting the school classes, receiving the remains of the deceased. It will simply be impossible to meet all these demands and expectations into the future and in the meantime one has to ask: what is the cost to the priest himself?

Secularisation
In an exploration of the beliefs and practices of the Irish people from 1980 to 2000, through the lens of the International Social Survey Programme and the European Values Study surveys, Eoin Cassidy says 'There is no doubting the evidence of a growth in the secularisation of Irish society and the increasing acceptance in the main of liberalism.'[8] Cassidy notes a significant de-

5. D. Vincent Twomey, *The End of Irish Catholicism?*, (Dublin: Veritas, 2003), 155.
6. Jan Kerkhof, 'Reorganising the Parish – a horizon of kindly light', in *The Furrow* LVI, (2005), 199.
7. Susan Wood, 'Priesthood: Forty Years after Vatican II', in Donald Dietrich, ed, *Priests for the 21st Century*, 3.
8. Eoin G. Cassidy, (ed), *Measuring Ireland: Discerning Values and Beliefs*, (Dublin: Veritas, 2002), 41.

cline in a belief in the moral authority of the church, attendance
at religious services and confidence in the Catholic Church.
While there is a constant acceptance of belief in God throughout
the relevant timespan it is interesting to note a significant decline in belief in a personal God. Jan Kerkhof has seen it all before: 'Some people are saying that the Catholic Church in Ireland
is catching up very quickly on the process of secularisation that
begun many years ago in a number of western European countries.'[9] Parish clergy are confronted with the reality of this secularisation on a daily basis. Parents regularly present children for
the sacraments of initiation with very little real understanding
of that which they are requesting from the church. Couples may
come looking for a church wedding motivated more by a desire
to please their parents or the aesthetics of the venue than any
faith conviction. Such attitudes confront and grate upon the
deeply and passionately held faith convictions of the priest.

Busyness
In assessing the shortage of clergy I have already discussed the
demands placed on a reduced workforce of clergy available to
the Irish church. Many of today's priests are extremely busy and
are often most busy in meeting the round of demands for sacraments. We have done little to reduce the number of Masses in
our parishes, the dead must still be buried, couples wedded and
babies christened. This leaves less space for reflection, prayer or
study and even recreation. In fact, there is less space to simply
'be'. As Brendan Hoban puts it:

> What is left when function consumes the person I am? What
> can I do now to live a human life in the time God gives me?
> … My contention is that the balance in priesthood between
> function and person, that would enable a more enriched and
> effective priesthood and a more normal personal life, is no
> longer there.[10]

Have we, in this age of functionality, lost our sense of being,
our ontological dimension? Are we so absorbed in what we *do*
that we have lost a sense of who we *are* at the deepest level of
our being? Is our identity entirely dependent on our role, task or

9. Kerkhof, 'Reorganising the Parish', 195.
10. Brendan Hoban, 'Elephants in the Living Room', in *The Furrow*, XLVII
(1996), 666-667.

function? In this consumerist age, is production the sole criterion by which we are measured? Even though recognition of change in the role and theology of priesthood seems to threaten the concept of an ontological change at ordination, I believe there is something in this teaching that needs to be retrieved. This teaching can be useful if it enables us to get away from a purely functional approach or understanding of ministry. Many writers on ministry are sceptical that such a teaching has anything to offer. Paul Bernier says:

> One of the main ways that Trent's strong emphasis on ordained priesthood has come down to us is in the Tridentine teaching on the sacramental character. This does not seem to be the best way to ground a theology of ministry, however. Not the least problem here is that it tends to make the issue a question of either/or: Does ordination confer something ontological, or is it merely a function within the church? This leads to minimalism. It has also led to widening the split between clergy and laity and relegating all ministry to the ordained. It is also the underpinning for the priesthood as a superior state of life over the lay 'state'.[11]

However, Bernier also recognises that: 'The essential continuity between the two councils (Trent and Vatican II) is that both taught that ordination is a true sacrament that confers a special grace and "character".'[12]

John Macquarrie does much to redeem the 'ontological argument' when he outlines how the ontological dimension of priestly ordination is best expressed in terms of this priestly 'character'. He argues that such 'priestly character' is best understood in anthropological terms. 'Character' is the traditional word used to describe the peculiar being of the ordained minister. Character is a pattern, traced in the behaviour of a person. It signifies the way in which one's behaviour is dominated by one all-consuming purpose or direction, or at least by an ultimate concern; it signifies 'purity of heart'. Character is built by formation, education, a personal choice, genetic inheritance and of course, grace. In terms of a vocation to priesthood we can trace the beginning of character to the first moment of discerning a call; it is built

---

11. Paul Bernier, *Ministry in the Church: A Historical and Pastoral Approach*, 2nd ed., (New London: Twenty-Third Publications, 2006), 199.
12. Ibid., 231.

upon through seminary training and priestly formation and is developed over a lifetime.[13] Rahner is also helpful here as he encourages us to see the distinctive character of the ordained ministry in a sacramental way, seeing in the priest a tangible sign of the ministry of Christ.[14] Many contemporary writers on ministry see the ontological change in terms of a relational change. However it is understood, our identity as priests must not be reduced to being entirely dependent upon that which we do.

Popular Caricatures of Priests
In many of the communities in which he ministers, the priest has ceased to be relevant to the lives of significant numbers of people and is in various ways marginalised. Indeed the clericalised priest has become a parody of himself as so brilliantly depicted in TV shows like 'Fr Ted' or 'Killinascully'. There are many young adults in Ireland today whose only real exposure to priests is through such comedy. More tragically, many see the priest as someone who is no longer to be trusted as the phrase 'paedophile priest' trips off the pen in so many media reports. Perhaps it is to the individual priest himself that the most damage is done by clericalism. It is too easy to believe the clericalist propaganda and eventually end up isolated with no clear sense of identity, lacking intimacy and struggling to live out of an idealised notion of what one should be. 'The person we are is central to our pastoral role. It is as men that we are called to be priests. If our manhood gets lost in a clericalist role, is Christ's priesthood also crushed?'[15]

Clerical Child Sexual Abuse
I have outlined a number of factors which contribute to the crisis in diocesan priesthood. However compelling these examples may be, the most devastating symptom of all in the current malaise is clerical child sexual abuse. I deliberately use the terms

13. See John Macquarrie, *Theology, Church and Ministry*, (London: SCM Press, 1986) 172-178.
14. Paul D. Murray, 'The Lasting Significance of Karl Rahner for Contemporary Catholic Theology', in Eamonn Conway, ed, *The Courage to Risk Everything … Essays Marking the Centenary of Karl Rahner's Birth*, (Louvain Studies, Vol 29, [2004]) 23, 24.
15. Jerry Joyce, *The Laity: Help or Hindrance*, (Dublin: Mercier Press, 1994), 65.

'symptom' and 'malaise' for as Thomas O'Meara reminds us 'Ministry, like liturgy, is a sign of the church's health.'[16] It is too easy and journalistically lazy to link the issue of sexual abuse and clericalism as direct cause and effect. I accept all the defensive arguments about the percentage of clergy involved being no greater than the wider male population.[17] This does not excuse us, however, from forensically examining our particular clerical culture to see what lies there that may be contributing to or colluding with the problem. There are aspects of the priestly life and the clerical culture which may not be directly causative of child abuse, however they may be conducive to creating an environment in which such abuse can emerge and avoid detection or punishment.[18] Such self-examination and personal scrutiny are painful as we need to reassess the loneliness factor, the lack of intimacy, the way in which sexuality has been dealt with in formation, the lack of accountability, the male environment, the disproportionately placed trust, the unlimited access to children, the issues of power, celibacy … the list goes on. Eamonn Conway captures the pain of relinquishing that which may have been formerly enjoyed: 'Much of our current pain has been caused by a model of priesthood in which individuals are presented as sacred personages with sacred powers. The priest was understood to represent in his person the perfect body of Christ … This understanding of priesthood is now clearly bankrupt, and has been for some time. Both priests and people are suffering as a result.'[19] The shame, fear and confusion generated by this crisis have led to further isolation in the lives of priests. The crisis is deepened by the fact that the institutional church has lost credibility and the trust of the people to whom it ministers.

---

16. Thomas F. O'Meara, *Theology of Ministry*, Completely revised edition, (New York: Paulist Press, 1999), 26.

17. '"Fathers also abuse their children." Understandable as this argument is it misses the heart of the matter; when a priest or religious abuses a child it is as if God has allowed the abusing, so revered and sacred was and still is the priest in the lives of many members of the church. He was and still is for many "God's man on earth".' Marie Keenan, 'Child Sexual Abuse: The Heart of the Matter', in *The Furrow*, LIII (2002) 602-603.

18. See David Ranson, 'The Climate of Sexual Abuse', in *The Furrow*, LIII (2002), 388.

19. Eamonn Conway, 'Touching our Wounds', *The Furrow*, LIII (2002) 269.

A People of Hope

In the midst of this context we are called to be a people of hope. Karl Rahner reminded us towards the end of his life: 'It is part too of a Christian hope that we don't interpret these wintry times as a prelude to death. Each one of us should instead see these times as a personal challenge to work so that the inner core of faith comes alive. Then of course the church itself will again shine radiantly.'[20] The context demands of us serious self-reflection and this can be painful but as another theological giant reminds us: 'It is no bad thing when the Christian minister is, from time to time, compelled to reconsider his fundamental *raison d'être*.'[21] The Second Vatican Council presents us with a direction for priesthood which may well provide a road-map to guide priesthood through this hazardous journey.

Vatican II

On the one hand, the council may offer us a way forward but in another sense it is part of the problem. The council, it seems, had much to say to bishops and lay people (although a cogent theology of lay ministry is distinctly absent) but it lacked any clear direction for priesthood. Indeed there are those, such as Andrew Greeley, who insist that the council further confused a priesthood already in turmoil. 'Vatican II did something to the priesthood from which it is yet to recover. I don't know what that is. The crisis in the priesthood today, remains to a considerable extent inexplicable.'[22] The re-establishment of episcopacy to the sacrament of orders is a major change but the way in which the bishop is described as having the 'fullness of priesthood' has generated its own difficulties for the identity of the priest. Of course there is also uncertainty as there exists in this post-conciliar time, a struggle between acceptance and non-acceptance of the teaching of Vatican II. 'After every major council of the Christian Church, a prolonged time of uncertainty has inevitably occurred.'[23]

20. Paul Imhof and Hubert Biallowons, eds, *Faith in a Wintry Season – Conversations & Interviews with Karl Rahner in the Last Years of His Life*, (New York: The Cross Road Publishing Company, 1990), 76.

21. Macquarrie, *Theology, Church and Ministry*, 156.

22. Andrew M. Greeley, in Tim Unsworth, ed, *The Last Priests in America – Conversations with Remarkable Men*, (New York: Crossroad, 1991), 122.

23. Kenan B. Osborne, *The Permanent Diaconate – Its History and Place in the Sacrament of Orders*, (Mahwah, NJ: Paulist Press, 2007), 16.

A re-examination of the role of the priesthood and an enhanced theology of the laity has generated a level of uncertainty
among priests. Indeed Yves Congar, who recognised that much
of his earlier writings defined the laity in terms of their relationship to clergy, said later in life that 'it is no longer the layman
who stands in need of definition but the priest.'[24] Many theologians recognise the lack of a complete theology of ministry in
Vatican II: 'A uniformly developed theology of ordained priesthood, consistent with this vision does not regularly spring forth
from conciliar writings'[25] and similarly 'commentary on laity
and ministry is very limited in the documents of Vatican II, and
what we now call lay ecclesial ministry is barely envisioned.'[26]

The sixteen documents of Vatican II were trying to appease
different viewpoints and one needs to be wary of selecting pas-
sages from documents to suit one's purpose. The story of the
council clearly evidences a struggle between those who are influenced by movements within early twentieth-century Catholic
theology such as the *nouvelle theologie* and those defending a
post-Tridentine understanding of the church as articulated
within neo-scholasticism. A purely literal reading of the texts results in an incomplete interpretation of the true intention of the
council which can only be articulated by taking into account the
various rejections of *Schemata* and assessing the various inter-
ventions by the bishops. Within the historical event that is the
council, we see unfolding broad directions, pointers and trends
which reveal significant theological shifts.[27]

---

24. Yves Congar, 'My Pathfindings in the Theology of Laity and
Ministries', in *The Jurist*, 2 (1972) 178.
25. Thomas R. Whelan, 'Clergy and Laity: Fragmentation or fellowship?'
in Seán MacRéamoinn, ed, *Ministry, Clerics and the rest of us*, (Dublin:
Columba, 1998), 29.
26. Zeni Fox, 'Laity, Ministry, and Secular Character' in Susan K. Wood,
ed, *Ordering the Baptismal Priesthood: Theologies of Lay and Ordained
Ministry*, (Collegeville: Liturgical Press, 2003) 135. Susan Wood, 'Priesthood: Forty Years after Vatican II' in *Priests for the 21st Century*, examines
the implications for the relationship between the ordained priesthood
and the priesthood of the baptised.
27. To gain a further insight into the historical context and storyline of the
council, see John W. O'Malley, *What Happened at Vatican II*, (London:
Harvard University Press, 2008) and David G. Schultenover, ed, *Vatican
II: Did Anything Happen?*, (New York: Continuum, 2008).

There is in the conciliar documents a sound basis on which to construct a theology of ministry appropriate to our current situation. One needs to assess all the texts, but also attend carefully to whole work of the council in arriving at the final drafts of its documents, because all of these reveal a significant shift in the theology of priesthood.

A helpful starting point may be the intervention of Bishop François Marty, made at one of the plenary sessions:

> The commission cannot agree with those Fathers who think the position paper should have followed the scholastic definition of priesthood, which is based on the power to consecrate the Eucharist. According to the prevailing mind of this Council and the petition of many Fathers, the priesthood of presbyters must rather be connected with the priesthood of bishops, the latter being regarded as the high point and fullness of priesthood. The priesthood of presbyters must therefore be looked at in this draft as embracing not one function, but three, and must be linked with the Apostles and their mission.[28]

Tria Munera

The council recognised that the ministerial priesthood is not to be defined solely by its eucharistic role but is related to the entire mission and ministry of Christ.[29] The council marked an expansion of the role of the priest from the rather narrow scholastic understanding which dominated prior to the council and which was in fact a contraction of the early church's expression of the ministerial task.

> For centuries in Roman Catholic theology and piety, the priest has been viewed above all as the one who has 'the power to say Mass' ... this almost exclusively sacramental definition of priesthood has had far-reaching effects on both theology and pastoral practice ... The historical tendency to place sacramental power before pastoral leadership represents a reversal of the pattern one can discern in the New Testament.[30]

---

28. Osborne, *Priesthood: A History of the Ordained Ministry in the Roman Catholic Church*, 318.

29. See Bernier, *Ministry in the Church*, 226.

30. Nathan Mitchell, *Mission and Ministry: History and Theology in the Sacrament of Order*, (Delaware: Michael Glazier, Inc., 1982), 303.

Priesthood had come to be defined in a narrow 'sacramental' way, in terms of the power to confect the Eucharist and forgive sin. The Council Fathers developed and expanded this definition. This renewal of the theology of priesthood also marked a movement away from a cultic model of priesthood. As Wood says:

> The bishops at Vatican II broadened the theology of the priesthood from its Tridentine forerunner, which was predominantly a cultic and priestly theology with an emphasis on the priest's role in the Eucharist. Vatican II expanded this theology through its use of the threefold office of priest, prophet and king corresponding to the sanctifying, teaching and pastoral leadership duties of a priest.[31]

The priestly, prophetic and kingly roles ascribed to the priest in Vatican II marked a broad and expansive understanding compared to the scholastic definition which was limited to a sacramental focus.[32] The threefold task – the *tria munera* – witnesses to the mission and ministry of Jesus himself. It is the task of each generation of priests to translate the priestly, prophetic and kingly role to their own particular circumstances. Practically, we need to ask ourselves what style of leadership is required in the church today, how can we best communicate the Word, how can we enable communities to grow in holiness?

While one would imagine that this change would be broadly welcomed there has been some resistance. Osborne (rather kindly, I think) attributes this to a lack of understanding:

> Not all priests have reached an understanding of what this change implies, but priests generally find this approach to priesthood far more nourishing than the scholastic view, which dominated the Roman Catholic Church from 1150 to Vatican II. The change was sudden and dramatic, but nonetheless one that has been encouraging and nourishing.[33]

However, he also has a strong word for those who resist the implications of this change: 'Any definition of priesthood today that is not clearly elaborated within this framework is a definition that the Second Vatican Council has clearly rejected.'[34]

31. Susan Wood 'Priesthood: Forty Years after Vatican II', in Dietrich, ed, *Priests for the 21st Century*, 4.
32. I am using the term 'sacramental' here in its narrowest sense.
33. Osborne, *The Permanent Diaconate*, 128.
34. Ibid., 77.

The context within which the priest in Ireland is ministering today has made it difficult for those priests who wish to embrace the vision of Vatican II. As I have already outlined, the sacramental demands placed on the priest as a result of the shortage of clergy and the expectation that an unchanged rota and workload can be delivered by fewer priests means that in practice the priest in today's Irish parish often finds himself living out of a scholastic model of priesthood. When he has fulfilled the demands to baptise the babies, marry the couples, bury the dead, celebrate the daily and Sunday Masses he has time for little that is prophetic or kingly.[35] A priestly ministry that has a purely sacramental focus is a distortion. Priesthood can never be adequately understood on a purely cultic or liturgical basis; if the sacramental aspect is divorced from the other aspects of the ministry, such as preaching or pastoral care, it is a reduced and marginalised ministry which will become increasingly irrelevant in the lives of people.[36]

This limited understanding of priesthood is to settle for the concept of a 'sanctuary priest' and a way of life which is less than fulfilling or life-giving, which does not allow the full potential of the life of a priest to be expressed. Twenty years ago Enda Lyons recognised the dangers: 'There can be no doubt that saying Mass, and administering the sacraments … are essential to the priest's ministry. However, the priest's role in the parish does not consist merely in performing these sacred actions.'[37] He noted the comments of Rahner from twenty years earlier: 'This narrowly ritualistic interpretation of the specifically priestly task is not only humanly intolerable, but also theologically wrong.'[38]

The context within which priests minister today has resulted in an increased anxiety among clergy to define their role and clarify their identity. I have observed many diocesan clergy conferences discuss the 'essential' role of the priest. Invariably, the agreed consensus centres on celebrating the Eucharist. Many priests feel threatened and insecure by the increased status and

---

35. See comments by Wood in 'Priesthood: Forty Years after Vatican II' in Dietrich, ed, *Priests for the 21st Century*, 5
36. See John Baldovin SJ, 'The Priest as sacramental Minister – History and Theology', in *Priests for the 21st Century*, 19
37. Enda Lyons, *Partnership in Parish*, Revised Edition, (Dublin: Columba Press, 1993) 86.
38. Ibid, 87.

profile of lay ministry[39] and are thus inclined to define their ministry in terms of that which lay people cannot do.[40] This brings us again to the question of the difference between ordained and lay ministers, between the ministerial priesthood and the priesthood of the faithful. Many priests feel threatened and diminished as they struggle to maintain a distinct identity and role but it is not a positive development when we define ourselves over and against others in ministry. When writing of the 'Priestly Image of Today and Tomorrow' Rahner said:

> The basic question with regard to the basic essence of the priestly office, therefore, is not 'What is it which the priest alone can do?' but rather this: Let us say that what assumes and brings to its fullness in his office is a complex of tasks and functions deriving its meaning from the nature of the church herself, so that it is this that gives the priestly office its justification.[41]

Of course part of the confusion which exists between ordained and lay ministry was the renewed understanding of the priesthood of the faithful – or the common priesthood. 'Though the common priesthood of all believers was said to differ 'in essence' from the ordained priesthood, we were never told convincingly what this essential difference was.'[42] Vatican II has left us with the task of clarifying this distinction.

In the meantime, this confusion has resulted in defensive definitions of priesthood. The challenge before us now is to let go of our fears and allow a new understanding of what it is to be a priest to emerge. This will allow a new ecclesiology to develop

39. Edward Hahnenberg noted: 'Vatican II's reluctance to apply the term "ministry" to the laity soon gave way to an expansive use of the term. In the years following the council, the language of the lay apostolate, which had dominated theological treatments of the laity since the early twentieth century, all but disappeared. In its place came "lay ministry".' ('One priestly people: Ordained and lay ministries in the Church', in *Priests for the 21st Century*, 104).
40. 'There is a tendency on the part of some key Roman Catholic Church leaders to emphasise the radical and specific difference of each ministry over against a foundational interrelationship of all institutional church ministries.' Osborne, *The Permanent Diaconate*, viii.
41. Karl Rahner, *Theological Investigations*, Vol 12, 48.
42. Bernier, *Ministry in the Church*, 223.

which sees all church members called to ministry through baptism and who share in a common priestly identity.[43] An ability to relinquish a defensive stance on priesthood, a willingness to cease from defining ourselves 'over and against' others in ministry brings us to another change in priestly identity which Vatican II presented. Once we begin to change perspective, we begin to acknowledge the primordial radical relationship between all ministries as the appropriate starting point.

Inter-Relatedness
The *tria munera* theology of Vatican II implies an interrelated base for all ministry; all the baptised share in the mission and ministry of Christ who has himself been sent by the Father. Vatican II insisted on a collegial understanding of priesthood.[44] Osborne says:

> A collegial understanding of bishop and priest indicates that one cannot have a theological, pastoral, or personal (self-identity) view of priesthood that is nonrelational. The older scholastic view, which was based on the power to consecrate and to forgive sin, was individualistic.[45]

He regards all ministry as inter-relational and asserts that this is the current teaching of the church on the issue.[46] Wood sees a similar shift in the teaching of the council as she recognises that Vatican II 'also identified priesthood as a communal ministry.'[47]

In tracing the history and development of *Presbyterum Ordinis* it is interesting to note the eventual outcome whereby the preferred term for priest was presbyter. This can be interpreted as a commitment on the part of the bishops to develop a collegial style of ministry among priests.[48] This emphasis on inter-relationality makes it clear that priests are meant to act as a group rather than as individuals. However, this inter-relationality is not confined to the priest-to-priest relationship but to all in ministry:

43. See Macquarrie, *Theology, Church and Ministry*, 157.
44. See Eugene Duffy, 'Presbyteral Collegiality: Precedents and Horizons', *The Jurist* 69 (2009), 116-154 for a fuller discussion of this topic.
45. Osborne, *The Permanent Diaconate*, 84.
46. Ibid., 135.
47. Susan Wood, 'Priesthood: Forty Years after Vatican II', 4.
48. See Osborne, *The Permanent Diaconate*, 75.

Priesthood, theologically, is not individualistic but interrelational, and this interrelational dimension includes a collegial or presbyteral relationship with the bishop as the fullness of the priesthood, with fellow priests and with all fellow ministers.[49]

John Paul II also emphasised this communal dimension of priesthood in *Pastores dabo vobis:*

The nature and mission of the ministerial priesthood cannot be defined except through this multiple and rich interconnection of relationships which arise from the Blessed Trinity and are prolonged in the communion of the church.

The ordained ministry has a radical communitarian form and can only be carried out as a collective work.[50]

We have already seen reluctance within the priesthood to embrace the implications of a model of priesthood based on the *tria munera*; we see a similar failure to realise the call to communal ministry among diocesan clergy. Many feel they were formed to work as 'lone rangers'; a rugged individualism was seen as a virtue and indeed, so-called 'particular' friendships were discouraged within the seminary. Priests find themselves living lives of increasing isolation with few skills for developing true and appropriate intimacy; where once presbyteries may have accommodated a number of priests and parishes were staffed by a team of clergy, priests increasingly find themselves living and working alone. Priests often feel threatened by increasing numbers of lay ministers and respond by emphasisng the dividing line between ministries. This has not served us well and will certainly not sustain a church into the future. Seán MacRéamoinn observed some years ago, 'As we face a new century, a new millennium, a new world, and hence a new agenda for the church, we must work and pray to be rid of all divisions which serve only to inhibit and frustrate our discipleship.'[51] Until priests themselves move away from a theologically individualistic understanding of priesthood towards a more interrelational and communal understanding, we will become increasingly isolated

---

49. Ibid., 88.
50. See John Paul II, *Pastores dabo vobis*, English trs (Washington DC: USCCB, 1992), paragraphs 12 and 17 respectively.
52. Seán MacRéamoinn, 'Stoles, Collars and ...' in Seán MacRéamoinn, ed, *Ministry, Clerics and the Rest of Us*, (Dublin: Columba, 1998), 25.

and less able to support and bond with each other or work with
lay colleagues. As Osborne says: 'No wonder the morale of
many priests has plummeted downward. When the communion
aspect of priestly ministry is minimalised, the individual priest
is marginalised.'[52] There is plenty evidence of such marginalisation and isolation among clergy and also of its devastating consequences.

Implications

A Contemporary Role for Today's Priest

In the midst of the confusion created by the context in which
the secular priest ministers today, there is a very clear role
emerging for the ordained. The *Catechism of the Catholic Church*
reminds us that 'the ministerial priesthood is at the service of
the common priesthood. It is directed at the unfolding of the
baptismal grace of all Christians.'[53] If we can fully retrieve the
teaching on the priesthood of the faithful as Vatican II encourages us to do we will come to recognise the ordained priesthood
as belonging within the wider common priesthood; the ministerial priesthood is not something entirely separate or apart from
the priesthood in which all the baptised share. Paul Philibert
recognises that: 'The ministerial priesthood is entirely relative to
and finds its fulfilment in the cultivation of the baptismal priesthood.'[54] Paul Lakeland agrees: 'The special roles of ordained
ministry are exercised within the context of a truly priestly community.'[55] As mentioned earlier, towards the end of his life,
Congar developed an understanding of the clergy in relation to
the laity rather than vice-versa and also recognised a continuum
of ministries into which priesthood is inserted. The criteria for
living out the common priesthood of all the baptised are expli-
cated in the prophetic, priestly and kingly dimensions of the
baptismal anointing into the priesthood of the faithful. A definite and necessary role is emerging for today's priest as he is
called to free up the gifts available to the church through the
laity and empower all to exercise the ministry appropriate to

52. Osborne, *The Permanent Diaconate*,85.
53. The *Catechism of the Catholic Church*, no 1547.
54. Paul J. Philibert, *The Priesthood of the Faithful: Key to a Living Church*,
(Collegeville, MN: Liturgical Press, 2005), 72.
55. Paul Lakeland, *The Liberation of the Laity: In Search of an Accountable
Church*, (London: Continuum, 2003), 90.

their calling. This is a truly kingly role and it requires skilled and collaborative leadership. 'Priests are in a unique position to facilitate or hinder the development of collaborative ministry, especially at the parish level.'[56]

Parish Clustering:
If today's diocesan priest is to fulfil the threefold aspect of his calling to be priest, prophet and king, if he is to minister in a truly inter-relational way and if he is to work at freeing up the vocation of all God's people allowing the charisms of each to flourish, then we need to develop a structure which will act as a supportive scaffold for priests and enable this model to flourish. Such a structural reordering must be a priority for the Irish church today. There is some urgency as the current model of priestly ministry is simply unsustainable. It is damaging to the individual priest, to the priesthood and ultimately to the wider community which the priest is called to serve. I believe parish clustering offers us a structure within which the Vatican II model of priesthood can develop. However, parish clustering is not simply about amalgamating parishes; it must not be confined to a purely pragmatic system of managing resources. Earlier in this collection, Eugene Duffy has offered a theological rationale for clustering; it must be this broad understanding of what clustering means that we choose and nothing less. Clustering can easily become clericalised, being nothing more than an arrangement among neighbouring priests to provide holiday cover and sick leave, to ensure Masses and 'duty' are always covered. In fact clustering offers us a means by which we can develop a truly collaborative and inter-relational style of ministry. Ultimately, it would evolve into team ministry where full-time, part-time and volunteer, lay, religious and clergy would work together in a supportive and life-enhancing way. Over thirty years ago, Yves Congar developed a model of concentric circles of diverse ministries within the community. Priestly isolation would be reduced and the priest working in a parish would become less and less marginalised in his own community and in wider society. There is a wider theological rationale underpinning all of this but there is also a theology of

---

56. Loughlin Solfield and Carroll Juliano, *Collaboration – Uniting our gifts in Ministry*, (Notre Dame: Ave Maria Press, 2000), 180.

priesthood with which such a model is entirely congruent. Edward Hahnenberg reminds us that secular priesthood is a call to minister in the world:

> It seems we can no longer rely on the notion of 'sacred ministry' to identify or distinguish the priest, if by 'sacred ministry' we imply activity in a realm separate from the secular, a church apart from the world. To link identity to separation, to rest alone as 'a man set apart' for the things of God, is at best, a return to a French baroque spirituality and, at worst, a drift into clericalism. Every priest today is not called to be an agent for social reform, a spokesman for political causes, or a worker-priest one with the people, but disengagement from the world in which we live is not an option.[57]

---

57. Edward Hahnenberg, 'One priestly People – Ordained and Lay Ministries in the Church', in *Priests for the 21st Century*, 114.

CHAPTER ELEVEN

Sunday Liturgies in the Absence of the Eucharist

Thomas R. Whelan

It is only in recent years that we have begun to experience in Ireland a phenomenon that has been commonplace elsewhere for many decades, and longer: that of having to organise worship when we do not have an ordained priest available to us to preside at a eucharistic celebration. The very existence of the 'Sunday Celebration in the Absence of Eucharist' has been described as a 'liturgical solution to an ecclesiological problem',[1] and therein lies the predicament. Rome has offered guidelines on the matter and, quite rightly, has left to local churches the task of addressing the liturgical aspect of this dilemma (there is no prescribed ritual).

Serious reflection on issues relating to the experience of the contemporary Irish church and how it articulates itself at local levels is timely, and offers an important opportunity to open a much needed debate on the implications of having an increasing shortage of ordained priests in our dioceses. It supplies an occasion to begin asking hard questions. The goal is not the attainment of an administrative and operational solution to the running of the local church, but the creation of a new and vibrant communion of assemblies bearing witness to the mercy and love of God. This communion of communities, to be true to itself, engages fully with current social and cultural issues so that, through the encroachment of the Reign of God in our midst, we might be facilitators of justice and reconciliation, peace and prophetic challenge, enablement and compassion – and experience an enlivened sense of who we are called to be as Christians. This is our baptismal calling. The social ethic that worship requires for

---

1. To paraphrase James Dallen, *The Dilemma of Priestless Sundays* (Chicago: Liturgy Training Publications, 1994), 135 and 142. This American publication presents a most comprehensive overview of the question that is sensitive to both its pastoral and theological aspects.

it to be authentic flows from this calling and is the measure of its legitimacy. The implications of the actions we undertake to address the shortage of ordained priests must be informed by our kingdom call, for they have ecclesiological, sacramental, ethical, and eschatological ramifications.

We need to place a few 'markers' as we begin the discussion.

a) Currently, with few exceptions, all Catholics on these islands who wish to celebrate Eucharist every Sunday, can do so. As we are beginning to find out, this will not always be the case and many dioceses are reflecting seriously on this issue today. However, we need to place this in context. For the vast majority of Catholic Christians throughout the world today, the celebration of Sunday, the day on which Christians gather in order to celebrate the death and resurrection of the Lord (see Constitution on the Sacred Liturgy [= SC] 106), is without Eucharist because local churches do not have sufficient numbers of ordained priests to preside in these Sunday assemblies.

b) There seems to be a certain level of unhealthy concern in Ireland at present around the difficulties that members of the Catholic faithful have in not being able to celebrate *daily* Eucharist because of an increasing shortage of priests. A number of locally devised 'liturgies in the absence of a priest' and 'Communion Services' have emerged to address this situation.[2] At the outset we need to be clear that daily Eucharist, as commendable as it is, is devotional and optional, and that, not only do weekday Communion Services not offer a pastorally credible solution, but they tend to muddy the waters![3]

---

2. A good example is that produced by John McCann, *Weekday Celebrations for the Christian Community: A Resource Book for Deacons and Lay Ministers* (Dublin: Veritas, 2000). This publication responds to an Irish pastoral situation, and the rituals contained therein, as well as the brief introductions to the various sections, show a depth of theological, pastoral, and liturgical balance.

3. See the recent Pastoral Letter of Bishop William Murphy of Rockville Centre diocese, New York, issued on 9 May 2008: 'Communion Not to be Distributed at Weekday Word Celebrations,' *Origins* 38:2 (22 May 2008): 28-31. This pastoral, which came into effect in the diocese on 1 July 2008, sets out the reasons why, when a priest is unavailable for Mass, the practice of weekday communion services is not commendable.

There is a rather complex set of traditions in both the Western as well as Eastern Churches with regard to the question of the frequency of Eucharist (and the related question of the frequency of reception of

The problem becomes more focused – both pastorally and theologically – when we begin to speak of *Sunday* liturgies in the absence of Eucharist. And this is the focus of discussion in this paper. It will only be a matter of time before Sunday celebrations without Eucharist will become a pressing issue in Ireland. As liturgy is itself primarily an ecclesiological act, so too will any solution we develop around this emerging pastoral problem have ramifications for how we mature as church.

c) Local experience and context is important, and this is what we must address. If being 'catholic' means anything, it first of all refers to our belonging to a church that is 'universal'. However, most significant is the underlying reference to the paschal faith which we share and which finds expression in a common understanding of Eucharist, of church, and of ministry. As 'Sundays without Eucharist' is an issue that has been dealt with for over seventy years by some local churches, we, in our search for insights, might best place our experience in that wider frame. We need to take seriously their experience, be they long established or developing churches: their decades of theological reflection, lessons learned, and informed practice will offer a guide to us to find the best way to respond to the changing face of our Irish church.[4]

d) Reflections offered here will employ theological frameworks for reference. This does not mean that pastoral, historical and other considerations will not feature. We are doomed to fail if we do not allow serious and at times difficult theological questions to challenge our ministry. A theology which cautions is in turn enriched in its encounter with living communities. The faith context within which we 'live and move and have our ecclesial being' must inform and critique our theo-

Communion outside of Mass), although there are some important points of theological convergence. A good introduction to the issue can be found in Robert Taft, 'The Frequency of the Eucharist throughout History,' *Beyond East and West: Problems in Liturgical Understanding* (Washington, DC: The Pastoral Press, 1984), 61-80, and John F. Baldovin, 'Reflections on the Frequency of Eucharistic Celebration,' *Worship* 61 (1987): 2-15. A large number of more recent publications address one or other aspect of this issue.

4. By comparison with other Catholic countries, Ireland still has a high number of ordained priests and a relatively small and healthy ratio of priest per head of Catholic population (even if this ratio is increasing).

logical reflection and worship practices, just as these in turn influence our experience of faith and pastoral ministry.

The first exercise we undertake is to explore the many names by which these Sunday celebrations are called in various places, as this gives us insight into local ecclesial self-understanding as well as highlighting other issues that we may need to take on board. We will then overview the Roman Directory of 1988 which seeks to offer guidelines on the development and use of such services in local churches. Finally, a critique will be offered, using a traditional understanding of Sunday as a framework for discussion.

PART ONE: RESPONDING TO A PROBLEM

1. Choosing Words to Name a Reality

The most common title found for these extraordinary ecclesial gatherings is 'Sunday Celebrations in the Absence of a Priest'.[5] In a properly theological sense, it is impossible for Christians to celebrate liturgy in the absence of a priest, so this title is a misnomer. We keep forgetting that through baptism we share in the priesthood of Christ, and that, if we wish to use cultic vocabulary to describe our understanding of what happens when we 'do liturgy', then we will need to be clear that our act of worship involves, at its heart, an exercise of the priesthood of Christ, in, through and with whom we offer praise and thanksgiving to God (see SC 7). We should therefore note that the preferred designation for ordained priests in Roman documents is 'presbyter', and this is in fact the term employed in the Roman Directory which speaks of 'Sunday Celebrations in the Absence of a Presbyter', thus redressing any of the theological issues that the unqualified use of 'priest' might present.[6] Leaving aside a consideration of the terms 'priest/presbyter', another difficulty occurs with this title in that it draws attention to the absent (ordained) priest, thereby shifting the focus away from the local assembly within which presbyteral ministry finds its meaning and purpose. As we will discuss later, the theological importance of the worshipping assembly, even without Eucharist and without a presbyter, cannot be minimised.

---

5. This is the term adopted, among other places, in France: *Assemblées dominicales en l'absence de prêtre.*
6. See note 15, below.

Some have suggested that a better title might be 'Sunday Celebrations in the Absence of Eucharist' – acknowledging, importantly, the difference between Eucharist (by which is meant, the Mass) and the reception of Holy Communion (outside of Mass). In its favour, this designation highlights, albeit negatively, the core issue, that a particular Sunday assembly is unable to celebrate Eucharist, and that its absence compromises in some way the integrity of the Sunday act of worship.[7] We will have occasion to look at this point again. Some French speaking countries have tended to use a title that gives expression to this lacuna: 'Sunday Celebrations in the Expectation of the Eucharist'.

The Canadian Episcopal Conference, after many years of experimentation and serious theological reflection, developed interesting forms of celebration. Its *Sunday Celebration of the Word and Hours* tries to move away from the prospect that a Communion Service will necessarily be part of the Sunday service.[8]

A number of other designations are employed and all have in common the difficulty that they describe the event in terms of what is not happening, or in terms of who the presider is or is not:

Non-Eucharistic Liturgies
Lay-led Liturgies/Sunday Worship
Sunday Assembly Led by (*animée par*) Lay People

---

7. This is the perspective that is to be found in the Roman Directory of 1988: 'It is imperative that the faithful be taught to see the substitutional character of these celebrations, which should not be regarded as the optimal solution to new difficulties nor as a surrender to mere convenience' [21]; communities 'will come to realise that their assembly on Sunday is not an assembly "without a priest", but an assembly "in the absence of a priest", or, better still, an assembly "in expectation of a priest".' [27]

8. The Canadian preference is the celebration of the Liturgy of the Word (to which a Communion Service may be added) or the celebration of Morning/Evening Prayer when Sunday Eucharist is not possible: the ritual book is published as *Sunday Celebration of the Word and Hours* (Ottawa: Canadian Catholic Conference of Bishops, 1995). A pastoral and theological study of the Canadian text has been made by Veronica Rosier, *Liturgical Catechesis of Sunday Celebrations in the Absence of a Priest*, Liturgia condenda 13 (Leuven: Peeters, 2002), 211-252. The German Archdiocese of Freiburg made a similar choice and its revised *Liturgy of the Word on Sundays* (1995) shows a clear preference not to have the 'Service of Distribution of Holy Communion' added to any of the three Forms of liturgy that it proposes.

Sunday Celebrations in Anticipation of a Priest
Stational Celebrations (*Stationsgottesdienst*)

Titles do not allude to the fact that the assembly which celebrates operates as the Body of Christ and desires to be sustained
so as to be a witness in its world to God's great and sustaining
love.

2. *Initial Roman Response*

The Liturgy Constitution of Vatican II, *Sacrosanctum concilium*,
responding principally to a call from Argentinean bishops, spoke
of the possibility of having 'Bible Services' on Sundays in those
communities which could not have a celebration of the Eucharist.[9]

Within a few months, a Roman Instruction, *Inter oecumenici*
moved the emphasis from a 'Bible Service' to

> ... a sacred celebration of the word of God with a deacon or
> even a properly appointed layperson presiding ... the plan of
> such a celebration shall be almost the same as that of the
> liturgy of the word at Mass ... ending with the prayer of the
> faithful and the Lord's Prayer.[10]

The first Roman text to address the question of Communion
'when Mass cannot be celebrated because there is no priest
available', was issued in 1967, and permitted 'the distribution of
communion by a minister with the faculty to do this'.[11] Some
five years later the Instruction *Immensae caritatis* (1973) permitted
laypersons to distribute communion as special ministers and
stated that this permission was readily applied to the Sunday

---

9. See *SC* 35 §4, 'Bible services should be encouraged, especially on the
vigils of the more solemn feasts, on some weekdays in Advent and Lent,
and on Sundays and holydays. They are particularly to be recommended
in places where no priest is available; when this is the case, a deacon or
some other person authorised by the bishop is to preside over the celebration.' Translation taken from ICEL (ed), *Documents on the Liturgy 1963-
1979: Conciliar, Papal, and Curial Texts* (Collegeville, MN: The Liturgical
Press, 1982), document number 1, par 35 (= *DOL* 1:35).

10. SC Rites, Instruction, *Inter oecumenici*, September 1964, art 37, in *DOL*
23: 329. Two other Roman documents which dealt directly with this issue
are Congregation for the Doctrine of the Faith, *Sacerdotium ministeriale* (on
Certain Questions concerning the Minister of the Eucharist), 1983; and the
Code of Canon Law, CIC 1248 §2.

11. See SC Rites, Instruction, *Eucharisticum mysterium* (1967), 33 c; see *DOL*
179: 1262.

liturgy in the absence of a priest.[12] The intervening years between the first and last Roman Instructions referred to here witnessed the issuance of several Rescripts to local churches, having been requested by them, to permit lay people to distribute communion.[13]

So, the Roman response moved from a more cautious encouragement of the use of 'Bible Vigil Services' to a realisation that something more was needed. The extension of permission to religious and lay people to distribute communion came quickly over a period of a few years, and developed on the back of other ministerial issues, especially that of the shortage of ordained priests.[14]

3. The Roman Directory of 1988

Some twenty five years after the conciliar discussion on the impact of a shortage of priests for Sunday eucharistic worship, the Congregation for Divine Worship published a *Directory for Sunday Celebrations in the Absence of a Presbyter*.[15] The document addresses the *de facto* situation and has benefited from the pastoral wisdom of many bishops' conferences throughout the world. It also readily availed of the theological insights which emerged from reflecting on this experience in various local churches since the 1940s.[16]

12. See SC Discipline of the Sacraments, Instruction, *Immensae caritatis* (January 1973); see especially Ia, *DOL* 264: 2075.
13. These were often granted with explicit statements that, among the conditions necessary for such a permission, was the 'scarcity of ordained ministers in some regions' (SC Discipline of the Sacraments, Instruction, *Fidei custos* (1969), in *DOL* 259: 2043), or, as it was stated in relation to a Rescript issued in favour of Brazil, when the 'sacred minister of the eucharist is to be absent for a foreseen period of at least eight days' (SC Extraordinary Affairs, in April 1965; in *DOL* 253: 2035).
14. Rosier gives a very good historical overview from the 1940s onwards in her, *Liturgical Catechesis of Sunday Celebrations in the Absence of a Priest*, 91-127.
15. The Directory was issued on 2 June 1988, the Solemnity of the Body and Blood of the Lord: '*Directorium de celebrationibus dominicalibus absente presbytero,*' *Notitiae* 263 (1988): 366-378. A presentation is made by Pere Tena on pages 362-365. English translation can be found in *Origins* 18 (1988): 301-307 and in *National Bulletin on Liturgy* 22 (June 1989): 108-119. (When referring to the Directory in the body of the text, paragraph numbers will be given in square brackets.)
16 In the comments that follow, only two issues will be picked up on, the question of the 'shortage of priests' and the proposed forms of celebration of Sunday without Eucharist. For a thorough analysis of the Directory see Rosier, *Liturgical Catechesis of Sunday Celebrations in the Absence of a Priest*, 128-154.

(i) Shortage of Ordained Priests

The basic reason why certain communities cannot celebrate Eucharist regularly on Sundays is because of the shortage of ordained priests. The Directory lists three different ways in which this primary cause manifests itself in different places. The solutions which can be proposed in each case will be influenced not just by the particular circumstances which caused the shortage of presbyters, but also by a particular ecclesiology and eucharistic theology as well as by the histories, traditions, expectations, and human/economic resources of the local churches concerned.

The first type of situation listed describes what would seem to be the pastoral context for the vast majority of Catholic Christians throughout the world. In the younger churches in Asia and Africa, as well as in the slightly older churches of Central and Latin America, the number of those baptised has grown faster than has the number of priests available to minister among them.

> (a) In some regions, after their first evangelisation, the bishops have put catechists in charge of gathering the faithful together on Sunday and, in the form of a devotional exercise, of leading them in prayer. In such cases the number of Christians grew and they were scattered in so many and such widely separated places that a priest could not reach them every Sunday. [3]

The first record of Sunday prayer gatherings and catechetical meetings without a priest comes from a letter of Francis Xavier (1506-1552), written in January 1544 from the Indies. There is also evidence coming from China, Japan and Mexico of prayer books composed for the use of the newly developed ecclesial communities which could only be visited occasionally by missionary priests. These prayer books served to deepen the bond among Christians in the new communities into which they had been incorporated through baptism. One of the convictions that drove this was the belief that these devotional prayers provided 'a school of faith'. They also opened up an opportunity for allowing the local cultural ambience to influence the missionaries in the composition of prayers.[17]

---

17. These gatherings for 'Sunday communal worship with prayer and catechesis' predate the reforms of the Council of Trent whose principal

We find the first trace of Sunday gatherings, presided over by a lay catechist, in Burundi in Africa in 1898, and in 1943 these gatherings became mandatory in places where missionary priests did not regularly serve. In 1930 Togo follows the example from Burundi, after which the practice seems to become increasingly common. In more recent decades the practice spread quite rapidly among young churches in Asia, Africa and Latin America.[18] In many of these churches today, Christians do not celebrate Eucharist for months at a time, and sometimes only on an annual basis. The norm for them is the celebration of Sunday without Eucharist.

A second reason for the shortage of priests, according to the Directory, relates to restrictions of religious freedom; and a third, to a more contemporary phenomenon among the older churches.

(b) People blocked from gathering on Sunday, either because of the persecution of Christians or because of other severe restrictions of religious freedom. Like the Christian of old, who held fast to the Sunday assembly even in the face of martyrdom, the faithful today, even when deprived of the presence of an ordained minister, also strive to gather on Sunday for prayer either within a family or in small groups. [4]

(c) On other grounds today, namely, the scarcity of priests, in many places not every parish can have its own eucharistic celebration each Sunday. [5]

liturgical books were published between 1568 and 1614, and which sought to unify the form and content of worship in the Latin church. See Johannes Hofinger, 'Communal Worship in the Absence of a Priest: Its Importance and Structure,' in Johannes Hofinger, ed, *Worship: The Life of the Missions* (Notre Dame, IN: University of Notre Dame Press, 1958), 125-145; for a general survey of 'liturgical creativity' in Mexico, China and Japan in the sixteenth and seventeenth centuries, see Dominic Jala, *Liturgy and Mission*, Bibliotheca 'Ephemerides Liturgicae' Subsidia 41 (Rome: CLV Edizioni Liturgiche, 1987), 3-19.

18. See Anscar J. Chupungco, *Liturgies of the Future: The Process and Methods of Inculturation* (New York / Mahwah, NJ: Paulist Press, 1989), 192-3. Along with the article by Hofinger cited above, see also Constans F. G. Kramer, 'Religious Services in the Absence of a Priest,' in Johannes Hofinger, ed, *Liturgy and the Missions* (London: Burns & Oates, 1960), 157-163; and William Joseph Duschak, 'Sunday Services Without the Priest,' in Johannes Hofinger, ed, *Teaching All Nations: A Symposium on Modern Catechesis* (New York: Herder and Herder, 1961), 251-64.

The Directory [5] makes reference to a phenomenon of the past 60 years or so that principally affected the European and North American churches rather than the younger churches,[19] the result of which has meant that these places have also come to know the practices of Sunday worship in the absence of a presbyter. Germany and France were among the first countries in Europe to engage with a liturgical response to this pastoral dilemma.[20] Today decreasing numbers of priests means that many parishes no longer have resident presbyters while in other places there are communities which have never known pastors to reside in their midst.[21]

(ii) Solutions Proposed

The Roman Directory proposes a number of temporary solutions to address the worship needs of assemblies in these circumstances. They can be grouped under two headings: when a priest can be made available; and when there is no ordained priest available.

A: When Ordained Priests are available, but in small numbers:
1. Ordained priests, where this is possible, can be 'assigned to celebrate Mass several times on Sunday in many, widely scattered churches.' The document goes on, however, to note that 'this practice is regarded as not always satisfactory either to the parishes lacking their own parish priest or to the priests involved'. [5][22]

---

19. We need, however, to place this *datum* in a global context. In 1995 Jan Kerkhofs was able to state that (without counting the many European religious priests working in Latin America and Africa), 'Europe still has the largest number of priests, about 60% of the diocesan clergy of the whole world and 47% of religious priests': 'The Shortage of Priests in Europe,' in Jan Kerkhofs, ed, *Europe Without Priests?* (London: SCM Press, 1995), 2.
20. For a general survey in relation to Germany and France see especially Dominico Sartore, 'Assemblee Senza Presbitero,' in D. Sartore, A. M. Triacca and C. Cibien, eds, *Liturgia* (Milan: Edizioni San Paolo, 2001), 171-178.
21. A recent study (2002) shows that in both the United States of America and in Europe there is one priest per 1,375 Catholics, whereas in East Asia this number is one priest for every 2,473 Catholics, in Africa for 4,694 Catholics, and in South America for 7,138 Catholics: see Dean R. Hoge and Aniedi Okure, *International Priests in America: Challenges and Opportunities* (Collegeville, MN: The Liturgical Press, 2006), 30.
22. See *CIC* 905 §2: 'If priests are lacking, the local ordinary may permit priests, for a just cause, to celebrate twice a day and even, if pastoral need requires it, three times on Sundays and holy days of obligation.'

2. People go to Mass in a nearby parish. This solution 'is to be recommended and to be retained where it is in effect'. [18] While probably not initially intended as such, this proposal contributes to the creation of a *modus operandi* when neighbouring parishes form a cluster or grouping.

Other options, not found in the Directory, include the following:
- The use of 'Anticipated Sunday Masses'. While this option is not formally listed in the Directory, it was permitted as an option as early as 1964.[23]
- A second option, sometimes proposed, is to substitute Sunday Eucharist with Eucharist on a weekday (weekly or monthly), for which occasion an ordained minister would come.[24] However, this practice has the effect of lessening the importance of Sunday (which might come to be celebrated increasingly without Eucharist), and creates a rupture between Eucharist and Sunday.[25]
- The redistribution of priests 'in a diocese, if their work-loads were readjusted, if more lay persons were employed to help in parishes and at diocesan level, if the number of Sunday Masses in parishes was reduced, then we could cope and would not need lay-led liturgies.'[26] A similar solution was encouraged by Pope John Paul II who, in the early 1980s, also asked for a redistribution of clergy at a worldwide level.[27]

23. The term 'Anticipated Sunday Mass' ('Saturday evening Masses') refers to a legal concession, granted for pastoral reasons for the first time in June 1964, by which participation in Eucharist on Saturday evenings is taken to be a fulfilment of one's obligation to celebrate Eucharist on Sundays: see *DOL* 444: 3829 ff. Among the reasons cited were the shortage of priests; tourism; and facilitation of Catholics who were obliged to work on Sundays (as in Israel and the then East Germany).
24. See Gabe Huck, 'Many Other Things: Priestless Sundays: Are we looking or leaping?', *Liturgy* 80 18/7 (1987): 5.
25. The importance of the link between Sunday, Eucharist, and Assembly will be discussed in the second part of this paper.
26. J. Frank Henderson, 'Priestless Sundays: What are the Questions?' *Liturgy* 80 19:3 (1988): 8.
27. In 1980 Rome issued 'Norms for the Distribution of Priests', requesting a sharing of ordained priests by churches which have a large number of clergy with those churches and nations where numbers are small. This was reiterated by John Paul II in his encyclical of 1990, *Redemptoris missio* 67-68.

B: Where Ordained Priests are not Available:

When people cannot celebrate Eucharist on Sunday, no canonical obligation exists to attend other forms of assembly prayer. However the Code 'specially recommends' that people spend some time in prayer, in their family or with groups of families.[28] Pastoral practice also suggests that it is beneficial to communities that they meet to pray on Sunday, even when there is no Eucharist: otherwise they will die altogether.[29] The Directory takes up this last point, expressing the general pastoral desire that, even in the absence of an ordained priest, 'in the best way possible the weekly gathering of the faithful can be continued and the Christian tradition regarding Sunday preserved. ... The faithful ... aware of the importance of the Lord's Day ... gather to listen to the word of God, to pray, and, in some cases, even to receive communion'. [6]

The Directory lists some options here:

1. *Celebration of the Word of God* [20];
2. *Celebration of the Word of God with Eucharistic Communion.* The text refers to a celebration of the word, 'and also its completion, when possible, by eucharistic communion. In this way the faithful can be nourished by both the word of God and the body of Christ' [20];
3. When neither of the above two forms of gathering are possible, the faithful 'are strongly urged to devote themselves to prayer, either individually or in family or in small groups.' [32];
4. Celebration of Eucharist transmitted by radio or television can provide useful assistance [32];[30]

---

28. See Huck, 'Many Other Things: Priestless Sundays,' 4. See *CIC* 1248 §2: 'If because of the lack of a sacred minister or for another grave cause participation in the celebration of the Eucharist is impossible, it is specially recommended that the faithful take part in the liturgy of the word if it is celebrated in the parish church or in another sacred place according to the prescriptions of the diocesan bishop, or engage in prayer for an appropriate amount of time personally or in a family or, as occasion offers, in groups of families.'

29. Pope Paul VI expressed a similar concern when addressing the bishops of Central France: see note 46, below.

30. While this option can be helpful it can never adequately substitute for the communal gathering on a Sunday that is so important for the sustenance of the assembly, even in the absence of Eucharist. It also speaks of an individualism in worship that is anathema to a Christian understanding of worship, and the fact that we are called and saved as a people (see *Lumen gentium* 9). See John Paul II, *Dies Domini*, 54.

5. Liturgy of the Hours [33]
6. Liturgy of the Hours with Sunday Readings [33]
7. Liturgy of the Hours with Sunday Readings and Communion [33]
8. Liturgy of the Hours with Communion [33]
9. An act of 'Spiritual Communion' [34].

An alternative to the above includes employment of the *Rite of Holy Communion outside Mass* (from the Roman Ritual, and different to no 2 above). However, this Rite has a different pastoral circumstance in mind and presupposes that it is carried out by an ordained minister. The selection of readings supplied by this Rite is centred on Eucharist and the Liturgy of the Word is not as elaborate as that celebrated at Mass. In contrast, the second option listed above would use a form of Introductory rite not unlike that found at Mass, and the Liturgy of the Word used will be that as given in the Lectionary for a particular Sunday. The Directory favours this option and it seems to be more at ease when a Communion Service is included in the celebration.

While liturgical theology, rightly, has problems with the frequent celebration of Liturgies of the Word with Holy Communion, most particularly on Sundays, we need to note that this practice is not unknown throughout the two thousand history of the church, although, we must emphasise, as acts of piety, and not as a substitute for Sunday celebration of Eucharist.[31] The Directory encourages the use of the Liturgy of the Hours (morning or evening prayer) [33], and this represents the most ancient form of popular daily prayer (not daily Eucharist).[32] The invitation is there for us to introduce it in some form into the lives our Christian communities, following the example of Canada.

Who presides at these? The Directory envisages that the leaders of these Assemblies would be, in order, a deacon [38]; instituted acolytes or lectors [39]; or other lay women or men [30;

---

31. Communion outside of Mass existed at the time of Tertullian, and is referred to, among other places, in the *Apostolic Tradition*. The practice survives in the Liturgy of Good Friday.
32. See the comment of Robert Taft, 'Before the Western Middle Ages no one would have dreamt of preferring daily private Mass to the common hours on weekdays': *The Liturgy of the Hours in East and West: The Origins of the Divine Office and Its Meaning for Today* (Collegeville, MN: The Liturgical Press, 1986), 305.

40].[33] These ministers (other than the deacon) must not become a source of confusion by way of their vesture, the gestures they employ, or in the use of forms of greetings that are reserved to those in Orders [39-40].

It is ultimately up to the bishop, working collaboratively with clergy and people of the diocese, to regulate and design the forms of Sunday celebration that best serve local needs, always keeping in mind the extraordinary nature of these gatherings. The Directory offers an outline of what these liturgies might look like, but leaves it to the local churches to create their own [41-49].[34]

It is evident that situations such as those described here will not arise in Ireland in the near future. As already stated, in comparison with other churches, there is still a relatively large, if declining, number of serving clergy in Ireland, and, before other forms of Sunday worship are introduced, it is necessary to ensure, as is required by canon law, that a 'shortage of priests' (*penuria sacerdotum*) does exist, that all other possible avenues are explored so that the celebration of Sunday Eucharist is a reality for as many of the parish communities as is possible.[35] The clustering of parishes is one of a number of structural possibilities being explored at present to ensure that this will remain the case in Ireland for the foreseeable future.

---

33. In 1991 The Association of National Liturgy Secretaries of Europe issued a document, *Leading the Prayer of God's People: Liturgical Presiding for Priests and Laity* (Dublin: Columba Press), the final text of which was agreed at a meeting at the then Irish Institute of Pastoral Liturgy in Carlow. This was in response to a growing need, addressed also by other episcopal conferences throughout Europe, for appropriate training in the leading of Sunday Services.

34. While the Lectionary readings for the Sunday are not mandated, they are presumed [19 and 36].

35. See *CIC* 517 §2 and 526; see also John Paul II, Post-Synodal Apostolic Exhortation of 1988, *Christifideles Laici*, 23. This may very well mean that as many of the diocesan and parish administrative posts as possible are given to lay people, and that there is a greater degree of collaborative ministry at both parish and diocesan levels than is currently the case. Chapter Two of the Directory ('Conditions for Holding Sunday Celebrations in the Absence of a Priest', [18-34]) sets out the conditions required for a decision to be made in a diocese to schedule regular Sunday celebrations which would replace Mass.

PART TWO: THEOLOGICAL ISSUES FOR REFLECTION

The celebration of Sunday Liturgies in the absence of Eucharist is a short-term measure for what will be a long-term problem (a 'permanent short-term solution'). If not dealt with in a thoughtful way, it can produce other long-term problems. In an exercise which I hope will be useful, I would like to use 'tradition' as a criterion for evaluation of the various implications of celebrating Sunday. Tradition, which is not above being questioned and can never enslave – and is above all a living ecclesial entity – acts nonetheless as a safeguard to us as we move forward by pointing out concerns, practices and theologies from our two thousand year history – concerns, practices and theologies that faith communities thought important in their day, that we may have forgotten but might now need to remember. In the light of tradition,[36] the practice of Sunday Celebrations in the Absence of a Presbyter sets off alarm bells, principally in three overlapping areas: the relationship between Sunday and Eucharist; the nature of Eucharistic celebration; presbyteral and other ministries and ecclesiology.[37]

1. Sunday and Eucharist

Nowhere is the theology of Sunday more clearly outlined than in the Liturgy Constitution of Vatican II:

> By a tradition ... having its origins from the very day of Christ's resurrection, the church celebrates the paschal mys-

---

36. Tradition cannot be confused with history. 'Liturgical history does not deal with the past, but with tradition, which is *a genetic vision of the present*, a present conditioned by its understanding of its roots. And the purpose of this history is not to recover the past (which is impossible), much less to imitate it (which would be fatuous), but to *understand liturgy* which, because it has a history, can only be understood in motion, just as the only way to understand a top is to spin it.' (Emphasis in original): Robert Taft, 'The Structural Analysis of Liturgical Units,' *Beyond East and West: Problems in Liturgical Understanding* (Washington, DC: The Pastoral Press, 1984), 153-4.

37. I offer these reflections, not necessarily in an attempt to elicit full agreement on the part of the reader, but rather as a modest contribution – anything else would be pretentious – to a discussion that is badly needed in Ireland in relation to how we understand liturgy, church, and ministry. This cannot, however, be divorced from a larger conversation, also badly needed, on the social, cultural and ethical implications of being Christian in Ireland at the beginning of the twenty-first century.

tery every eighth day ... For on this day, Christ's faithful must gather together so that, by hearing the word of God and taking part in the Eucharist, they may call to mind the passion, the resurrection, and the glorification of the Lord Jesus and may thank God, who 'has begotten them again unto a living hope through the resurrection of Jesus Christ from the dead' (1 Peter 1:3) ... the Lord's Day is the [original feast day] and should be proposed to the devotion of the faithful ... in such a way that it may become in fact a day of joy and of freedom from work. Other celebrations ... shall not have precedence over the Sunday, the foundation and core of the whole liturgical year. (*SC* 106).[38]

The importance of the Sunday assembly as the occasion for hearing proclaimed through scripture and celebrating through sacrament the memorial of the Lord's death and resurrection until he comes, is reiterated in the Directory [1, 8-11]. The centrality of Eucharist to the life of the community is also emphasised, using a citation from the conciliar document, *Presbyterorum ordinis* 6:

No Christian community is ever built up unless it has its roots and centre in the Eucharistic liturgy. [25][39]

The theologian James Garcia has spoken of the unity that exists within tradition between Sunday, Eucharist and Assembly. If any of these three components is omitted, deficient, infected or imbalanced, the whole Sunday observance suffers distortion.[40] We then begin to speak of a practice that is not normative for the church, and this fact alone permits us to ask about the theological implications of celebrating Sunday without Eucharist. The Liturgy Constitution 106 brings these three elements together:

Sunday: For on this day
Assembly: Christ's faithful must gather together
Eucharist: so that, by hearing the word of God and taking
            part in the eucharist ...

---

38. *DOL* 1: 106.

39. It might have just as easily cited *Ad gentes* 39 (the Conciliar Decree on the Church's Missionary Activity) which states similarly that young churches cannot mature without the Eucharist.

40. See James Garcia, 'Contributions and Challenges to the Theology of Sunday,' *Worship* 52 (1978): 369-374. This same triad underpins the theology of *SC* 106 and is also to be found in the Directory, especially art 12.

The imbalance is evident if we look at the various relationships that can exist within this triad.

(i) So, the practice of celebrating Eucharist with Assembly on a day other than Sunday is not normative.[41] Some churches of the Reformed tradition only celebrate Eucharist (Holy Communion Services) once a month or maybe every quarter. Taking into consideration the two thousand year tradition of the church, this is an extreme. Likewise, another extreme is found in the Roman Catholic practice of celebrating Eucharist daily.[42] Representative of a middle point in the tradition is the practice of the Eastern Churches as well as the Orthodox Church which celebrates Eucharist rarely on weekdays, and only for special occasions, but always on Sundays, the Day of the Resurrection. The traditional form of daily prayer in the churches (East and West), for two thousand years, remains prayer at morning and at evening hours.[43]

(ii) To omit Assembly from a celebration of Eucharist on Sunday is forbidden by Canon Law, and so requires no comment.[44] While Irish Catholic Christians differ little from those in other local churches with regard to an individual sense of salva-

---

41. 'Normative' in the sense that, if we are to believe tradition, Eucharist is what marks the Christian celebration of Sunday.

42. These comments serve, not to denigrate weekday Eucharist, but simply to place it in relation to the Sunday celebration of Eucharist, as understood in tradition. This in turn will help us consider the seriousness of a situation wherein Eucharist cannot be celebrated on Sundays, for whatever reason.

43. The commendable practice of daily celebration of Eucharist does not have the same hold over Christians as does Sunday Eucharist: in fact, the daily celebration of the Hours is to be preferred and this practice goes back to the earlier strata of the lives of different local churches. This practice is reflected in the current *Code of Canon Law* (CIC 904) where it 'strongly recommends' that ordained priests celebrate daily Eucharist (reflecting a practice that has been used as a touchstone of priestly piety since the 1600s) when there is no pastoral obligation to do so (*CIC* 276 §2 no 2 says that they are 'earnestly invited'), but requires that priests, except for just cause, celebrate the Liturgy of the Hours daily (*CIC* 276 §2 no 3: 'are obliged').

44. *CIC* 906: 'A priest may not celebrate without the participation of at least some member of the faithful, except for a just and reasonable cause.' The form of the Order of Mass *sine populo* supplied in the Roman Missal presupposes the presence of at least some form of ministry apart from that of the presiding priest.

tion and its acquisition, a balance is required in which the wider
social and ecclesial aspects of the baptismal calling are set forth.
The *ecclesia* is at once a transcendent and incarnated reality. It is
not an end in itself and exists to serve the kingdom and be 'an
instrument of salvation for all', and this salvation is achieved in
and through the communion of the assembly of believers.[45] And
this communion of believers is most visible in the Sunday assemblies for Eucharist (see *SC* 40-41).

(iii) To celebrate Sunday in Assembly, but without Eucharist
is equally unrepresentative of the normative, which is why it
raises some very serious questions. Sunday is the day on which
the church traditionally has assembled in order to keep the
memory of the Risen Lord. The Lord rose on the first day of the
week, and appeared to his followers. The giving of the Spirit
happened on Easter Sunday, as did the commissioning to mission and the gifting to the church of the other fruits of the resurrection: peace and the forgiveness of sin (see John 20:19-23). The
celebration of Eucharist – the breaking of the bread (Acts 2:42) –
is tied to the appearances of the risen Jesus which took place on
the first day of the week (Luke 24:13ff.): it is the celebration of
Eucharist that makes of Sunday the Lord's Day.

The Lord's Day is also the eighth day (see John 20:26), the
day outside of time and yet fully lodged in time – a strongly eschatological dimension that gives to 'Sunday-time' a sacramental dimension. This is the day on which, through the Eucharist,
the Christian assembly renews that experience of Christ's continual presence through Word and sacrament. This tension between the 'already' and the 'not-yet' reflects the pull that exists
between incarnation and transcendence, as well as the challenge
to see the *kairos* of God intersecting with and transforming our
chronos. Eucharist can be understood as the crowning event of
Sunday, giving visible form and ultimate meaning to both
Sunday-time and the worshipping assembly, and calling it beyond itself to become the *sacramentum mundi* which facilitates
the breaking forth of the justice of God in our social milieu.

---

45. See *Lumen gentium*, 9: '[God] has willed to make men and women
holy and save them, *not as individuals without any bond or link between
them*, but rather to make them into a people who might acknowledge him
and serve him in holiness ...'. Emphasis added.

2. Eucharist as a Verb

The centrality of Eucharist to Sunday is fully acknowledged in the Directory. As far back as 1977, Paul VI, in an address to the Bishops of Central France, said:

> Let all realise that these Sunday assemblies [in the absence of a presbyter] could never be enough to rebuild communities that are alive and outreaching amid a populace that is barely Christian or in the process of dropping the observance of Sunday. ... [therefore, the goal of such Sunday assemblies] must always be the celebration of the sacrifice of the mass, the only true actualisation of the Lord's paschal mystery.[46]

Note here the fear that Sunday celebrations without Eucharist might become the norm. The Directory [21] underlines the fact that these celebrations can only be understood as a substitute, and states that:

> i) such celebrations cannot be held where Mass has already been celebrated, is to be celebrated or was celebrated on the preceding Saturday evening (even if Mass is celebrated in a different language);
> ii) there cannot be more than one assembly of this kind on any given Sunday.

The Directory acknowledges that people will feel the pain of not having an ordained priest and of not being able to celebrate Eucharist. Among the solutions it suggests are: praying for vocations [23, 44]; that people who want to but cannot participate in the Sunday celebration of Eucharist receive its fruits by virtue of their desire for Eucharist ('Spiritual Communion') [34]. A central issue in many local churches has been making sure that Communion Services are not confused in the minds of people with Celebrations of the Eucharist (Mass). The principal contributing factor to such confusion is a lack of appreciation of the meaning of Eucharist as paschal mystery and active participation of the assembly in the self-offering of Christ that takes place as the assembly does *anamnesis* of all that God has done for us in Christ Jesus. The reception of Holy Communion is seen solely as a private encounter with the Real Presence (often understood in the narrowest sense).[47] Some theologians today speak of the differ-

---

46. *DOL* 449: 3842; also in *Notitiae* 13 (1977): 151-153.
47. See Philippe Barras who speaks of the experience in France, 'Taken outside its normal ritual context (the eucharistic celebration), receiving

ence here being between understanding Eucharist as a *verb*, that
is, something that we 'do', an activity of the believing assembly
which engages through efficacious memorial with the living
paschal mystery of Christ and his self-offering, rather than as a
noun which connotes something static, already completed, non-
dynamic.

Often the way in which Eucharist is celebrated will lead to
such misunderstandings. Unfortunately we in Ireland have a
feeble understanding and experience of Eucharist. For many of
us the distribution of Holy Communion at Mass could be easily
done outside of Mass, as – disregarding the General Instruction
of the Roman Missal (GIRM)[48] – we still take the consecrated
hosts from the tabernacle. The GIRM 85 states that:

> It is most desirable that the faithful, just as the priest himself is
> bound to do, receive the Lord's Body from hosts consecrated
> at the same Mass …

The normal Sunday experience is that, while the priest-
presider receives a large host, only some members of the assembly
can receive from the token number of smaller hosts or breads
placed on the plate/paten which have been consecrated at Mass.
The remainder of the assembly – the majority – will receive from
consecrated hosts reserved in the tabernacle. The ritual message
communicated is that the purpose of Mass is to consecrate hosts.
The logic of this is that Mass can be dispensed with when we are able
to receive directly from the reserved Eucharist in the tabernacle.[49]

communion can lead to, or promote, an individualistic understanding of
the eucharist and come to appear as a personal right. The absence of *epiklesis*
and of consecration puts, ritually for the congregation, the eucharistic bread
outside the reciprocal movement of a gift and counter-gift which is made
real by the Spirit and which leads us to giving up our lives for our brothers
and sisters': 'Sunday Assemblies in the Absence of a Priest: The Situation
and Trends in France,' *Studia Liturgica* 26 (1996): 102-103.
48. *General Instruction of the Roman Missal* (Dublin: Irish Liturgical
Publications, 2005). This edition includes adaptations approved for the dioceses of Ireland.
49. The SC of Sacraments, in its Instruction of 1949, *Quam plurimum*, referred back to the Council of Trent's Decree on the Eucharist, chapter 4,
when it stated: 'It would be a good thing to recall that the primary and original goal of the reservation in church of the sacred Species outside of Mass is
the administration of Viaticum. The secondary goals are the distribution of
communion outside Mass and the adoration of Our Lord Jesus Christ hid-
den under the same Species.' The normative use of the tabernacle to supply

The same article (GIRM 85) states the second element that is 'most desirable' in receiving Communion at Mass:

> … in the instances when it is permitted, (the faithful) partake of the chalice, so that even by means of the signs Communion will stand out more clearly as a participation in the sacrifice actually being celebrated.[50]

A recent American commentary on the Rite of Mass offered an eschatological reading of reception from the cup, and stated that 'drinking at the Eucharist is a sharing in the sign of the new covenant and a foretaste of the heavenly banquet'.[51]

The bishops of the American State of Kansas issued a 'pastoral message' in 1995 on Sunday Communion without Mass.[52] In their listing of many aspects of Christian life that were 'blurred' as a consequence of regular Communion Services when Mass could not be celebrated, they referred to the confusion created between these Services (which, according the Roman Directory [21] have a substitutional character) and the Eucharistic celebration. In their pastoral judgement the best option was to forbid their continued use, 'except in emergencies':

> We, the bishops of Kansas, have come to judge that Holy Communion regularly received outside of Mass is a short-term solution that has all the makings of becoming a long-term problem. It has implications that are disturbing: a blurring of the difference between the celebration of the Eucharist and the reception of Communion.

The celebration of the Eucharist is an action of Christ the Priest, present and active in the assembly gathered in his name (see Mt 18:21). It is an action of efficacious memory by which,

consecrated Hosts for distribution during Mass was never an intended purpose of Eucharistic reservation.

50. See also *GIRM* 283. Permission to receive Communion under both kinds was granted for Ireland in 1991: see *New Liturgy* 76 (Winter 1992-93), 6. See also a pastoral note in that issue by Brian Magee, Idem, 16-18. A helpful comment and guide is found under 'Liturgical Note 16' in the *Liturgical Calendar for Ireland*, published each year by Veritas (Dublin).

51. Introduction to the Order of Mass, issued by the (US) Bishops Committee on Liturgy in 2003, par 134; cited in Ed Foley *et al*, eds, *A Commentary on the General Instruction of the Roman Missal* (Collegeville, MN: Liturgical Press, 2008), 188.

52. Bishops of Kansas, 'Sunday Eucharist – Do This in Memory of Me,' *Origins* 25:8 (July 13, 1995): 121-124.

through the invocation of the Spirit of God, we are plunged ever more deeply into the paschal mystery of Christ's saving life and ministry'… until he comes again in glory'. This action alone has social and ethical consequences, but that is a discussion for another time. There is an identity created between the 'memory' command of Jesus at the Last Supper and the 'memory' action of the local church in Eucharist, which changes the 'you' of Christ's mandate ('[You] do this in memory of me') to the 'we' in the Eucharistic Prayer ('We re-call Christ's death, his resurrection from the dead …'). There is a vast difference between this and a Holy Communion service.

3.Ministry and Church
(i) Presbyteral and Other Forms of Ministry

The underlying problem, to which Sunday Liturgies in the Absence of Eucharist is offered as a temporary solution, is the shortage of priests. The obvious solution here is to work towards a situation where there is a sufficient number of ordained minis-ters to offer leadership in Christian communities. Until that day arrives, there will be large sections of the church throughout the world deprived of the central sacrament, the sacrament which creates church, the Eucharist.[53] The Directory [22 and 44] quite rightly suggests that prayer for vocations is an absolute necessity if this problem is to be addressed. However, there are other areas relating to ministry that would need serious study to see if these provide blocks to ordained priesthood and would better serve the church if removed: mandatory celibacy; the question of gender and orders;[54] the use of viri *probati*; and the form and nature of formation for ordained ministry.

---

53. The concern that a community might have a right to an ordained priest occasioned a number of writings in the 1980s: see the entire issue of *Concilium* 133 (1980), 'The Right of a Community to a Priest'; Edward Schillebeeckx, *Ministry: A Case for Change* (1981); and the revised edition of this book, *The Church with a Human Face: A New and Expanded Theology of Ministry* (1985); and Raymond Hickey, *A Case for an Auxiliary Priesthood* (1982). The Roman response, indicating why its discipline cannot be changed, came out in the form of a document from the Congregation for the Doctrine of the Faith, *Sacerdotium ministeriale: Letter to the Bishops of the Catholic Church on Certain Questions Concerning the Minister of the Eucharist* (1983). See also Jan Kerkhofs and Paul-Michael Zulehner, 'Where Now? Possible Scenarios,'in Jan Kerkhofs, ed, *Europe Without Priests?*, 163-188.
54. This question was addressed by the Apostolic Letter of John Paul II, *Ordinatio sacerdotalis* (Pentecost 1994).

The Directory [38] lists deacons, in the first place, as being appropriate leaders of these assemblies. In the late 1990s, the Irish Episcopal Conference requested from the appropriate Roman Dicastery permission to ordain suitable male candidates to the permanent diaconate. It took quite some time before the rest of the local church heard about this initiative and there has not been as much discussion and debate around this issue as one would like. The initiative seemingly came from the Conference's Vocations Commission, immediately raising a question as to the motivation: we were, forty years after most other churches, beginning to do something that was potentially good, but for the wrong reasons. The thinking behind *Lumen gentium* 29 when it re-introduced permanent deacons was to create a wider variety of ministries in the church and to restore to an important ministry its own dignity. In the years that followed, local churches did not always seem to take on board the very changed character of diaconate in relation to the early centuries when they performed a sacramental role in the community. By 'sacramental role' I refer to the fact that they did, in the thinking of the time, what Christ did: be with the sick and infirm as well as with those cast out of society, so as to allow people gain a sense of self-respect in the knowledge that they, although on the margins, were at the centre of God's love and attention. That is why they ministered also at the Table, beside the bishop. They guaranteed that the voice of the voiceless would be heard at the central act of the believing community, the Eucharist. It is unfortunate that today the Irish church has not learned from the mistakes made over a number of decades in other local churches where it would seem that a diaconate ministry grew that is centred on liturgy almost to the exclusion of other aspects of this ordained ministry.[55]

---

55. There is much to be learned from how various local churches experience and adopt the ministry of permanent deacons. It is a practice that developed more on the North American continent than elsewhere: in 1992 there were more permanent deacons in the USA than in the rest of the world put together (11,040 out of a total of 19,939), while the next largest number was represented by the European continent with just 5,329 permanent deacons. Some important reflection on the role and ministry of deacons has been undertaken in France and Germany and needs to be accessed in Ireland. 'In 1992, 133 parishes without a resident priest were entrusted to a permanent deacon. The greatest concentration is to be found in Italy (57), Switzerland (28), and Germany (21). Markedly more parishes have been entrusted to lay people (853) and to sisters (198)', (see Jan Kerkhofs, *Europe Without Priests?*, 35-36). See Gearóid

Any movement forward in the preparation of Sunday Liturgies in the Absence of Eucharist should have other forms of leadership ministry in mind to complement that of the permanent deaconate, ministries that emerge from the assembly. The practice of co-presidency by lay people is one that could be profitably explored.

(ii) Ecclesiology
a) The President of the Assembly

In what is now regarded as a seminal study, the French theologian, Hervé Marie Legrand, demonstrated how in the first millennium the person who presided over the life of the community was the person who presided over the Eucharistic celebrations of that community.[56] In the second millennium this practice was reversed, and a person now presided over the life of the community because first of all he presided over the Eucharist. Stated differently, up to the medieval period, people were ordained to positions of leadership, and a central part of their leadership function related also to prayer and presidency of the Eucharist. From the medieval period onwards a person was understood to have been ordained in order to preside at Eucharist and they presided over the community because of this fact.

There is need for us today to re-evaluate presbyteral ministry in the light of tradition, as well as in the light of some of the documents of Vatican II, especially *Lumen gentium* and *Presbyterorum ordinis*. There is a clear tension in the conciliar texts between a medieval theology of ordained priesthood and an older theology which places the ordained in a primary relationship with the living Body of Christ, the church community. At the risk of over simplifying the positions, one could state that the medieval tradition sees the ordained priest as relating directly and primarily with the priesthood of Christ. The faithful, present at Mass, offer the sacrifice vicariously through the hands of the priest, whose power (*potestas*) includes that of consecration and absolving from sins. The Dogmatic Constitution on the

Dullea, ed, *Deacons: Ministers of Christ and of God's Mysteries* (Dublin: Veritas, 2010).

56. See Hervé-Marie Legrand, 'The Presidency of the Eucharist According to the Ancient Tradition,' in R. Kevin Seasoltz, ed, *Living Bread, Saving Cup: Readings on the Eucharist,* revised and expanded ed, (Collegeville, Liturgical Press, 2002), 196-221.

Church (*LG* 9) places the ordained firmly in an ecclesial role and describes their ministry as a participation in the triple office of Christ: prophetic, priestly and pastoral (see also *PO* 4-6). The importance of this is underlined by the preferred choice of the term *presbyter* to name the person in the second rank of orders rather than the more common term *sacerdos* – even if the documents are not consistent in the employment of this term. The Latin *sacerdos* only describes one of the three 'offices' of Christ, whereas *presbyter* embraces all three.[57]

The role of the presbyter is to offer leadership at local level through a sharing in Christ's prophetic ministry, that is, pointing out the presence of the Reign of God in the life of the local church, with the counter-cultural and personal challenges that this brings, along with the comforts offered through the Spirit. It includes the ministry of preaching. In the exercise of the priestly office the presbyter leads the local assembly to a deeper insertion into the Paschal Mystery of Christ through the various sacramental rites and other forms of prayer, principal among them being the Sunday Eucharist. Sharing Christ's pastoral office, the presbyter offers guidance and leadership in the assembly, ordering and bringing forth the various gifts that have been bestowed by the Spirit in the community, and that must be used and cherished for the benefit of all. As pastor, priest and prophet the presbyter *must* allow that those on the margins of society and the community be brought into the centre, for it is among them that Christ is to be found.

We are in danger of making of the presbyter, once again, a 'Mass-priest'. When we separate the liturgical from other forms of leadership, we move towards a form of sacramentalism that borders on the apotropaic. When much of the time and energy of the ordained priest is caught up with a sacramental ministry, understood in the narrowest sense of this term, then the self understanding of the Christian assembly (which cannot celebrate regular Sunday Eucharist) becomes distorted. It sees the periodic or occasional celebration of Sunday Eucharist as being associated with an infrequently-seen presbyter, separated from a Eucharist-less community which is otherwise under the guidance of a lay-leader who takes care of other matters in the life of the community.

---

57. This is discussed more fully in my 'Clergy and Laity: Fragmentation or Fellowship?', in Séan MacRéamoinn, ed, *Ministry: Clerics and the Rest of Us* (Dublin: Columba Press, 1998), 26-53.

The Directory [27] goes some distance in acknowledging the abnormality of such an ecclesial situation. An assembly cannot actually exist 'without a presbyter'. Hence the difference is underlined between that and a situation of 'expectation of a priest'. Lay people who preside at Sunday Services act as substitutes and the Directory emphasises that their role is:

> not an honour, but a ... responsibility and above all ... a service to their brothers and sisters under the authority of the parish priest. For theirs is not a proper office but a supplementary office ... [31].

b) Pastoral Leadership in the Assembly

The question then arises as to how the church community perceives itself. Is the church community something that exists because of the ministry of the priest and on which it is theologically dependent? Or is it something that is theologically prior to the ministry of the ordained priest, and therefore which calls forth, in union with the wider church, the ministry which is required for it to grow and function as the living Body of Christ? Should the local church call forth other creative solutions to ensure that it is able to bear witness as a community of believers gathered around the Banquet table of the Risen Lord?

As there is no sign that an increase in vocations to the ordained priesthood will happen any day soon, and, in the absence of other ways that will allow all Christian communities to celebrate Eucharist every Sunday, we will have to acknowledge that the structures that we will put into place now will be there for quite some time to come. We therefore need to be very careful about what these structures might be and be happy that they are underpinned with the best of our theologies of church – an ecclesiology that is not introverted but that makes us look outwards.

Whatever happens with regard to new forms of leadership, the last thing we need is for a group of people to assume a new form of clericalism. We will need to model new forms of pastoral leadership that are less autocratic than those experienced in the past, that emerge from the community of believers and are answerable to them, not in the sense of popularism or seeking affirmation – for the measure of ministry is nothing other than the Reign of God – but in the sense of accepting responsibility. As with all forms of leadership, those accepting such responsibility must enable others, create the context for a flourishing of gifts that will benefit the growth of the community, and not the self-enhancement or the soothing of the bruised egos of individuals who offer their Spirit-given gifts within the community.

iii) Ownership by the Assembly

The Liturgy Constitution describes liturgy as being a celebration of the local church and of the local parish (see *SC* 40-41). The official title used by Rome, *Sunday Celebrations in the Absence of a Presbyter* does not bring to the fore the nature of the gathered local assembly as found in the Liturgy Constitution, nor the fact that it is, with Christ, the principal celebrant of its own worship, that it assembles as the living Body of Christ to join its voice with that of Christ in his self-offering of praise and thanksgiving to God in the Spirit for all that God has done for our sake and for the salvation of the world.

Sunday celebrations without an ordained priest have repercussions for ordained ministers and our perception of them. There is a danger that, because of an increased workload over a wider geographical area and moving, of necessity, from one community to another, ordained priests will quickly become dispensers of sacraments bereft of a more wholesome context of pastoral leadership. Henry de Lubac summarised an ancient ecclesial sense that 'the church makes Eucharist; Eucharist makes church'. The singularity with which the ordained priest is forced to the fore in the situation of Sunday Worship without Eucharist creates a danger of substituting the ecclesial subject (the assembly which lives 'in Christ') with the person of the priest, any priest, irrespective of an association with the local church. The Eucharist can easily become something that happens through the consecratory actions of the priest rather than thanks to the all-embracing Mystery which flows from the central liturgical action of the assembly, within which the priest presides.

PART THREE: CONCLUSION:

SUNDAY LITURGIES IN THE ABSENCE OF EUCHARIST

By way of conclusion, I pose an important question: are we dealing here with 'celebrations', understood broadly and in a non technical sense? Or can we speak of true 'liturgies' being celebrated in the absence of a presbyter? And what are the theological and pastoral implications of referring to these celebrations as 'liturgies'? If we take a theological lead from *Sacrosanctum concilium*

then we must say that the Sunday assembly without Eucharist
has a claim to the title 'liturgy' (a term employed by some local
churches to designate this type of Assembly).

Through no fault of its own, the local parish community has
no resident ordained priest. Yet, in order to remain part of the
local *ecclesia* it must retain its links with other neighbouring assemblies, and with other parts of the local church or diocese.
This it does, in many ways, through periodic visits from a presbyter belonging to the local church or from the bishop himself,
as also, importantly, through the (lay) pastoral leadership that
has been appointed and ratified by the local church.[58] It assembles on a Sunday morning in the name of Christ, under its own
form of pastoral leadership, and hears the Word proclaimed in
its midst, using the church's Lectionary readings of that Sunday.
The manifold presence of Christ is experienced by this faith
community, not just in its leadership, but in its very gathering,
in the Word proclaimed, and in Communion received (see *SC*
7).[59] In fact, this assembly forms part of the living Body of
Christ, whose priesthood it exercises (*SC* 10). It exercises this
priestly office 'in Christ' principally and primarily through
mediation and its prayer of intercession for the salvation of all
humankind, as well as through its self-offering in, through, and
with Christ (see *LG* 34). This act of worship – through praise,
Word, intercession and thanksgiving – is a participation in the
salvific paschal mystery of Christ.

Theologically, some of the central elements which help us to
identify a worship environment as being 'of the church' are present: local assembly formally gathered as 'church' under leadership formally designated; Word proclaimed; praise and thanksgiving centred on the saving paschal mystery of Christ; exercise
of priesthood of Christ (through intercession).[60] This assembly

---

58. The Directory [30-31] requires that the parish priest or the bishop appoint
appropriate leaders to this task, thus ensuring an 'ecclesial' character to this
ministry.
59. For more on this, see Michael G. Witczak, 'The Manifold Presence of
Christ in the Liturgy,' *Theological Studies* 59 (1998): 680-702; and, Judith
M. Kubicki, 'Recognising the Presence of Christ in the Liturgical
Assembly,' *Theological Studies* 65 (2004): 817-837.
60. There is more here than is required by the *Code of Canon Law* for it to
be designated as a formal liturgy of the church: *CIC* 834 §2: 'This worship
takes place when it is offered in the name of the church, by persons law-
fully deputed and through actions approved by ecclesiastical authority'.

cannot be denied the fact that its worship is authentic, if less than complete: it does not enjoy the iconic role of the ordained presbyter who sacramentally represents Christ to the assembly and mirrors the assembly back to Christ, and its participation in the paschal mystery of Christ in worship does not reach its most intense, complete, and epicentric form of liturgical expression in Eucharist.

However, sight must never be lost of the fact that, in the words of the Bishops of Kansas, we are dealing with 'a short-term solution that has all the makings of becoming a long-term problem'. The 'solution' produces bad liturgy and bad theology, and any attempt to suggest otherwise is disingenuous. All that theology can do is assist us to name the issues and indicate a temporary pastoral way forward, warning us of the dangers before they occur. The real solution would be to deal with the issue of insufficient ordained priests with all of the theological and pastoral urgency that we can muster. In the meantime we are left with a highly unsatisfactory pastoral 'solution' to a problem not of our making. And we must address it as responsibly as we can. Parishes are best served when they appreciate the conundrum that is created by the severe shortage of ordained priests and yet must be supported as fully as possible in their task of leading the local churches to embody the paschal mystery as a *sacramentum mundi*, for the salvation of all.

The implications of our 'solution' are primarily ecclesial. They call for a re-evaluation of the ecclesiological ramifications of celebrating on a Sunday, in Assembly, but without Eucharist. It is incumbent on all of us to tease out: the meaning of 'priestless'; new forms of church organisation; and creative ways of pastoral leadership that are inclusive, ecclesial, and kingdom-oriented.

CHAPTER TWELVE

Experiences of Clustering Parishes

A. THE DIOCESE OF ACHONRY

Dermot Meehan

Background

The diocese of Achonry consists of twenty-three parishes and a population of about 35,000, with thirty-eight priests in active ministry. It has no big centres of population and remains a relatively rural diocese. In 2003, following a series of meetings of the bishop and priests it was decided to divide the diocese into four clusters with a view to providing a better pastoral service to its people. The cluster that we reflect on in this paper includes five parishes: Ballaghaderreen, Ballymote, Bunninadden, Gurteen and Keash. In many respects it is typical of the other clusters that operate in the diocese.

Beginnings

The work of this cluster began with a series of 'Listening and Learning' sessions held in the Spring of 2004, which were facilitated by the Western Theological Institute (WTI). In all, there were about six of these sessions and they were attended by more than 100 people each evening. These sessions provided opportunities for priests and people from all of the parishes involved to identify their current pastoral needs and to begin to formulate possible responses to the more urgent issues.

Out of the 'Listening and Learning' sessions, a smaller group of lay faithful met with the priests of the five parishes from autumn 2004 to summer 2005. The meetings took place approximately every five to six weeks. They were informal initially and discussed topics which, generally, had been raised at the original 'Listening and Learning' sessions. These included: liturgical celebrations, adult faith formation, care of the youth of the area, pastoral visitation, prayer and spirituality, care of the elderly and housebound. Most of these smaller group meetings were again facilitated by a member of the WTI staff. Eventually, it was agreed that the group would appoint a chairperson and secretary from among the members.

One of the issues that had been raised in the 'Listening and Learning' sessions was the pastoral care of young people and how to minister to them in the present climate. To carry that issue forward, it was agreed that the parishes would carry out a survey of young people to try to ascertain their needs. With the assistance of a member of the WTI staff, much energy and time went into preparing, executing and collating this survey.

The second project was around preparing families for the baptism of a child. The working group, with representation from all the parishes, invited a member of the Baptismal Preparation Team in Castlebar parish to come and speak at a meeting. Her presentation was followed by a very lively and interesting discussion on the pros and cons of having a similar team in our cluster.

Problems

When this working group resumed after the summer holidays in autumn 2005, it seemed to be suffering from a lack of energy and focus. Attendances were down and occasionally some parishes had neither clerical nor lay representation. At that stage, the two projects which the group had been working on seemed to be 'parked' and people came away from meetings feeling quite frustrated. There seemed to be a lot of talk without any concrete or worthwhile decisions being made. This malaise, on reflection, was due to two things not happening in order to support this working group. Firstly, the priests of the cluster only met once as a group between September 2004 and April 2006. Secondly, the parish representatives on the working group were supposed to meet regularly with a bigger group in their own parishes. This only happened in one of the five parishes with any regularity. So, something needed to happen to give the cluster some new energy.

Steps towards a solution

The first step was a meeting of the priests of the cluster. That took place in June of 2006 and was chaired by a member of the WTI staff. It was a very constructive meeting and has proved to be a real turning-point in the story of our cluster. At that meeting, the priests agreed to meet every month. The meetings since then have helped the priests in the five parishes to see how clustering can work – something that this reflection will return to later.

The next step came in September/October 2006, when meetings were held in each of the thirteen church areas that comprise the five parishes, to select delegates to work as a Steering Committee for our cluster. The decision to hold a meeting in each of the thirteen church areas came out of a growing conviction among the priests that our greatest challenge was to put structures in place that ensure that the natural communities in the cluster maintain their identities and their strong sense of community into the future.

Meetings of priests in the cluster

The monthly meetings of the priests in the cluster are structured meetings with a chairperson and a secretary, an agenda and minutes which are circulated in advance of the meeting. The meetings take place in a meeting room with the type of chair that helps to keep the mind focused! The meeting follows a simple format. It begins at 11.30 am with a short period of prayer. Then it works through the agenda and tries to finish around one o'clock. There's lunch afterwards and we're ready to disperse and move on to our own schedules about 2.15 pm or so.

Regular meetings of the priests have had a number of beneficial results. For a start, we've begun to harness the talents within the group. For example, one of the priests has good communications and IT skills. He has produced, out of the discussion at the working group on baptism preparation, a leaflet to give to parents when they come to arrange their child's baptism. This leaflet is colourful, simple and accessible. It's the sort of thing that most of the priests in the group admit that they would never be able to produce if left to their own devices and it has certainly proved helpful to all of us in our ministry.

Another of the priests has good ecumenical contacts. Through his contacts with the Church of Ireland, an invitation was issued to the Catholic congregations in the cluster to join in the Harvest Thanksgiving Service in the Church of Ireland Parish Church in Ballymote for the past two years. There was a good response from the five parishes and for some of those who came along, it was their first time attending a service in another Christian church, not surprising since none of the other parishes has any Church of Ireland or other Protestant church in their area. Those who attended were very appreciative of the hospitality offered by the Church of Ireland community after the

Service. Over the past two years, we've also held ecumenical Carol Services in the cluster, to which the Church of Ireland communities have been invited, thus affording further opportunities for common worship.

The regular meetings have also given us a good sense of support and of working together as priests, particularly so for those ministering in parishes on their own. This has taken a number of practical forms. For example, it was agreed to appoint one priest in the cluster with responsibility for arranging cover for a priest who is sick. It was felt that if a priest is sick and can't manage his duties, then he shouldn't have the added burden of trying to arrange cover for himself. It has also been agreed in principle that the priests in the cluster will co-ordinate their holiday times so that, in so far as possible, holiday cover might be provided within the cluster.

The monthly meetings of the priests have brought a new focus and energy to the idea of clustering. They ensure that things get done and build in a level of accountability. Regular meetings of the priests helped to get our cluster back on track. They've gone a long way towards convincing us how clustering can be beneficial to us as we constantly face new challenges in our ministry. You could say that we've taken ownership of the idea of clustering and are prepared to work at it. WTI has facilitated us to work at our own pace and not according to any blueprint. While we are aware of the great work being done in other clusters in the diocese, we don't feel under any pressure to do exactly what they have done.

Obviously, the agenda of the Steering Committee influences the meetings of the priests in the cluster – and *vice versa*. One of the things we greatly appreciate is the commitment of the members of the Steering Committee to their task, and working together, people and priests, has greatly enriched the lives of our communities, even in a short space of time.

The Steering Committee
The Steering Committee for our cluster is made up of one representative from each of the thirteen church areas in the five parishes and also one priest from each parish. This committee first met in February 2007. Initially meetings were chaired by one of the priests and facilitated by a member of the WTI staff. However, from the outset it was agreed that the roles of chair-

person and secretary would be taken by lay members of the committee once the group had become established and the members were familiar with each other. This took place about six months after the first meeting of the group. One of the priests was appointed vice-chairperson and liaises between the Steering Committee and the priests' group.

The Steering Committee meets once a month, usually the first Tuesday, except in July and August. The meetings open with a scripture reading, prayer and reflection. Then the minutes of the previous meeting are read, we close out any outstanding issues and deal with the items on the agenda for that meeting. We aim to keep the meeting to an hour and thirty minutes maximum. We always have a cup of tea and light refreshments afterwards, and this can be a good time for networking and sharing of ideas.

A Sample of Activities
Over the past year the Steering Committee has spearheaded the following activities:
- A Penance Service for the parishes of the cluster in preparation for Christmas and Easter – a different parish hosting the service each time
- An Ecumenical Carol Service
- Publishing of a baptismal preparation pack
- A Youth Pilgrimage to Croagh Patrick
- A rescheduling of Mass times within the five parishes
- A Sunday evening Mass during the summer holidays
- A Prayer Service for the Dead in each parish during the month of November
- A letter to local sporting clubs highlighting the sacredness of Sunday and encouraging them to keep Sunday Mass times free from games and training
- The production and distribution of Easter cards for all the homes of the parish giving the times of the Easter Triduum liturgies
- Ongoing discussion on adult faith development and reaching out to those who no longer attend church or do so infrequently

What we feel is working well
The meetings of the Steering Committee run to schedule each

month and, so far, there have been no cancellations or un-
planned breaks. By and large, there is a good attendance at these
meetings. The delegation of the chair and secretary to lay members of the committee has worked very well and, at this stage, all
the members of the committee have found their voice within the
group, leading to good and genuine discussion. The agendas for
the Steering Committee and for the meetings of the priests'
group feed into each other, to the enrichment of both.

The Challenges
As with all groups, one of the great challenges is maintaining a
good level of energy, motivation and interest within the group
so that members feel it is worthwhile attending meetings. There
is always a tension between discussion and planning, turning
suggestions into concrete action and bringing closure to as
many items on the agenda as possible. People obviously like to
see results! When committee members feel frustrated at a perceived lack of progress, it is good to take stock and remind ourselves of what has been achieved and accomplished. To this end,
we found a review at the end of the year, facilitated by a staff
member from the WTI, most helpful.

The big challenge ahead of us is the establishment of Parish
Pastoral Councils in each of the five parishes of the cluster. We
feel certain that this will deepen and enrich greatly the work of
the cluster.

So, after a slow and somewhat shaky start, we're on firmer
ground now, more convinced of the value of clustering and willing to take small but confident steps into the future, whatever it
may bring.

B. THE DIOCESE OF LIMERICK: THE THOMOND CLUSTER

(i) Noirin Lynch

Bishop Donal Murray, speaking in March 2007 said:

The challenge is for the parish to help create a community in
which the deeper questions can be addressed, in which
there's room to reflect and to contemplate, to celebrate with
real reverence, dignity and beauty, in which the conscious-
ness of being Christ's body grows and in which people can
learn together how to live the gospel; not agreeing on every

detail of political and social life, but agreeing on the vision of God and the human dignity in Christ, which inspires everything we do and we are. The Cluster is at the service of that.[1]

The diocese of Limerick has a long term commitment to parish pastoral development. Over the past ten years the diocese as a whole has been engaged in an on-going process of reflection and action in order to empower and challenge the whole faith community to respond to God's vision for us.

As one part of this process, the diocese has put in place a Diocesan Pastoral Centre, led by Fr Noel Kirwan. The team at the Pastoral Centre work to support parishes and clusters of parishes as they stretch and grow in response to this call. As a member of this team, my role is to co-ordinate resources and training for parishes, so that all parishes and clusters have access to the supports they need to develop healthy pastoral leadership and ministry structures.

When we speak of clustering of parishes, we need to be alert to the fact that the term has a variety of meanings or applications. In some cases it means that priests in neighbouring parishes are working more collaboratively, and in other cases it means that whole parishes are working more closely. Most are somewhere in between.

The process of clustering took an interesting route in Limerick in that, over ten years ago, clustering of parishes had begun to happen in a very unstructured way. As part of our ongoing pastoral development, there was a need for training for parishioners. Rather than trying to go to every single parish and train people, it was decided that parishes might gather together for training. From that start, parishes realised that they got energy from working together. A more formal structure began to emerge, and pastoral consultation began to happen through the cluster meetings, as well as through parish pastoral councils. For example, in Lent 2004, Bishop Murray issued a Pastoral Letter[2] inviting us to reflect on how we celebrate Eucharist, and to consider how this affected how we organised Mass times and other liturgical celebrations in the cluster. The time and number

1. March 2007, Speaking to the Parish Pastoral Councils and Cluster meeting groups of the Clare Island and Thomond clusters. These parishes cover the north side of Limerick city and stretch into county Clare.
2. *To Rekindle the Amazement*, 2004. http://www.limerickdiocese.org/publications/pastorals/18022004.htm

of Masses in each parish was to be discussed in the parish, in the light of this pastoral letter. Final decisions were to be made after discussion in the cluster groups. Decisions would bear in mind that each parish would so arrange its Masses that it had some possibility of being able to offer help to a neighboring parish whose priest was on holidays, or ill, or who has to be away for any reason.

It's now almost eight years since clusters were formally established, and yet you could almost say that we're only at the beginning, because all the time we're being challenged to 'push out into the deep'. It's no longer enough to be able to say that we have a cluster in place, structure alone is not sufficient. We're still tweaking some of the clusters' boundaries – looking at what worked and what didn't, what seemed to work in theory didn't always work in practice. When something changed (like the number of priests or the interests and talents of those working in the cluster), we realised that actually one of those parishes doesn't fit so well within that cluster. Then it became necessary to try something different. So, there is a significant amount of 'learning as we go'. What makes Limerick diocese unique is the fact that this development comes very much from our relationships 'on the ground'. It's about people who choose to co-operate, and who are open to gradually becoming more connected – a process that sometimes goes smoothly and sometimes struggles.

By the spring of 2008, there were 13 clusters established, covering the 60 parishes of the diocese. Each cluster of parishes is different. The Thomond Cluster in Limerick City consists of the four north side parishes. Together they originally formed the parish of St Munchin and now comprise the parishes of St Munchin's/St Lelia's, Our Lady of the Rosary, Christ the King and Corpus Christi.

In my opinion, the key thing that the meetings of the Thomond Cluster identified was its need to clarify its role. The role of the cluster meeting is not simply to become a new layer of meetings, but rather to support, compliment and be of service to the parish.

Thomond cluster meeting decided that there are tasks that are appropriate for parish and tasks that are appropriate for a cluster. Certain questions and concerns are really better dealt with by a larger group like a cluster, which can take on issues that an individual parish couldn't attempt. For example, a parish pastoral council would be overwhelmed if it were to look at the issue of 'how do we support the older people in our community, given that there's no retirement home on this side of the city?' However a cluster can say, together let's look at the wider issues, the demographics etc; let's see where that brings us, and let's reflect and identify solutions that can work for all the parishes together.

(ii) John Kernan

The Thomond Cluster – north of the river Shannon – is a fascinating area stretching from old urban Thomondgate in the parish of St Munchin to the outer suburban reaches of Caherdavin and Moyross. With approximately 20,000 to 22,000 people it includes some of the wealthiest areas of Ireland with some of the most travailed areas, including Moyross. We have an interesting and challenging cross-section.

The Cluster meeting group of approximately 24/26 people meet 4 times a year and is hosted in one of the four parishes. A smaller executive, consisting of about half a dozen members including the priests from each of the four parishes, meet to plan the cluster meetings.

Sometime in 2003, as the Thomond Cluster, we set ourselves some priorities. These were –
- To develop space and skills for prayer and reflection
- To identify ways of reaching out and building community
- To establish a demographic survey of the Cluster
- To identify means of support for older people

The idea behind 'Space for Prayer' was a move at that time to open a prayer space in one of the shopping centres and while effort and time were put into the proposal, it never really got off the ground.

The priority 'to identify ways of reaching out and building community' actually came from our experience within the process of developing cluster meetings. We found that the experience of lay people and clergy from the four parishes talking to one another and sharing ideas has strengthened the social relationships in the cluster. I think there is now a relationship that wasn't there a few years ago, between priests and people and between people themselves and between priests themselves. I know our priests are meeting more socially than was the case in the past.

The demographic survey of the cluster was an interesting experience. Our Lady of the Rosary parish had already carried out a survey of the people in their own parish which they shared with us. We decided to try and carry out a survey for the whole cluster of approximately 20,000 people. To do this, we were assisted by Professor Des McCafferty, of the Geography Department in Mary Immaculate College and by Dick Tobin, Senior Executive Planner with Limerick City Council. Because our cluster area coincided exactly with the electoral areas on which the 2002 census was based, the survey could use the census figures. In the cluster we were then able to tweak the figures, to break them down into the statistics for each of the four parishes. I think the experts would be quicker to stand over the figures for the totality of the cluster because of its coinciding so much with the electoral areas than they would be for our parish statistics. But in actual fact we cannot be too far wrong.

We ended up with about 8,000 people in St Munchin's parish; about 6,000 in Our Lady of the Rosary parish; about 4,000 in Corpus Christi parish; almost 4,000 in Christ the King parish. These were again broken down in terms of age, gender, marital status, household size and social classe. It was an interesting exercise but you might wonder where it was going.

The survey was picked up in a very interesting way. First, it was taken up by Professor Stiofán de Búrca, the retired head of the old Health Board, and now a Professor in the University of Limerick (UL). The survey was then used under the direction of Dr Eileen Humphries (UL) to carry out a study of the older age groups in the cluster. UL has identified samples of people over 65 in our parishes and held 'one to one' interviews with them. Then Professor Lyons in St Camillus' Hospital used the survey as the basis of a medical survey. Those over 65 who were surveyed were asked if they wished to have a medical survey – my wife promptly said 'no' and I said 'yes' and that's the way it went. I understand that in St Camillus' they have given a medical examination to hundreds of people for free, an examination that would cost a lot of money if you paid for it privately – and it was great fun – neighbours were meeting, fasting early in the morning and then sharing breakfast and stories following the examinations. The medical people in St Camillus' also enjoyed the exercise. They are used to people arriving in serious ill health and finding all these healthy elderly people coming in looking for craic was a new experience for them!

Meantime, the results of Professor de Búrca's survey will be ready for publication later with the demographic figures updated to the 2006 Census. I understand that the medical survey is on-going and that while the results are being sent to our GPs the final report will be published later.

In 2006 we elected new officers to the Cluster and added some more priorities to those of 2003. To the list we added:

- That at our meetings four times a year we should reflect on the bishop's pastorals to keep in touch with the thinking of the diocese
- Greater collaboration among priests
- Greater collaboration among parishes
- A newly formed group called *Eaglais Óg* – the Young Church

Reflecting on the bishop's pastoral is fairly obvious. All past-oral initiatives must be grounded in prayer and reflection if they are to be of value.

Greater collaboration among priests is being achieved in a number of ways. One was a decision that all the priests within the cluster would, at certain times during the year, celebrate Mass in the different parishes in the cluster. On the surface this achieved a positive variation for both priests and parishioners. Our bishop makes the point that in times when there were more priests around and available, just having one priest every Sunday or even knowing who is coming next every time, was just not the real experience of most people! However, the deeper meaning of the experience was that people began to see that all the priests of the cluster, and all the parishes, are inter-connected and at the service of one another. The church is more than 'my priest' and 'my Sunday Mass' – by getting to know one another, and by risking change, we recognise ourselves as the one Body of Christ, and we reduce the isolation we sometimes feel.

Eaglais Óg – the Young Church – is a new movement working at developing a 'sense of church' in young people. It is being de-veloped by Canon Mícheál Liston and Father Chris O'Donnell, of the Diocesan Youth Service, with young people and using the facilities of the new Dominican Bible Institute. This is not a 'youth' thing, not about youth clubs. It is about together finding a relevant sense of church with room for craic. We are also hop-ing to work with parents from the 'Do this in Memory' pro-gramme to see if there is anything on-going that can be devel-oped.

Our cluster now has a completely new issue to address – 'Regeneration' – which is a very live issue in one of our cluster parishes, Corpus Christi, in Moyross. Regeneration is a government initiative to renew both physically and socially disadvantaged communities and their districts. Bishop Murray has exhorted us all to remember that the people where regeneration is happening are our brothers and sisters. How can we focus all the talent we have in the cluster to help the people who are facing and going through such substantial change? At a recent cluster meeting, a young woman, working in Moyross, explained how threatening the experience can be. It sounds great – they are going to knock all the houses and start with a clean slate. Everything will be new. Attitudes and everything else will be revived. But, as she pointed out, when you have been living and raising your family in a house for all those years the notion that the bulldozer is going to come to knock it is a threatening one. We have to try and think how can we help. The people of Corpus Christi asked us, as neighboring parishes, if we can do something. They asked us to think about it and to pray hard for them in what they have to do. Regeneration can be a fantastic experience. It requires a huge effort on the part of all involved and please God it will work. The bishop is exhorting us to get in there but as it is unknown territory. We'll have to plan the way as we go along.

Other challenges that now face us will be to maintain and develop the momentum of the cluster and its meetings, especially when members of the meetings change, and that's life.

To finish with another comment from our bishop – speaking to parish pastoral councils on Pentecost Sunday, he said:

And so we are here to give thanks for all the endeavours and all that has been achieved, and to give thanks also for the initiatives that have struggled or fallen through. Nothing that we do in our effort to follow the way of Christ is ever lost. That is the source of the joy that should mark not just our celebration today, but the whole life of our parishes and clusters.

CHAPTER THIRTEEN

Leadership and Management Skills in a Pastoral Context

Eamonn Conway

In times of change learners inherit the earth; while the learned find themselves beautifully equipped to deal with a world that no longer exists. (Eric Hoffer)

Introduction
This paper sets out to explore what can be learned from contemporary secular experiences and practices of leadership and management for pastoral leadership in the church by clergy and laity. It focuses on the dynamics of the process of leadership and what makes for effective leadership rather than upon the concrete challenges faced by pastoral leaders today as such, though some of these will be examined.

Two objections to this exercise need to be dealt with at the outset. First, resistance to such learning is sometimes mounted on the basis of the unique nature of the church as an institution, and in particular the fact that the church is of divine origin. How can secular experiences of leadership therefore be of any value or relevance to the life of the church?

The reality is that the church is essentially both human and divine.[1] Though instituted by Christ, it nonetheless exists in history and thus 'has the appearance of this world which is passing.' The activity of the church is the activity of men and women, using their God-given gifts and talents in the service of the church's mission. As creatures, our gifts and talents are enhanced and liberated the more in tune with and responsive we are to our Creator; they do not have to be set aside or somehow supplanted in order that God can act in and through us. God's support to us in enhancing and developing our gifts comes in and through the wisdom of the age in which we live and serve.

---

1. See *Sacrosanctum Concilium*, 2; *Lumen Gentium* 48; *Catechism of the Catholic Church*, p 178; Karl Rahner, 'The Church of Sinners' and 'The Sinful Church in the Decrees of Vatican II,' in *Theological Investigations* 6, (London: DLT, 1969).

Indeed, God is co-experienced, co-known and co-loved in our encounter with and response to all created realities, so much so that the term 'secular' is somewhat of a misnomer as it can be a privileged place of graced encounter and response.

It is also the case that the manner in which the Spirit is present to those who exercise leadership in the church is not such as to make unnecessary the process of learning how to do things better, including learning from what is perceived as the secular world. Recently, we have seen, for example, the Catholic Church in Ireland accepting to comply fully, some would argue even obsequiously, with the demands of the state's Health Service Executive in terms of internal ecclesial governance with regard to child protection. Similarly, psychological testing, counselling and personal development courses have become a key part of seminary formation and few today would argue that prayer and spiritual direction, while indispensible, are enough to equip clergy for their pastoral responsibilities.

A second, related objection argues that the church is not a democracy and therefore patterns and principles of governance and leadership which one finds in secular bodies do not apply.[2] Joseph Ratzinger, for instance, has warned against viewing the church as 'a human invention ... which could be reorganised according to the needs of the historical cultural variables of the time'.[3] At the same time, Walter Kasper argues that 'to take up some democratic structural elements and procedures today in a manner both critical and creative' is not simply to pay tribute to the *Zeitgeist* but rather to seek to implement the ecclesiology of Vatican II.[4]

Just as the church in the past adopted a number of feudal and monarchical elements, elements that still persist in the church though long abandoned elsewhere, it is legitimate to explore what contemporary wisdom and insight into leadership and governance can be gleaned from secular society.

---

2. For a recent debate on this compare Donald Wuerl, in Francis Oakley and Bruce Russett eds, *Governance, Accountability and the Future of the Catholic Church*, (NY: Continuum 2004), 16-18, with Paul Lakeland, *The Liberation of the Laity*, (NY: Continuum, 2003), 207-219.

3. See Ratzinger, 'Pastoral Constitution on the Church in the Modern World', in Herbert Vorgrimler ed, W. J. O'Hara (English trs), *Commentary on the Documents of Vatican II*, Vol V, (London: Burns & Oates, 1969), 118-119.

4. Walter Kasper, *Leadership in the Church*, (NY: The Crossroad Publishing Company, 2003), 63.

At the same time, we will keep in mind that we are here discerning principles for leadership in the Christian community,
for whom Christ remains, 'the way, the truth and the life' (John
14:6), and thus, *the* model of Christian leadership. Maintaining a
focus on Christ while considering secular experiences of leadership will not, in fact, be a problem, because what is best in
human experience we inevitably also find in Christ.

Who are leaders?

We might begin by asking whether leaders are born or made.
Sometimes people who find themselves in leadership positions
in the church do not really consider themselves to be leaders
and may be somewhat daunted at the demands that the position
they hold seems to make of them.

Given the considerable flexibility that exists in most church
leadership positions, as well as the absence in some instances of
effective systems of accountability, the temptation is to 'reduce' the
role to what we are good at, or consider ourselves to be good at,
and to 'shelve' the rest or deem it unimportant. It is in the interests
of the individual, and of the mission of the Christian community,
that those who find themselves in pastoral leadership would begin
by asking themselves soberly and honestly if they have the necessary talents and gifts, as well as energy and enthusiasm, to exercise
the level of leadership the position requires. The recognition of our
giftedness, and the evaluation of how it matches up to the demands
of the leadership context, demand a process of prayerful discernment and continual growth in honest self-awareness.

At the same time, we should not underestimate the power of
God's grace to draw forth from us in particular circumstances
energies, gifts and talents that we did not know or might not
have recognised that we possess. Oscar Romero is an example of
this. He was considered for most of his life to have been a rather
reserved, scholarly, orthodox and devout priest and later bishop,
known if anything for his criticism of the more progressive elements in Liberation Theology. Confronted with the horror of the
senseless and brutal murder of one of his closest co-workers
along with other innocent members of his flock, and unavoid-
ably faced with the suffering of his people, a level of courage
and conviction was drawn out of him that became the source of
confidence and hope for a whole nation. We can think of many
other examples like this.

This brings us to our first leadership attribute: empathy. If this is missing, then all the leadership techniques we might acquire will be useless; if we have the capacity to empathise, then the best leadership techniques will come to us naturally. The Oxford Dictionary defines empathy as 'The power of projecting one's personality into (and fully comprehending) the object of contemplation.' This reads a little too clinically. The sense of 'suffering with' belongs to the etymology of the word. Empathy is about the ability to be disturbed by others; to see as far as is humanly possible, the situation from the perspective of others. It requires gentleness with ourselves, and especially, in the leadership context, with regard to our own projects and ambitions, if others are to be taken seriously and not merely be 'objects' to be integrated into our plans.

From a Christian point of view, we can add two observations. The first is that empathy is fundamentally about love. It is true, as the history of Christian spirituality bears out, that we can only change that which we first love and accept. This is true of ourselves, but also of others. Love alone can heal; love alone can give the confidence to let go; love alone provides the courage to see things differently, or to move forward, as is often the case, when things are anything but clear. It is critical in leadership to bear this in mind: we can only change what we love.

By way of contrast, we know how criticism unless properly mediated can be crippling. In management circles it is recognised that 'negative feedback' in the workplace is only ever effective, and can only really be heard, if it is offered within a context of general respect and mutual regard.

I remember many years ago hearing a very short homily at a priest's ordination by the late Cardinal Basil Hume in which he said simply, but profoundly, that a priest's first responsibility was to love his people. If we are without love, or if we fail to bring love to bear on a particular pastoral task, then, despite all out talents and techniques, we will be, as St Paul said, like 'a gong booming or a cymbal clashing' (1 Cor 13:1). The well known saying from St Augustine, *'Ama, et fac quod vis'* (Love, and do what you will) applies also to leadership.

The challenge, as St John of the Cross noted, is to persist in love when we find ourselves in anything but a loving situation. 'Where you do not find love', he says, 'put in love so that you will draw love out.' In a leadership context where we run up against conflict and even hostility, the challenge is to avoid reciprocating with hostility, out of a sense of our own vulnerability. The challenge is not to allow one's own empathetic disposition to be altered or constrained by the attitude of the other. To be loving is not to be foolish: there is what is called 'tough love'. Being loving is not to be confused with being 'nice'. But the toughest love of all is an unconditional love that does not allow itself to be limited or determined by the rejection or hostility of another.

We can make a second observation from a Christian point of view. 'Christ plays in ten thousand places' (Gerard Manley Hopkins), and God reveals God's self in the minds and hearts of all God's people. By being empathetic, listening to others, relating to them with respect and with reverence, we also listen to, respect and respond to God's will present and active in their lives.

In summary, then, the first challenge good leaders face is to have sufficient love to accept people and situations as they find them, not in order to leave people and things as they are but in order to create the spirit of acceptance, trust and confidence which allows and enables change to happen.

So what can leaders do to help people to have confidence and trust in their leadership?

Earning People's Confidence and Trust
Most pastoral leaders are appointed rather than elected. The people we work with seldom choose us and are unlikely to be able to get rid of us if they do not like us or if we are doing a bad job. While we may have automatic authority by virtue of our appointment, increasingly our influence and effectiveness are not guaranteed and we have to work hard for these. So what approach to leadership can we take that is likely to earn people's confidence and trust in us?

The first thing to realise is that earning confidence takes time and effort and is not to be confused with being considered popular or being liked. For instance, we can have confidence in people in leadership positions whom we do not particularly like but nonetheless whom we consider to be doing a good job. The following approaches are helpful in terms of building confidence:

- *'Not lording it over them'*

It is very important to make time to meet with those whom we work, informally as well as formally, and to meet with them in circumstances where they feel comfortable to communicate freely.

We have all had the experience of being summoned by our 'boss' to his/her office. Whether intended or not, from the very outset there is a built in sense of the 'superior' meeting the 'inferior'. Little things like not revealing in advance what the meeting is about, making contact through a secretary or by email rather than personally, sitting behind a desk, all tend to reinforce the boss's authority. We may be told in such circumstances that we are free to speak our minds but it is likely to be the last thing we would feel safe to do. Meetings in such circumstances tend to breed fear and compliance rather than build trust and confidence. At least twice in the New Testament, Christians are admonished not to 'lord it' over those entrusted to them (See Matthew 20:25 and 1 Peter 5:3).

Formal meetings have their place in working relationships and are unavoidable. At the same it is important to make time to meet with those we lead apart from formal agendas, and in an environment and context in which they feel comfortable and secure. It can be invaluable simply to drop in to people's offices, to enquire how their work is going, to show interest and openness with regard to their tasks. We usually learn more from such informal interaction than from formal meetings. We also build relationships and foster trust and confidence. Given that pastoral leaders seldom have formal means of receiving feedback, in such circumstances people also feel more confident to tell us things we need to hear.

- *Offering a clear sense of direction*

It is very important for leaders to get the balance right between, on the one hand, offering a clear sense of vision and direction, and, on the other, doing this in such a way that people feel invited and empowered to become involved and give of their best. I have heard this described as 'the light grip on the throat' approach.

- *The willingness to take responsibility*

It is important to be willing to take responsibility for one's decisions as a leader, and not to seek to hide behind those with whom we work. Good leaders will take responsibility not only for their own mistakes but also for the mistakes of their team members. This is only fair, as they usually get the credit when their team is successful. Good team leaders will promise their team members that they will stand by them, and protect them from criticism or rebuke. However, leaders can legitimately ask in return for a commitment to be kept fully informed of what is going on, and especially of any difficulties or problems. It is not fair if leaders first hear of these from a third party. Shirking responsibility, criticising openly or blaming others, especially those with whom one works, utterly undermines confidence in a leader.

• *The toleration of failure*
The gospel urges us to be forgiving and so we could expect that in Christian leadership contexts there would be a high tolerance of failure, but this is not always the case. Entrepreneurs are generally successful because they have a high tolerance for failure. It is important to be able to forgive quickly one's own mistakes and failings as well as those of others. It is also important to have strategies in place in order to learn from failures and integrate such experiences into future planning. Leaders who cope well with their own failures and those of others are more readily trusted than those who appear never to make mistakes or who think that admitting to mistakes and failures is a sign of weakness.

A culture in which failure can readily be admitted is important so that there is no tendency to cover-up, and mistakes can quickly be identified and rectified. A tolerance of failure is also important in order to encourage creativity and risk-taking. It is important, especially in a time of transition, that leaders have created a context in which people on the ground feel free to explore solutions to emerging problems and do not fear criticism or punishment if they get things wrong.

The toleration of failure is important for another reason: most learning in life is stumbled upon through trial and error; it is rarely predicted or planned.

As a leader, sometimes it is important to let failures go without comment; to trust that people themselves will deal with the situation. There is a place for occasional benign neglect, provided it is not just avoidance of conflict on one's own part.

• *Follow-through*
Confidence and trust depend upon a leader's ability to honour decisions made or else explain honestly why they are not being

followed through on. Building confidence requires consistent implementation even of small commitments undertaken.

In conclusion of this section, it takes serious work to earn sufficient trust to bring people with you, and an investment of personal time and resources which is easy to underestimate. In what follows, we will examine approaches to working together that are particularly important in the effective leadership of others.

What Working Together Takes

• *Leading, not just managing*
The importance of recognising the difference between leading and not just managing is well noted in leadership theory. Whereas those with management responsibilities do not necessarily have to be leaders, leaders have to be both able to lead and, at times, in order to follow through on projects and commitments, to manage effectively both people and resources.

As Peter Drucker, author of the famous *The 7 Habits of Highly Effective People*, puts it, managers are entrusted the task of asking the 'how' and the 'what' questions, whereas leaders must also ask 'why' and 'when'. A manager, when examining a ladder placed against a wall will ask how high it is, consider if it is safely positioned and strong enough for the task in hand, and so on. A leader will also consider the more basic matter of whether or not the ladder is lying against the correct wall and ask if this is the right time to start using it. Managers set out to do things right; leaders, to do the right thing.

• *Communication*
Most experiences of working together that go well have excellent communication as their basis, and most projects that fail identify weak communication as the cause. Poor communication fosters distrust which in turn demotivates people and makes it easy for them to detach or disassociate from a project. Good leaders ensure that those for whom they are responsible never hear important information second-hand or inappropriately. Really important information should be given directly, and not even by email, letter or phone, so that questions can be asked and difficulties raised and addressed immediately.

It is also important for those who exercise leadership not to 'surprise' their superiors or to leave them to hear important information about their work from others. There are no compelling reasons as to why principles of freedom of information that apply in state organisations should not also apply in the church. People have a right to the timely dissemination of all information that pertains to them and this practice should characterise our working together in pastoral contexts. But communication is more than about the exchange of information: it is about a quality of presence to one another that is marked by mutual respect at the service of a common goal.

• *Unity, not uniformity*
It is tempting, but ultimately damaging to most projects, only to recruit people to a team who see things more or less as we do; to choose only those we think we will best get on with or be able to 'handle' – variations on the 'safe pair of hands' syndrome that very often characterises the church's way of doing business. We should not underestimate or be fearful of our own ability to lead a challenging team. A united team of people with diverse views is likely to be much more creative and visionary than a team comprised of people with uniform perspectives.

•*Trusting people*
It is important to strike a balance between, on the one hand, avoiding micro-managing, and on the other, delegating to the extent that we lose oversight.

We have all had the experience of working with people who simply cannot let go of responsibility for particular aspects of a project. Leaders who engage in micro-management may well be paying too little attention to 'the bigger picture', or be missing it altogether. They may well be compensating for their lack of vision or for the fact that they have lost oversight of what is going on.

Most people work best when they have delegated responsibility; when they experience being trusted; when they enjoy some freedom with regard to how they fulfil their responsibilities; when they operate within agreed procedures for accountability.

The Catholic principle of subsidiarity can be applied here: matters are best handled in the first instance at the lowest possible level of organisation. At the same time it is important to distinguish between delegating responsibilities on the one hand, and abdicating responsibility on the other. Leaders should have interest in all aspects of the work in hand and remain sufficiently informed so as to be able to co-ordinate and direct as required.

• *Clarity regarding decision-making*

People on pastoral councils often complain that they are given the impression that a decision is being taken jointly until it turns out not to be the decision that 'Father' wants, and then it emerges that they were only really being consulted. We cannot expect to be happy with every decision taken by our leaders or by teams of which we are a member, but we are entitled to be happy with how decisions are made and reassured that the decision-making process is clear and fair.

As leaders, we need to distinguish between situations in which we are consulting people, but taking responsibility ourselves for the decision and its implementation; and situations in which we are sharing the decision-making, and consequently responsibility for the decision, with others. The 'buy-in' we can reasonably expect of people differs in both of these situations: people feel a greater sense of identity with and responsibility for decisions which they themselves have taken.

• *Time management*

Usually when we think of the resources a project might need, we think in terms of finance, equipment, etc. However, the key resource in any project is always people and the time which they are able to put at the disposal of the project. Employees and volunteers in any organisation can have differing levels of commitment and different expectations, and careful management with regard to both is needed.

We usually underestimate the amount of people's time a project requires. It is a key leadership responsibility to ensure that people are clear from the beginning regarding the level of time and commitment expected of them, tempted as we might be to fudge this at the outset in order to win their co-operation. Understandably, people become resentful if they find out that we have deliberately understated the amount of work a project requires.

In managing our own time as leaders it is a constant struggle to rise above the 'fire-fighting'; to ensure that important issues are not neglected as we deal with what presents itself as urgent and in need of immediate attention. The challenge is to work 'smart, not hard'. If we ourselves or fulltime employees reporting to us cannot accomplish the work expected within a normal working day and instead have to work evenings and weekends over an extended period, something is wrong and a review is needed. Such a situation is unsustainable and burnout or melt-down will inevitably result.

• *Valuing what people do*
It is important to know what people actually do, and also to ac-knowledge it. In general, church leaders are good at saying thank you and at publicly acknowledging the work of volun-teers as well as professionals. But valuing what someone does is not just about saying thank you or giving plaudits publicly. It is about actually integrating people's work into the vision and planning; it is about taking their contribution seriously and al-lowing it to be influential, even if we are not always or necessar-ily fully in agreement with what they have achieved.

• *Dealing with middle-managers*
In large leadership contexts, the leadership of 'middle-managers' is always considered particularly challenging. In the church we are talking here, for instance, about parish priests. Generally speak-ing, these are people who, in career terms, have reached a plateau, or some would say, a ceiling. As a result, they may feel frustrated and resentful. They may also have more vested in maintaining the *status quo* and in avoiding change and innovation than others. The existing system has brought them this far and it is at least un-certain that significant change would bring them any further. In fact, younger more flexible people might well be more likely to benefit from a changed working environment.

Dealing with middle managers poses a particular leadership challenge. Very often, middle managers have learned to tell superiors what they think they want to hear and they tend to sieve out any information that they think might be unwelcome. This is a communications challenge that needs to be addressed.

The first task is to earn their confidence. It is important to lis-ten to them and to be prepared to learn from them. Insofar as they are dealing with people 'on the ground', their input is vital. Many of them will have been in middle-management roles for several years and will have immense experience. It is important to support them, to give them voice and to back them up when appropriate.

It is also important that leaders make clear to them that they value hearing the truth and in fact expect to hear it from them. In terms of helping them to 'buy in' to change, it is vital that they are helped to see that they will have a valued and valuable role to play in the changed environment, one for which they are already well qualified and have sufficient experience, or else for which they will be resourced with appropriate training. It is also important to ensure that their basic human needs will be met regarding a sense of security in their work, a sense of identity in their role, and so on.

Above all it is important to build up with them and among them a sense of being part of a team with a shared responsibility. It is important to share with them how change is expected to improve things; how it will benefit not only them but also those they serve.

Insofar as many middle managers will have often already experienced failed attempts at restructuring and change in the past, it is important to build in measurable goals marking progress in implementation, and to be consistent in terms of follow-through.

No one should be appointed parish priest without some formal training. Those already parish priests should be fully involved in the making of decisions that affect them. At the same time the attitude that 'what is there will see me out' should be considered totally unacceptable. As long as parish priests hold office they are responsible not only for the community's present situation but its future also.

• *Dealing with conflict*
One of the most difficult things for those in leadership, and perhaps especially in the church, is to deal with conflict. We are not good at it. We frequently let things slide and avoid confrontation for as long as possible. Then, when avoidance no longer works and we have to act, we take the least painful way, which is usually the least personal way, of dealing with the issue, thus maximising the hurt and damage caused.

Very often when conflict arises there has, in fact, been some fault on both sides. As a leader I may not have seen things coming that I should have; I may have avoided dealing with an issue when I should have and when it was more manageable. The key is to act early. If trust and quality communication characterises working relationships then it should be possible to address and resolve matters before they get out of hand.

In dealing with a conflict situation the first criterion needed is honesty, both with oneself and with others. If we expect others to acknowledge culpability we have to be prepared to do so ourselves.

In many pastoral work contexts, especially where the state has influence, there will be guidelines for dealing formally and informally with conflict situations.

It is important to keep things in perspective, not to exaggerate, and to remain factual. Insofar as possible it is also important to distinguish between the person, and the role which they have to play in the exercise of which conflict has arisen. It is also important to accept that dealing with conflict is part of one's own leadership role and to get on with it.

• *Evaluation and Accountability*

Most dioceses and religious orders in the country will have a 'family history' of failed pastoral initiatives, and in many cases this has bred a cynicism that holds back contemporary attempts at renewal. Seldom are formal evaluations of pastoral projects conducted regardless of whether they are deemed successful or otherwise. Evaluation is important for a number of reasons: it may identify problems that can still be addressed; it gives all those involved or affected by initiatives an opportunity to voice their opinions; it can provide important information with regard to future planning. Evaluation is not something to be appended at the end of a project. It should be planned for and integrated into the project from the very beginning.

Accountability in the church has traditionally been understood only vertically or hierarchically – that is, the priest to his bishop, the bishop to the pope, the pope to God.

In the first instance we are always individually accountable to ourselves; to the standards and the expectations which we have set for ourselves. In the final instance, we are accountable to God in Christ. In between these, however, along with vertical accountability there is also room for horizontal accountability, that is, accountability to those with whom we work and those whom we serve. All those who invest in a project, whether through their time or through making resources available, all those affected by our efforts have a right to be kept informed of what is happening and to be given an opportunity to inform us of their views.

We will now look at the distinctive leadership challenges of leading change.

Leading change

Generally, people speak of two different approaches to change. Innovative change is where we 'dream the dream'. This is where we imagine a desirable future and develop strategies to attain it, only considering subsequently the limitations imposed by our starting-point or the present situation. In this context people like first to explore all the possible options, moving then to consideration of which options are preferable, and only then considering those that are most probable or likely given the limitations of the situation.

The contrasting approach is perhaps the more familiar and is known as conservative change. This is an approach to change which considers first and foremost where we are now and aims at reinforcing or re-establishing what was the *status quo*. The only changes envisaged are those which will restore the situation to what it was. Whereas the emphasis in the former, innovative change, is on discontinuity, the emphasis in the latter, conservative change, is on continuity.

In the church we are most familiar with conservative change, and most institutionally-led 'innovations' are in fact exercises in conservative change. Included here, for example, is the recent introduction in Ireland of the permanent diaconate which, no matter how theologically and sacramentally we might wish it to be otherwise, practically speaking and in the present context will have the effect of providing a limited reserve priesthood akin to the reserve police force. It would be worth reflecting on whether or not the clustering of parishes is also a form of conservative change. Is the matter of the radical transformation, and in some cases, breakdown of community, and the emergence of new forms of community, not just geographic but virtual, being sufficiently considered in pastoral planning? Is the driving issue meeting the canonical requirement of a priest pastor for each parish in face of dwindling and ageing clergy?

Few of us really relish change, and the reality is that conservative change is always more appealing than its more innovative counterpart. Generally, we only change significantly when we have to, either because of compelling external circumstances or because the situation in which we find ourselves is too painful to be allowed to continue.

The pastoral leader has a number of tasks specifically with regard to change. The first is to anticipate it and not wait until it simply becomes inevitable and something that has to be under-taken in panic or under undue pressure. It is helpful in this con-text to point out to people that in the rapidly changing world to which the church must respond, the choice is not between changing and not changing. The only choice is between choos-ing and directing change, and allowing changes to overtake us and force themselves upon us. When we pause to reflect, we know this to be true of our own personal lives. To live is to change, however reluctantly, and it is preferable freely to choose change than always finding ourselves having to change led by others and under pressure.

The leader must also discern courageously whether in partic-ular circumstances innovative or conservative change is re-quired, and bring people through a process of discernment in this regard. In the pastoral context, the fear around innovative change, with its emphasis on discontinuity, is that we would end up being unfaithful to an aspect of the church's core mission and identity. The issue is not, however, one of having to choose between being faithful or unfaithful. It is more complex. It is to discern carefully that to which we are obliged to remain faithful and then to undertake the changes that are necessary in order to remain faithful.

The New Testament is full of examples both of conservative and innovative change undertaken as the nascent Christian community sought to establish itself between what was experi-enced as the conflicting demands of continuity with its Jewish roots and the needs of Gentile converts. As Peter Neuner, for in-stance, has pointed out:

> In the encounter with Hellenism, Christianity was challenged by new questions and problems with which the earliest com-munity had not yet been confronted and which Jesus himself had not yet given an answer. These questions were new and the answer was given to them in faithfulness to the tradition in a creative process.[5]

The scripture scholar Peter Schmidt, has pointed out that:

> ... the 'will of God' does not impose any pre-existing and al-ready fixed structural mould on history. Rather, a particular

---

5. 'Ministry in the Church:Changing Idenity' in Jan Kerkhofs, ed, *Europe Without Priests* (London: SCM, 1995), 129.

development was accepted as the best translation of the gospel in certain circumstances in the church and it was therefore read as the historical expression of God's will (as tradition). An eternal immutability of structural forms is not part of this attitude of trust in the original inspiration – preparing a covenantal people for God.[6]

In the church today there is a real danger that we would be faithful to particular forms which the ministry of the church once took but which now are in danger of betraying the church's mission.

Sometimes fear is the problem. We know from scripture that there is no fear in love, that perfect love overcomes all fears (1 John 4:18). But our love is seldom perfect and our fears often imprison us, including the fear of infidelity. The parable of the talents is worth considering in this context (Matthew 25:14-30). This is not a parable about entrepreneurship; Jesus was not interested in how many talents the men managed to make. He was more interested in the fact that they had the courage to risk losing what they had. The message is that fear is the opposite of faith and trust and though disciples have to be aware of their fears, they should not be paralysed by them. Faith is all about risk-taking. It is about trusting that even in failure we are held and loved by God. This is why leaders who take their Christian faith seriously, regardless of whether they are working in the church or in industry, should be up there among their very best because of the liberating and empowering love of God in Christ which is freely given to them.

The parable of the talents is potentially a quite harsh judgement on us. As pastoral leaders we have to be vigilant that our personal fears, fears perhaps about how we might cope or be found wanting in a very changed pastoral situation, do not cause us to run away from necessary change under the guise of a false fidelity. Or it could well be plain laziness that underpins our loyalty to the *status quo*.

There are a number of what are sometimes referred to as 'lubricants' of change, factors or approaches that can be taken, which facilitate change, and which are helpful to bear in mind:

---

6. 'Ministries in the New Testament and Early Church', in Jan Kerkhofs *Europe Without Priests* , 45

- The first is to allow for the reality of a sense of grief at the loss of the familiar. All the stages of grief apply when people come to realise that the *status quo* is no longer tenable and that change is inevitable, and dealing with grief takes time. Unacknowledged grief can breed negativity and stifle new initiatives.
- In order to bring people along, it is important to communicate fully what is going on, and to ensure, insofar as is possible, that the purpose and the implications of the changes are clear.
- It is also important to make changes incrementally and at a pace most people can follow.

Prayer and Attentiveness

Each of the synoptic gospels warns against gaining the world at the cost of losing our souls (Matthew 16.26; Mark 8:36; Luke 9:25). In pastoral leadership, the end is not just important but the means as well. The manner of our working together, and not just the task we set out to achieve, should witness to the kingdom and mark its in-breaking in our midst.

The story is told of a bishop who had, as his episcopal motto, 'God is my helper'. It was joked that this was precisely the problem: the bishop saw God as *his* helper. Personal prayer and reflection, as well as occasional prayer together as a pastoral team, is necessary not only to keep us on track but also to keep us in our place.

The emphasis in recent writings on ministry is to see ministers as 'active receivers'. On the one hand, this emphasises that God's kingdom discloses itself as gift in our midst; we do not produce it by our efforts. At the same time we are 'active' receivers: we are called to be enthusiastic co-creators with God, energetic co-workers in the vineyard.

The paper began by emphasising the centrality of empathy and love. We can only change what or whom we love. This includes ourselves. We can only change if we first know ourselves to be loved and accepted as we are. This sense of being loved comes to us in prayer. We also come to know this in and through relationships with others, both our family and friends, as well as those with whom we work. David Steindl-Rast has said that the more we are alive and awake the more everything we do becomes prayer. Attentiveness and deliberateness in our daily interactions and taking time to reflect on our actions can play a big part in our growth as leaders.

Conclusion

Until the recent past, pastoral leadership was the preserve of the clergy, working together occasionally but on their own much of the time. Very occasionally, lay people were entrusted with particular tasks and responsibilities. The situation today is much different. Increasingly lay people hold full-time and part-time posts in the church and more people are becoming involved on a voluntary basis. It is important that the working context is as human, wholesome and mature as possible, not only for the success of particular projects but also because of the nature of the church as the sacrament of Christ to the world.

In the past, clerical culture appeared on the surface at least to provide fraternal support and encouragement, and no doubt in many instances did so. At the same time we have to acknowledge that all too often a shallow and superficial bonhomie masked the fact that genuine communication among priests was poor and co-operation minimal. It is important today that priests find support among fellow clergy and that they have a clear sense of their own distinctive role and identity. This, however, cannot be established at the cost of developing a vibrant and supportive working relationship among the new teams of diverse people who are being commissioned to work in the vineyard of the Lord.

Contributors

Patrick Connolly is a Senior Lecturer in the Department of Theology and Religious Studies at Mary Immaculate College, University of Limerick

Eamonn Conway is Professor and Head of the Department of Theology and Religious Studies at Mary Immaculate College, University of Limerick

Eugene Duffy is a Lecturer in the Department of Theology and Religious Studies at Mary Immaculate College, University of Limerick

Eamonn Fitzgibbon is curate in Raheen Parish and a Vicar General of the Diocese of Limerick

Liam Irwin is Head of the Department of History at Mary Immaculate College, University of Limerick

Nóirín Lynch is a Pastoral Co-ordinator for the Diocese of Limerick

John Kernan is an architect by profession and the first chairperson of the Thomond Cluster in the Diocese of Limerick

Desmond McCafferty is Professor and Head of the Department of Geography at Mary Immaculate College, University of Limerick

Dermot Meehan is now Parish Priest of Swinford, Co Mayo

Donal Murray is the former Bishop of Limerick

Brendan O'Keefe is a Lecturer in the Department of Geography at Mary Immaculate College, University of Limerick

Eoin O'Mahony is a Social Researcher with the Council for Research and Development, at the offices of Irish Episcopal Conference, Maynooth

Catherine Swift is a Lecturer in the Department of History at Mary Immaculate College, University of Limerick

Thomas R. Whelan is Associate Professor of Theology and Dean of the Faculty of Theology and Spirituality at the Milltown Institute, Dublin

Myriam Wijlens is Professor of Canon Law at the Catholic Theological Faculty, University of Erfurt, Germany

Henk Witte is Associate Professor of Dogmatic Theology at the Catholic Faculty of Theology, University of Tilburg, The Netherlands